Don Mason A.G
90 & 196 Sqdn

LE (Bill) Lucas S/Ldr D.
9. 15. 162. 139 Pilot

John E.
40 & 12 Sqdn.
Hal Gardner NAV
106/'89 Sqan
Lancaster

Dave Fellowes W.O a/g.
460Sqn RAAF
Roy Smith NAV.
199 Sqdn Stirlings

IN MY ELEMENT

Group Captain
E A Johnston
OBE, FRAeS, RAF Ret'd

IN MY ELEMENT

An Old Pilot's Tale

George Mann *of* Maidstone

Group Captain E.A. Johnston
OBE, FRAeS, RAF Ret'd

IN MY ELEMENT

First published 1999
by George Mann

Hardback Edition   ISBN   0   7041   0283   8
Paperback Edition   ISBN   0   7041   0289   7

Printed and bound in Great Britain
and published by
George Mann Books, PO Box 22, Maidstone
in the English County of Kent

*To My Beloved Wife Isobelle who lived calmly through
all the turbulence and anxiety of Service life,
giving me unstinted support
and, when it was over, encouraged the scribbling
which brought forth my books.*

CONTENTS

ILLUSTRATIONS

*All photographs, with the exception of No. 14, which is
reproduced by kind permission of Short Brothers,
are either the copyright of the author or of
various friends whose permissions have been sought*

The cover illustration is taken from a watercolour
by the late Flight Cadet Ronnie Rotheram
depicting the author in *Annabelle,* January 1937,
on his first solo flight at Cranwell.

IN MY ELEMENT

1

Fledgeling

I WAS BORN WITH BOTH EARS COCKED FOR THE SOUND OF aero engines. So far as I am aware, there never was a time when I was not going to be a pilot. My father, a distinguished non-rigid airship captain in the Royal Naval Air Service, had been given the new Royal Air Force rank of Major and put in command of the Airship Station at Luce Bay in the middle of 1918. There my mother, Janita Daisy, gave birth to me on October 9th.

At the beginning of 1919 my father took command of the airship station at Longside, near Aberdeen, and my mother and I followed him there. With the signing of the Peace Treaty, however, there seemed to be no further use for the non-rigids which had performed such sterling service in countering the U-boat threat, and after the brilliant double crossing of the Atlantic by the rigid airship R34 under the command of Major G.H. Scott that midsummer, it looked as if there was a great future for the big rigids. Longside's complement of blimps was deleted and the station was closed down. Major Johnston became Flight Lieutenant Johnston and was found an ill-defined job, nominally 'for Royal Air Force Communications Duties', in the Air Ministry's new Controllerate-General of Civil Aviation. My parents took the lease of a flat in Highbury which became our home for the next five years or so.

My father was the scion of a long dynasty of shipmasters with roots in Fife. Himself a certificated Master Mariner, he had come into the RNAS via a commission in the Royal Naval Reserve. He brought to the job at Air Ministry an immense enthusiasm for the development of air navigation methods and equipment based on his talent, skill and experience both at sea and in airships. Finding that this was not a field adequately catered for in the Department, he soon made for himself a niche from which he was able to exert considerable influence.

Captain Frederick Tymms MC, who had been an Observer Officer in the Royal Flying Corps and had completed the RAF Long Navigation course before being demobilised, was appointed as his assistant. Just before joining my father he had navigated a Handley Page O-400 Bomber in the contest to be the first aircraft to fly from Cairo to Cape Town and had been lucky to survive a mid-air failure of its structure. These two men got on extremely well together; both were intensely practical and articulate; Johnston extrovert, inventive, by far the more skilled and experienced; Tymms reserved, curious of mind, exceptionally logical and deep-thinking.

Increasingly my father was pulled into the heady world of civil aeroplane operations which, throughout 1920 and 1921, were in constant operational and financial flux. During 1921, however, the transfer of rigid airships R33 and R36 to the Controller-General of Civil Aviation to evaluate their commercial potential gave him the opportunity to fly in them regularly from Pulham as a Navigation Officer. This brought him once again in a close working relationship with Major Scott, who had been his Commanding Officer at Anglesey in 1916, and many other former friends and colleagues of the old airship service, and was to have an important bearing on his future.

The disastrous crash of R38 in August 1921 put an immediate end to all airship programmes. Two months later, my father's short service commission in the RAF was terminated. With a wife and two children in a London flat to support, there seemed to him no option but to go back to sea. In those tough times his old Company gave him a berth as Chief Mate of their latest deep-sea bulk freighter, and some of my earliest memories relate to being taken on board her when she lay in port at Swansea and North Shields between voyages East of Suez.

After a dashing career in airships and in the Civil Aviation Department, my father found serving at sea under an Old Salt who was both opinionated and thick was something of a trial, so he was immensely pleased when he received a letter from Freddy Tymms in the summer of 1923 asking whether he would be interested in a job as

Navigation Officer with Daimler Airways. He leapt at it, and within a fortnight of taking his discharge from his ship at Avonmouth was flying as navigator of a DH34 on the new London-Berlin service.

In those days pilots did not 'navigate'. They always stayed below cloud and either followed railway lines or hopped from easily identifiable feature to feature. This promoted neither the regularity required by timetables nor reliability of service, and my father's mission was to convert the stubborn young pilots to using formal navigation methods and making the best use of what few aids existed. At first they were against him.

They soon discovered that he really knew what he was talking about and could and did put it into practice in the air with remarkable results. He could tell them where they were, what courses to steer, when they would arrive at the next destination - and he was always right. They were converted to his methods in no time.

Daimler was absorbed into Imperial Airways in April 1924, and my first real memories of aeroplanes date from the ceremony of naming the Handley Page W8s at the Plough Lane terminal of the old Croydon aerodrome. My father often took me to Croydon during the next few years, and by scrambling about the DH34s and the Handley Pages in the hangars I became thoroughly at home with aeroplanes. Nobody who was an official seemed to mind me, but occasionally a mechanic would warn me not to touch any switches in the cockpit because the landing flares were attached to the wingtip carriers.

The DH34 in particular appealed to me and probably was the biggest influence in making concrete my intention to become an aeroplane pilot. The cockpit was very high up in front of the wings, immediately behind the engine, and you had to climb a ladder on the outside of the fuselage to reach it. Perched up there, with nothing but the long nose in front, you seemed to be on top of the world. For years, whenever I climbed into bed at night I imagined I was climbing into the cockpit of a DH34, and dreamed of deeds of derring do in the skies before going to sleep. Later I transferred my dreams to the cockpit of Alan Cobham's DH61.

During 1924 the Government decided to embark on a large rigid airship development programme to forge commercial links with India, South Africa and Canada. My father readily accepted the invitation of Major Scott, who was appointed Officer in charge of Flying and Training in the new Directorate of Airship Development, to join the team as his Special Assistant, for the navigation problems of the long range routes on which airships were to operate offered a real challenge. So towards the end of the year my parents and I left the London flat and moved into an official Royal Airship Works quarter, 7 The Crescent, Shortstown, which we occupied for nearly three years.

This was by no means the end of my father's connection with the world of aeroplanes, for he had made a reputation among the pilots and with the people who mattered in flying operations and his services continued to be called upon in many capacities until the last few weeks of his life. Among other things he played a leading role in founding the Guild of Air Pilots and Air Navigators, of which he became the first Deputy Master and Chairman of the Court.

Soon after we arrived at Cardington my father took me down to the airship shed to see R33. There was a guard hut outside the entrance, manned by old Mr Keep, who asked us if we had any tobacco or matches. My father handed over his, and I had to declare none. R33 was hanging suspended from the roof of the enormous shed, about to be reconditioned and prepared for an experimental flight programme. As I went through the door of the shed I was confronted by an unimaginably vast wall of whitish canvas that curved out of sight to left and right and seemed to stretch up to the very roof of the huge building. This was my first and lasting impression of R33, which in time became a huge playing frame for me. I came to know her structure and her control car almost as intimately as I knew my own bedroom.

She was nearly 650 feet long, and at the very tip of her tail there was a tiny observation cockpit where I used to go and huddle and watch the workmen forty feet below me on the floor of the shed.

All around her were the wooden tower platforms and the long firemen's ladders used for working on her hull. The floor was littered with the half-hundredweight iron weights and sandbags by which, when she was inflated with hydrogen, she was tethered to earth like a monstrous Gulliver.

The control car was a magic, compact place for a youngster. At the steering coxswain's control wheel right forward were panoramic window-panels spreading right round from beam to beam. Just behind and to starboard was the height cox'ns wheel mounted athwartships, and on the port side were all the toggles for controlling the release of ballast and for valving gas, and below them the four engine-room telegraphs (smaller and lighter versions of what I had seen so often on the bridges of ships).

In the after part of the car was my father's big chart table. A narrow aluminium ladder ran up through a fabric cylinder from the control car to the keel of the ship, and this was more fun than almost any tree to climb. To get into the engine cars you had to use ladders which were not protected from the slipstream like this. I used to wonder whether this was because engineers were rated lower than riggers, let alone Officers. I thought the little engine cars, crammed full of machinery, were very dull places compared with the control car where my father, his fellow Officers and the two coxswains lorded it over all creation. Engines never captured my interest; they remained always just things at the end of a throttle linkage which delivered power on request.

Once inflation of R33 began, I was no longer free to play in her, but was allowed into the control car when my father was working there. Early in 1925 she flew off to Pulham. Our lives now oscillated between Shortstown and Pulham where the flight trials programme of R33 continued until she was permanently grounded at the end of 1926. Alongside R33 in the shed at Pulham I found a new playground in the uncovered hull of R36. Aft of the control car she had a long narrow passenger cabin which, in her unkempt state, was a rather spooky place, consisting as it did of many little, unlit, fabric walled cabins and spaces. I rather frowned on R36 as being a sort of airborne bus, comparing her unfavourably with the purely military R33 which did such exciting things as carrying fighter planes and dropping them in mid air.

Whenever we were at Pulham we lived in the main hotel in Harleston. While we were there the Italian semi-rigid *Norge* arrived en route for the North Pole. Colonel Nobile, in command, and his mixed

17

Italian and Norwegian Officers joined us there overnight. Although he thought very highly of himself, the airshipmen at Pulham regarded him as a comic opera figure. I was with my father in the shed when Major Scott asked him to give Nobile a lift to the hotel. We had a little Singer car which bore the nickname of the great diva of the day, and my father turned to Nobile and said, "Come with me, Colonel, Tetrazzini is outside." Nobile, who had so far been extremely disdainful of the reception accorded him, immediately came alive and smartened himself up, only to be faced with an ancient two-seater car. I rode on the bench dickie seat behind a very boot-faced Colonel.

After this, Imperial Airways borrowed my father to navigate the first commercial aeroplane service flight to India, and then back to Egypt where he became temporarily the Air Ministry's Superintendent of the Cairo-Basra Air Route pending the arrival of his friend Captain Freddy Tymms. For the first half of 1927, therefore, I lived with his mother at Wallasey and, through my Uncle Jim who was a Marine Engineer with the Bibby Line, was given the run of their big ships in Birkenhead docks.

By the time we got back to Cardington, R33 and R36 were all decommissioned and Pulham was no longer operational. By now, Cardington had its second airship shed as well as its weird looking mooring mast designed by Major Scott. The Officers and men were trained in operating the airship mooring system with the aid of kite balloons, and when my Father was involved in this I spent many a happy hour dashing up and down the stairs to the top of the 200 foot tower and clambering around the structure at the top. I even understood the complex mooring procedures which were to be used on the big airships. But although work had started on the construction of R101 there was nothing in the shed to interest me yet.

One day, however, my father said he had something to show me: it was the first test bay of R101, fully rigged and inflated, standing up against the west door of the shed. It was an astonishing sight not only because of its size but because of the revolutionary nature of its construction compared with the orthodox Zeppelin structure of R33 and R36. Colonel Richmond – 'Uncle Dope' - was the Chief Designer; he explained to me the concept clearly and without the slightest patronage. He and his wife were great friends of ours. His Chief Assistant, Flight Lieutenant Rope, was both a brilliant engineer and a much-loved man.

During the hiatus between the dismantling of R33 and the first flight of R101 my father was much involved with aeroplane people and operations. For a short while he taught navigation at the De Havilland School of flying at Stag Lane, sometimes taking me with him to watch the flying. Outside the hangars there was a line-up of DH 51s, a hybrid somewhere between the revolutionary Moth and the legendary old DH9, and I thought that they looked immensely dashing. One day the Chief Flying Instructor (C.F.I.), Clem Pike, asked me if I would like a flight. I was rather disappointed when he took me over to the little Moth standing nearby. I was put into the front cockpit without a helmet. During take-off I was dazed by the noise, the buffeting of the slipstream and the bumpy ride over the grass, but the moment the wheels left the ground I felt an immense surge of almost peaceful wonderment as the ground receded and became ever more unreal. The only reality was the little Moth whose wings sustained me and whose cockpit enclosed me. After a while Pike throttled back the engine and put the machine into a glide: all was silence save for the whistle of the wind in the flying wires and an occasional pop from the engine exhaust. I was entranced.

In addition to the dial of the airspeed indicator in the cockpit there was a simple device on the starboard wing strut: a vertical metal plate pivoting on a long arm which rotated as the air pressure built up, indicating the airspeed on a calibrated quadrant. I watched this with great interest as the pilot slowly lifted the nose of the Moth above the horizon, letting the speed drop until with a thud the new-fangled leading edge slats popped out into the anti-stall position and the nose fell gently below the horizon again. This, my first flight, in my eighth year, solved the problem whether to become an airship pilot or an aeroplane pilot when I grew up.

We were now living in Harrowden House, just on the edge of the Royal Airship Works, and I was at Bedford School, much to the delight of my father, for that had been the alma mater of his hero General Sir Sefton Brancker, the legendary first Director of Civil Aviation. One day a well-known barnstorming pilot, Captain Percy Phillips of Cornwall Aviation, popped down into a field at Fenlake, barely a mile away from our house on the way into Bedford, and he was naturally invited to enjoy our hospitality during the week he spent flying people around in his old rotary-engined Avro 504 at five shillings a go. I spent a lot of time in his camp at the edge of the field watching the proceedings and helping his mechanic carry cans of petrol.

There is something extraordinarily romantic in the memory of these primitive field operations carried out by a pilot, a couple of faithful mechanics and a decrepit van full of miscellaneous spare parts, a stack of petrol and oil drums and a small tent for office. The smell of burnt castor oil remains with me today, equalled only by the later memory of kerosene when the jets came. Towards the end of his stay my reward came. "I think you have flown before", Phillips said. I nodded. "Then we can have some fun," he announced.

The pilot occupied the front cockpit under the upper wing. The cockpit behind him had been enlarged to carry two or three passengers, but as this flight was special for me, I was alone in what seemed a large open space. After the usual drill – 'switches off' – 'suck in' – 'contact' - the mechanic swung the propeller and the engine burst into life. With a mechanic pushing backwards at one wingtip the pilot opened the throttle and swung the machine into wind. And off we went. Once again I experienced that intense feeling of release as the machine left the ground. This time we climbed quite high, and then, after an exhilarating steep S-turn while he searched for other aircraft in the proximity, Phillips dived her steeply and pulled her up into a loop. This was the first of a bewildering series of manoeuvres which made me absolutely terrified of falling out. I concentrated fiercely on hanging on to the longerons, but I need not have worried, for Phillips maintained positive 'G' even when we were upside down.

Afterwards he told me that we had done loops, Immelman turns, and spins. "Did you enjoy it?" my Father asked when I climbed out of the cockpit. "If you want to be a pilot you will have to take aerobatics in your stride." Having publicly declared my intention of being a pilot I was not now going to back down, so I lied, but truth to tell for a long time after that I was distinctly nervous whenever I was offered a flight.

Phillips took me up once in the next summer but didn't throw me around as I shared the cockpit with a fare-paying passenger who had paid his five shillings for a simple joyride. My next flight took place at Hanwell in one of National Flying Service's Dessoutter monoplanes. The cockpit was fully enclosed under the leading edge of the high wing; the pilot and his pupil sat side by side and two passengers could sit behind them. It was all rather luxurious. My father's influence got me a place in the co-pilot's seat, and for a few short, ecstatic minutes I was permitted to handle the 'joystick' in flight. When Alan Cobham brought his 'circus' to Cardington he visited us at home and offered me a free flight, but with all these experiences under my belt I found it very dull to be herded with many other kids into the cabin of his big DH61.

Meanwhile R101 was a-building in No 1 shed at Cardington. I did not have the same freedom of her developing structure as I did of the earlier ships, but my father took me with him often enough to inspect progress and I did come to know her in considerable detail. In common with the rest of the airship community, I was immensely proud of her, but though I fully understood the proposed place of these big airships in the aviation scene I did not for an instant feel that I wanted to be an airship pilot. Several times I was permitted to board both R100 and R101 while they were moored at the mast, and on one memorable occasion I was allowed on board R100 while she was walked out of No 2 shed, then hooked onto the mooring wire which was stretched along the ground from the masthead, and floated up to several hundred feet before being hauled down onto the mooring mast. That was as close as ever I came to flying in an airship until I was an old man.

My father was killed in the crash of R101 on October 5th 1930, four days before my 12th birthday. Although the disaster immediately snuffed out my interest in airships for the next half a century, it only strengthened my determination to follow him into the air. When my beloved mother died barely eighteen months later, Captain Tymms [1] became my guardian. By then he was Director of Civil Aviation in

---

[1] His contribution to the organisation of international civil aviation from its earliest days is the subject of my book *To Organise the Air*

India, but he happened to be back in England on business at the time. We had a long talk, as a result of which we decided that my best bet was to go for a Flight Cadetship at the Royal Air Force College at Cranwell as soon as I reached the minimum age of seventeen and a half. He spoke to my Headmaster, the redoubtable Humfrey Grose-Hodge, and my school career was arranged accordingly. It was also arranged that for the school holidays I would live with Major Scott's widow Jess and her family of four. Jess not only gave me unfettered use of a room in the top of her house in Bedford, five minutes away from the school, and saved my sanity, but became my greatly loved and admired 'half-mother'. Through her I met Isobelle Linck, who was to become the incomparable and adored partner of my life.

Among my father's effects which came to me were his manuscript of a manual of air navigation which he had drafted while he was at the Air Ministry in 1920, three volumes of the *Admiralty Manual of Navigation*, and the two volumes of *Nicholls' Concise Guide* covering the navigation and seamanship requirements for the examinations for Masters' and Mates' Certificates. The manuscript fascinated me and, by dint of studying *Nicholls* and the *Admiralty Manual* I not only came to understand it but formed a resolve to update and complete it for publication under my father's name in due course.

I did in fact start work on it while I was a Navigation Instructor in Canada during the war, but the publication of the Air Ministry's unsurpassable *Manual* in the early 1940s made my own project redundant. Even while I was still at school, however, I acquired sufficient grasp of theory to give a lecture on the science of navigation to the School's Scientific Society and stand up to sharp questions from both my Sixth Form contemporaries and the Maths Masters in the audience.

I flew only twice more before going to Cranwell. In 1935 my Guardian arranged with Herr Wronsky of Deutsche Lufthansa for me to go to the airport at Cologne nominally as a trainee traffic clerk for the duration of the school holidays, some six weeks. My father's old friend Captain Lamplugh - the irrepressible 'Lamps' of British Aviation Insurance Group fame - procured for me a free return ticket by Imperial

Airways, and Whitney Straight, after giving me a very satisfying lunch at the Royal Aero Club, drove me in his exciting American Ford coupé to Croydon. With me I carried a map, a protractor, a ruler and my slide-rule, determined to put to good use my theoretical knowledge of navigation.

At Croydon I was rather disappointed to discover that I was to fly to Cologne in the huge, lumbering Short 'Syrinx', a remarkably ugly landplane derivative of the Kent flying boat, with four Jupiter engines. By dint of map reading as far as the Belgian coast, I was delighted to prove with my slide-rule that she could attain a groundspeed of 90 miles per hour downwind. Thereafter, without coastlines to help, my skill in fixing our position was insufficiently developed and I fell asleep.

My post at Cologne aerodrome amounted to little more than having the freedom of the tarmac and the offices in the terminal building, and running out to meet incoming airliners, the most common of which were the old corrugated aluminium Junkers 52s, and the most exciting the very advanced four-passenger monoplane Heinkel He70 'Blitz' which was capable of more than 220 mph. In the terminal there was a delightfully polyglot crowd of young clerks of both sexes from Air France, Sabena, KLM and Lufthansa, and life out of hours was full of fun. I fell in love in at least three languages. A merry bunch turned up on the tarmac to wave me away on my archaic old biplane when I boarded 'Syrinx' to return home, and I slept all the way.

2

Flight Cadet

ON THURSDAY 10TH SEPTEMBER 1936, ONE MONTH SHORT of my eighteenth birthday, I took my place as a Flight Cadet at the Royal Air Force College, Cranwell, housed in a splendid landmark building on a wide and windy, treeless Lincolnshire heath. The next morning at 08.30 an hour's foot drill marked the beginning of a regime of tight service discipline which, together with the liberal academic and cultural environment of the college, the diverse sporting activities, the strong unwritten etiquette that existed between the various Terms, and above all the flying, would infuse the superb *esprit de corps* of Cranwell into each one of us.

Within a very few days one had adjusted to the harsh discipline of the drill sergeant and a College Adjutant who, having played rugger for his country, expected us all to be fit enough to qualify too. The system expected us to be ready to do anything at any moment without notice, but I soon found that the regime was really far from being harsh if one was prepared to accept its outward forms. We flew; we were taught Service subjects; and under the aegis of Professor Rupert de la Bere - called formally 'The Prof' but inevitably nicknamed 'Bass' by generations of Flight Cadets - we were given a remarkably enjoyable education in the humanities. 'Bass' undoubtedly held more influence over us than anybody else at Cranwell. A cheerful old buffer who talked volubly but rarely to the point, he dominated to good effect the cultural side of the College, and I always thought of him as exemplifying a well-read, gentle but very persistent hunting parson straight out of Jane Austen.

Our Gods, of course, were the Flying Instructors. They had nothing

25

to do with our Collegiate life; their sole function was to teach us to fly; but the power of their personal example was immense. My first instructor was Flight Lieutenant L.W. Dickens – 'Uncle Louis' - of whom I stood in great awe and respect. He had an acid sense of humour which I appreciated, and was altogether a bigger man and a better flying instructor than might appear from my rather flippant diary.

Having been issued with Sidcot flying overalls, shiny brown leather helmets of standard sizes, leather gauntlets, a seat-pack parachute with harness, and goggles which, although functionally excellent, were of a pattern that had none of the glamorous appeal of those worn by the stars of flying movies, we started to fly exactly a week after arriving at the College. I was posted to 'B' Flight, which occupied a small black wooden hangar of wartime vintage towards the east end of the tarmac. The locker room where we stored all our gear was a dark little annex at the back. It was a very self-conscious Johnston who, kitted up, with his parachute pack bumping against the back of his knees, walked across the hangar floor to meet his instructor at the desk where the aircraft serviceability logs - Forms 700 - were kept. Outside, the Avro Tutors and Hawker Harts stood ranged on the tarmac in bright training-yellow livery. The Tutor on which we began was a single bay biplane with a 215 HP Lynx engine. The instructor occupied the front cockpit; the pupil occupied the duplicated cockpit behind him. By all accounts a 'Gentleman's aeroplane' not only very safe but a delight to handle, she seemed to me on that first morning to be full of menace.

My first flight with Dickens lasted just over half an hour. After flying around pointing out significant landmarks he demonstrated the effects of ailerons, rudder, and elevators and how to keep an aeroplane in level flight. Then he handed control over to me. I was surprised to discover how light a touch was needed on the controls, but got devilishly confused, giving her rudder when ailerons were needed, and generally muddling up in three dimensions. My concentration was so great that I lost my bearings completely. Nevertheless Dickens seemed fairly pleased, and I thoroughly enjoyed my little trip.

On the next day we were able to fly again though it was rotten weather for tyros; there was no horizon of any kind - nothing but lanes of cotton wool with curling alleyways between cloud masses. In the morning I was made to climb, stall and glide. At lunch I discovered that some chaps had not even started straight and level flying, and their conclusion was that I must have a decent instructor. By the afternoon flying period the visibility was lousy everywhere and I found it was really difficult to keep the machine in any position at all. There was literally nothing to go by; the ground was more often than not invisible. Before we landed Dickens demonstrated a spin which I very much enjoyed.

The visibility was considerably better for my next flight which was quite eventful. I was not able to hear much of what Dickens said. I did a little flying straight, fairly decently despite a slight tendency to bumpiness. Then Dickens demonstrated a landing while I followed him with my hand on the controls. He made me take the machine off. I have no clear recollection of what happened because I was so engrossed in the job, but I think that I bounced considerably. In making sure of not stalling her in the climb-out I nearly hit some houses!

Unfortunately my earphones came adrift just before I opened her up, so that Dickens was talking down his trumpet to no effect. His fury was awful to behold when, after he had talked for three minutes, I told him I hadn't heard a word. That settled, he put the machine into position at 300 feet and told me to land it. I throttled down and brought her to earth. I don't think it was too bad. My fault lay in not pulling the stick fully back, so that I did a two-point landing. Again, I was too engrossed in the job to remember the details.

On my next flight I was put onto doing medium and gliding turns with landings and take-offs. I took off, did a circuit, and landed, albeit pretty lousily, without any help from Dickens. He seemed devilishly bucked and said "Lord, man, we'll have to concentrate on low flying and spinning. Why, you are pretty well ready to go solo." But my self-esteem was wholly deflated next day, when it was foul up, with no visibility at all. As I kept swinging all over the place, Dickens said, "Fix your nose on a cloud or something." All very well, but there was nothing to fix the thing on.

I did my best to check by the turn indicator. Everything went wrong. I held the stick hard enough to crush it. My take-offs were clumsy. Once after gaining height I adjusted the mixture control instead of the throttle. My turns were pretty grim and my landings unmentionable - I pump-handled the stick fiendishly and flattened out several times before stalling five feet up. It was awful.

After gyrating about in the dim murk I became hopelessly confused and tried to land on the wrong aerodrome. Naturally while I was trying to spot the damned field through a real pea soup my flying suffered like blazes. Dickens was very brusque and sardonic, especially when I told him I that I had been going for the wrong field.

So the pattern of learning continued; one day I was quite good and above myself with joy, the next worse than a clown on a roundabout and down in the very slough of despond. I was terribly anxious to get on; and when, rarely, Dickens congratulated me I really felt life was worth living. But when I felt I had made an inane hash of things I wanted to kick myself again and again. I moved on to spinning and recovery from spins, low flying, and then did a loop.

On 1st October the great crisis came and was tamely over. I was flying fairly well. I managed a really good landing. "If you can do that again, I'll let you go solo tomorrow," said Dickens. I managed even better the next time. "Look here, there's time enough now for you to do a test if I can find another instructor," he said and off he went to get one.

He managed to get Sergeant Scragg.[1] I went up, did some low flying and spinning, and made two landings. The second time I landed near to the hangars. "Right," said Scragg, "Now go round again exactly as you did then. Taxi well over the aerodrome so that you will get plenty of wind, and look out for other aircraft. If you have any doubts about how you're going to land, open up and go round again."

I wondered why the hell he was saying all this. Then, when he started to climb out, I realised what he meant. I was to go solo!

But I had to wait while they got various papers and forms for me to sign. It was then that I felt devilishly afraid. I was shaking all over: there was a sick feeling in the pit of my stomach. The airman in

---

[1] Later, Air Vice Marshal Colin Scragg

attendance, however, was very encouraging: "Not many Cadets crash on their first solo."

After an age formalities were completed. As I taxied out, my concentration on the job became so fierce that I lost all feeling of nerves. Without even wishing myself luck, I opened the throttle and shoved the stick forward for a decent take-off. The only sensation I had was when I was about ten feet up: "By Gad," I thought, "this is really marvellous. Well, I'm up and I've got to get down, but who cares a fig?"

Round I went rather unsteadily, and before I could feel any sensation at all I had landed and was taxi-ing back. The riggers came out to my wingtips. I saw a group of instructors standing outside the hangar watching me. I taxied too fast, making the airmen at the wingtips run. They signalled me to stop. Unthinking, I put on the brakes hard. The kite all but nosed over and the tail came down again with a colossal bump. I had done my first solo! I was almost delirious with joy.

"Quite a nice solo Johnston," said Dickens. "A very creditable circuit and landing. But, my God, if I find you putting that bloody brake on again I'll ground you for a week. How many times have I told you it is only to be used for parking?"

I didn't give a damn. After five and a half hours dual exactly, I had been the second in my Term to go solo. I raced back to the College and told everybody. That night I was a little tin hero.

Of course the reaction set in the next day. We were doing right-hand circuits. My turns were execrable, almost no bank at all. My landings were bloody - straight into the ground. And my take-offs were unmentionable. Dickens was furious, absolutely livid. He cursed like blazes. In the end he sent me up for two solo circuits, hoping that the fear of sudden death would make me do a reasonable circuit and a fair landing. It worked. In the afternoon I went up with him again and behaved fairly moderately.

I did another twenty-five minutes solo after that - vertical turns and so on. It was grand to be alone in an aeroplane; I could just do what I bloody well liked: vicious turns, heartrending sideslips, screaming dives, frightful yaws and furious climbs at 43.6 mph with the nose hanging up on a cloud. I noticed that, as usual when I'm deliriously happy, I took spontaneously to thanking God for letting me go solo so soon and thus experiencing yet another new sensation before my life should come to an end. 'It is strange how in certain emotional conditions you feel you have to thank someone for something,' I wrote.

Barely a week later we First Termers had our first brush with the Grim Reaper. Flt Lieut Baines came in half an hour late for his lecture looking rather white about the gills. He was unusually subdued. During the period he told us about a crash. According to him our Under-Officer, Burton, was part of a formation in a Fury which collided with a Hart flown by Flt Lieut Bartlett. Both Bartlett and Burton bailed out, but Bartlett pulled his ripcord too soon and got caught up in the tail assembly. He was killed. The poor man was married. Most of us were more affected than we cared to admit; we were all outwardly rather callous. Barnard [2] and Co. ragged me about it, saying that it would be my turn next. In my cowardly soul I prayed that my end would be quick, nay immediate, and completely unexpected. I was more than a little bit upset by this affair, for I had an all too fertile imagination which many others lacked.

Dickens was away for the next session so I put in two circuits with Flt Lieut Sweeney, who was most mild by comparison. He even went so far as to say 'not bad' after one of my landings.

When I next went up with Uncle Louis I had control for only ten minutes, and for the remainder of the half hour he chucked me about in spins, rolls, loops, rolls off loops, stalled turns and falling leafs. It made life worth living.

On my way back from the gym that evening I stopped awhile to watch the night flying in progress. I found it all rather romantic. The black blanket of the night was lit up in patches by the smoky yellow flicker of the kerosene flares. In the circles of ghostly light small indistinct figures of aircraftmen could be discerned. Around the taxi-ing post stood the waiting pilots in flying clothes, looking very spectral in the dim, unearthly green light. Somewhere in the mysterious silence of

---

[2] Later, Air Commodore J.O. Barnard

the void there was an aeroplane; its engine and its wires, seemingly far away from its fast-moving lights, made a mysterious noise suggestive of plaintive hopelessness.

One day, flying solo, I tried a loop (quite decently) before settling down to the landings and take-offs for which the flight was authorised. The wind was coming from the southwest, which meant landing diagonally across East Camp and into the narrow width of the aerodrome.

I was put off by having to glide in over the camp, and after a couple of fast, bad landings (ballooned like hell) I got thoroughly rattled. I started coming in across the aerodrome, gliding downwind from the middle and doing a steep 180 degree turn into wind at about 300 feet, with the consequence that I hardly came out of the turn before I hit the ground fast and all askew. I did some terrible landings.

The more I did, the more rattled I got and the more I splitarsed. To crown all, when I came in I taxied right up to the petrol dump, which was verboten to us. Dickens came at me in livid fury. In all his experience as an instructor he had never seen such a disgraceful exhibition of thoroughly bad flying. I oughtn't to be alive. He had been expecting me to spin into the ground at any moment. And why the hell had I taxied up to the dump in contravention of all orders? He threatened to have me up before the Chief Flying Instructor (C.F.I.) if I didn't shake my ideas up pretty quickly.

He seemed to think I had been trying to be funny. He was quite wrong. I was thoroughly rattled and I had been trying to conquer myself. I had to throttle on at the last minute and go around again at least three times.

Later on I met the F/Sgt. He also said I was bloody lucky to be alive. By all the laws of flying I ought to have been lying dead under the ground. So I seemed to be pretty unpopular. I felt terribly down in the dumps and very shaken up. In retrospect, with many years of flying under my belt (including not a little experience as a Flying Instructor), I am somewhat critical of Dickens' reaction.

In those days we were taught to do a gliding approach from 1,000 feet starting just downwind of the landing area and heading at ninety degrees across the wind direction. This was to enable one to judge one's final turn into wind at the right height, about 500 feet, so as to make a straight glide onto the chosen landing spot. On this particular occasion I became disoriented because the wind was diagonally across the narrow part of the aerodrome. The crosswind glide was taking me away from the aerodrome boundary, and on the final glide I was not only overflying a heavily built-up camp but also converging at 45 degrees on the built-up edge of the aerodrome. It was really a situation outside my experience and beyond my ability, and in trying to resolve it I got more and more rattled.

Dickens ought to have explored the reasons for my crass performance so as to guide me for the future. I was, however, a young man who always walked his own path, and this perhaps gave people the impression that I was overconfident. Dickens certainly jumped to the conclusion that my behaviour was a simple case of showing off. It wasn't. I really was in trouble; but I was too diffident to tell him so.

The technique for forced landings played a very important part in our basic flying training. If you were flying very low, there was no alternative to landing straight ahead if your engine stopped. Otherwise, you chose the most suitable field immediately to windward and descended in a series of S-turns, always keeping the field in sight, and so judging the turns that you straightened out for a final glide into wind over the hedge to land in the best position.

There were half a dozen selected fields in the neighbourhood of Cranwell where we practised this; it was always an exercise that I enjoyed, particularly as you could embroider the turns with steep inward sideslips to lose height rapidly, and the final glide with rakish swishtailing to kill surplus speed. As my one great fear was stalling, I tended to stuff the stick well forward during gliding turns, thus coming over the hedge far too fast, and as often as not having to go round again.

When Uncle Louis went on leave I went up with a new instructor, Flt Lieut Rhys. 'He's a decent sort of fellow,' I wrote; 'very mild after L.W.D. and he takes a great deal of trouble over explaining your faults. Dickens doesn't; he makes you explain the remedies yourself. But I found Rhys was awfully nervous; he was always grabbing the stick out of my hand.'

The next time I really frightened myself was when I did a terminal velocity dive. It was most nerve-racking. On a beautiful morning Uncle Louis told me to go up to 4,000 feet and do some loops and spins. After half a dozen loops I thought I would try a flick roll, so I shoved the nose down, brought it up at 120 mph and rammed the stick hard over. Lord knows what happened.

Things whirled about and I got thoroughly befogged. I glanced at the airspeed indicator: it had passed 160 and was half way round the clock again. There was a hell of a row. Very gingerly I eased the stick back. I was glad to get her out of the dive, for my heart was in my mouth. I was expecting the wings to come off at any moment. In fact I had my hand on my harness clip, ready to loose it for a jump. Starting at 5,000 feet I lost 2,500. Of course I had forgotten about easing back the throttle and had the engine on at full revs all the time.

That was my last flight before the end of term. By the time we dispersed, we were a very different bunch from the anonymous lot who had been brought in RAF lorries from Sleaford railway station to the College merely three months before. Tony Major had become one of my two closest friends. It was he who sought me out, and I always felt rather paternal towards him. Intellectually we shared many interests.

Slight of build, red-headed, almost effeminate, he was great fun. At first I though him almost childish and, like a child, self-willed. Despite being a Wykehamist he had no 'side' at all. Always laughingly good-tempered - except that when in his cups he became bellicose - he seemed to me to be incompetent at most things except soccer, tennis and cross-country running, but his courage was like steel.

After a refreshing Christmas break, we all reconvened cheerfully at Cranwell. Tony arrived loquaciously tight, boasting that he had written off two cars during his leave. Flying started as soon as the fog cleared. Uncle Louis was in grand form. When I did a very splitarse forced landing - a steep turn into wind round a farmhouse at 100 feet - all he said was "Damn' lucky we had brakes or we would have hit that wall hard. And I'm sure I never taught you that method of splitarsing in!"

33

We went high and spun. Then we went down for a spot of low flying. I was thoroughly enjoying it when Louis suddenly cut the engine at 50 feet. My mind went blank. I felt a tremor on the stick which woke me up just in time to stop us burying our nose in a ploughed field. When we returned to the aerodrome I barely avoided overshooting. Louis' only comment was, "My God: two square miles of aerodrome!"

Towards the end of January, Miley was the first of our Term to pile up. After a few landings at Brauncewell he decided to come back. Visibility was bad so he flew by compass and got quite lost. Eventually he decided to come down but overshot his field and, being in a bit of a flap, didn't put on engine. He touched down, saw he was too near the windward hedge and braked. Unfortunately he skidded on the muddy ground, hit the hedge a wallop and went gracefully over on his back. It must have shaken him a bit, for, when he realised where the world was, he unfastened his harness and landed with a crack on his head on a road. Soon he was the centre of a large crowd.

Two of our lot lost themselves a few days later. I thought ground visibility was pretty poor, but certainly not bad enough to get lost in. One was Peter Cribb who ended up at Peterborough. The other was S.N. Goyal. He flew downwind of the aerodrome and ended up over Boston. He didn't have the slightest idea where he was so he came down in a field by the main road.

At the beginning of February there were two crashes, both advanced Training Squadron machines, a Fury and an Audax. The Audax undershot one of the fields, hit the leeward hedge, rolled a couple of times and wrote itself right off. No one was hurt.

It was now time to begin to learn instrument flying. My first exercise was 40 minutes with Sgt Simons. It was a bind. It was no fun at all watching obdurate needles and liquids, trying to keep things in their appointed places. Moreover I could have sworn that I was doing a steep turn, a spin, a slow roll or a bunt: but no, a surreptitious peep under the edge of the hood showed I was more or less straight and level.

On my last flight with Uncle Louis he was full of beans. His new posting as a Squadron Leader had arrived. "It's agin' the regulations to roll Tutors," he said when we had taken off, "but I'm going to teach you how to."

I had thought we were going to do some instrument flying, so foolishly I hadn't bothered to put on my harness at all tightly. Therefore I flapped about in the cockpit somewhat as we became inverted, and could hardly reach the controls. All the same, despite the terrifying experience of hanging several inches off my seat, I quite enjoyed the eight rolls we did. After that he let me have half an hour's solo, telling me to enjoy myself "But don't do any rolls." I really did like him despite his fearsomeness.

One day when most of us were out doing map-reading, Burt got hopelessly lost south of Grantham, so he decided to land. He picked a nice field, glided in and started to turn up wind at 100 feet over a ploughed field. Somehow or other he lost flying speed and stalled in on his port wing with a hell of a crash. The machine was broken up and he was pinned into the cockpit by the top wing which had folded back on him. He hit his face the deuce of a bang on the crash-pad. Result: a thoroughly bloody nose. It took five yokels to get him out. As he staggered bloody from the wreckage, a wench confronted him with a bit of leading edge and asked him to autograph it.

Standing on the tarmac waiting to fly one day, I saw Worcester, taxi-ing across wind, do a spectacular nose-over. He got hit by a gust and went right over on his back. I thought it highly amusing at the time. The Fourth Term gave us a further quota of excitement. Elsdon flying an Audax had engine failure near Northampton. He wrote his machine off in landing but wasn't hurt.

Before I went off on my first cross-country flight my new instructor, Flt Lieut Baines, gave me a Navigation test. Visibility was excellent but the wind was very strong. Before I had been flying for ten minutes I had him in a maniacal fury. I was an imbecile. Everything I could possibly do wrong I did. I got mixed up with the railways going out of Sleaford and nailed myself onto the wrong one, with the result that I kept edging off my course to such an extent that I got quite lost.

I couldn't fly straight. I got tied up in knots with holding my map, adjusting the compass verge ring, trying to find my card with the courses and times written on it, and waggling the throttle. Baines was in a fury with me: "I've flown with utter bloody nincompoops in my time, but never with a blasted God-forsaken imbecile!" and "If you can't take that ruddy grin off your face and if you can't keep on your bloody course, I'll give you 28 days' jankers." Finally, "Christ almighty, you imbecile, are you trying to be funny and doing this on purpose?"

Nevertheless I enjoyed myself but felt a fool afterwards. When the test was repeated a couple of days later with Flt Lieut Wightman, we had a very pleasant trip to North Coates and back over the Lincolnshire Wolds, rather reminiscent of the South Downs. Freddie was completely confidence-inspiring, so that I flew as well as ever I have done.

The next was quite an exciting day: Claude Wright and Tony Major both piled. Claude's was rather spectacular. He undershot the main aerodrome (the wind was from the east), chanced it and hit the tin shed in the hollow by the road - he hadn't seen it. He jammed on his engine as he bounced off the roof, but it was no good and he settled on top of it firmly and decidedly. In doing so he cut his tail clean off. I rumbled as low as I dared over the scene a couple of minutes later. It was a priceless sight. The Chief Flying Instructor landed immediately behind him. It must have been hilarious to see Claude standing precariously at attention on top of a corrugated iron shed before being handed down by the C.F.I.

Tony Major's pile was just bloody silly, sheer damn carelessness. He landed on Larch Plantation and before he stopped he took off again without looking ahead. In fact he buried his head in the cockpit to wind the trimwheel forward, then he looked back to see if it was OK behind. Just as he left the ground he hit one of the horse jumps in the far corner, knocking half his airscrew off. He said he didn't know that he had hit anything until Wightman told him afterwards. Anyway, everything vibrated heartily, so in a flap to gain plenty of height he did a partially stalled climb, flapped again (visions of tail falling off, wing flutter and God knows what!) and cut his motor. He stalled and just nosed in from about 50 feet. He made quite a mess of his engine and bent his top wing, but these Tutors must be strong.

I made my first solo cross-country to Bircham Newton on a perfect, albeit rather cold day; the wind was 16 mph from northeast, the visibility marvellous and the clouds broken cumulus at 2,500 feet. Freddy Wightman lent me the obligatory £1, and after reporting with Lambert to the Duty Pilot I took off at 14.20hrs. Old K3388 almost leapt into the sky. In a wide right-hand circuit I reached 2,000 feet and came over the aerodrome dead on my course, 119 degrees by compass.

I was soon over Sleaford. Then the deadly chocolate-brown of the Fen country slid slowly by until I reached Algakirk and soon after, Fosdyke. From then to King's Lynn I followed the edge of the Wash. To my left I could see some Harts from Sutton Bridge diving on targets on the sea.

Over King's Lynn I got a glimpse of Lambert circling onto his new course, but he had disappeared by the time I had circled round to get onto 064 degrees by compass. A few minutes later I passed over Sandringham, then I sighted Bircham Newton. By this time my feet and hands were numb. I circled once over the aerodrome and landed. It was just 15.00hrs. Lambert had come in about three minutes before me. We taxied up to the Duty Flight, ordered petrol and reported to the Duty Pilot.

After filling up it took us half an hour to start the wretched aeroplanes. The trouble was this: although the petrol cock in the rear cockpit was turned on, that in the vacant front one was still off. We live and learn. We left together at 15.40hrs. I did two circuits but Lambert only did one so he got away well before me. Just before King's Lynn, however, I ran into a heavy snowstorm. He went round it but I went through it, so we met just after King's Lynn and flew as far as Algakirk in formation. After that, since our courses seemed about 10 degrees different, we parted. We met again over Sleaford, put our noses down and raced for home. It was 16.30hrs when we landed.

The next pile up in our Term was a pukka one. Tony Payn undershot Barkston landing ground and throttled on too late to save his tail from hitting a tree. He careered along at 50 feet with no rudder control in a wide right-hand circuit and walloped into a bunch of trees. Luckily he hit the one big one in the plantation or he would have banged into the deck. I flew over the crash later: the machine was a frightful wreck. Tony was shaken up a lot. He was a gloriously sarcastic and pricelessly funny man who told lewd stories in a likeable way.

When Baines gave me my next check dual he was in a thoroughly benevolent mood, consequently I had a good time. The *pièce de résistance* was a couple of half rolls and a spell of inverted flying. It takes a bit of getting used to. I was hanging well out of the cockpit and couldn't see anything in the office and I was thoroughly uncomfortable, but it was wizard fun, though of course my handling of the aircraft was pretty rough. Later on, flying solo, I lost my prop as I finished my landing run on the forced landing field at Barkston. A solitary aeroplane flew over at 1,000 feet and joy of joys saw my frantic waving. It was Willis. He landed alongside me and we soon had my engine running, so I didn't have to walk back to Cranwell.

On my final flight with Baines he told me in measured calm tones that my flying was bad, I was careless, inaccurate and splitarse. Then he cut my engine at 1200 feet and I managed quite a creditable sideslip approach into a decent field. With my final landing on the aerodrome he was quite pleased: I touched down on three points after doing a steep sideslipping turn into wind. But he warned me not to do such split sideslip turns near the ground as my judgement was not perfect yet and if I tried it too often I might just put a wing into the ground. However, we parted friends. And that was the end of my Tutor phase.

As soon as we came back from the Easter Break in 1937 I started to fly the Hawker Hart, a two-seater tandem training version of the biplane day bomber. Powered by a Rolls Royce Kestrel IB engine of 525 hp it had a maximum speed of 165 mph and an altogether more exciting performance than the Tutor. Whereas the latter climbed to 5,000 feet in about six minutes, the Hart could reach 10,000 feet in only a few seconds longer. I was to discover that it was a superb aerobatic aircraft.

Not surprisingly it was a foul day for my first flight in a Hart with Flt Sergeant Simons as my instructor: visibility nil, cloud 800 feet. My being so high up under the wing in the front cockpit, plus the long sloping aspect of the nose and the lack of all but a formless grey pall in front of me combined to make me hopelessly confused. I found the take-off a bit tricky. On opening the throttle she swung sharply to the right, requiring a strong application of left rudder to keep straight, but as the torque started working you had to stand really hard on the right rudder. At the end of a circuit, you first wound the radiator in, then you throttled down, wound the trim wheel right back and let your speed drop to 75-80 mph. To keep a steady glide you had to shove like hell on the stick and keep it right forward. To break the glide you merely eased off pressure, but to hold the machine off you had to pull the stick back gently until she stalled, which she should do with wheels a couple of feet above the ground. As she dropped, you whipped the stick hard back into your tummy. If you touched your wheels before she stalled, you would bounce to the sky. You had to be on the alert all the time for dropping wings; if you stalled her too high, she was as likely as not to put a wing in.

Spinning was thoroughly enjoyable. Just before she stalled you kicked on full rudder and whipped the stick back. She reared up, toppled sideways onto her back, lazily dropped her nose and suddenly flashed round in a fast spin. It was rather grand. You got much more of a thrill low flying in Harts than in Tutors: there was more speed, more power, and you had a totally different outlook on the world, sitting perched up in the front cockpit.

I went solo on a Hart after 2 hours 50 minutes dual and a 25 minute test. Wightman tested me on a lovely day with woolly clouds at 2,500 feet. We took off and climbed through these and then I spun through a hole in them and dived to 1500 feet. After a few turns we went down for a spot of low flying. Then I did three landings.

"Do you think you could get round safely by yourself?"

"Yes, sir."

"All right, then off you go."

So I signed Form 700, loaded ballast and popped off. In my anxiety to do a perfect landing I touched my wheels slightly, too soon; but I got down decently.

Four days later, disaster struck. On Saturday evening Major and I decided to go and see a film in Nottingham, but when we arrived there we went on a pub crawl. He made a bit of a fool of himself in the bar of the Black Boy, and a Flight Lieutenant who recognised us told us courteously but firmly to be careful and behave ourselves. This only made Major drink more. On Monday the whole might of the law was brought to bear on us and we were both rusticated for one term for being out of bounds (Nottingham), for being in the bar of the Black Boy (forbidden) and for being drunk.

I was devastated. The likelihood of so severe a punishment had never occurred to me. I went straight home to Jess Scott, whose sole ironical comment on the incident was that the RAF must be losing its sense of proportion.

Needing space and solitude I holed up in the lovely country house of Mrs Richmond, the widow of the Chief Designer of R101. She treated me with great kindness and sympathy. My Guardian wrote me a thunderous letter of disapproval from India. He got in touch with Capt. A.G. Lamplugh who, with a much deeper appreciation of the needs of a lad not yet nineteen, arranged for me to do a navigation and engineering course at University College of Southampton.

I lived and studied in the Navigation School for a couple of months and enjoyed it hugely. Most of my fellow-students were Merchant Navy Officers of various ages who were studying for their Mates' or Masters' tickets, and I had the good fortune to share a cabin with a most engaging character called Percy Papps, small, jolly and quiet-mannered, a 'B' licence pilot who had just come back from fighting in Spain. He had flown Breguet two-seater bombers and Nieuport fighters. The only other aviator was Fisher, an RNVR man. The three of us reckoned that we were well able to hold our own as airmen against all the seamen.

Our instructors were qualified Extra Masters, breezy and enthusiastic men who bawled their lectures out as though on the bridge in a gale. It was all a very far cry from Cranwell where bored NCOs tried to keep us awake with rather poor dirty stories or supercilious Flight Lieutenants shot lines about flying. Conversation in the wardroom was always interesting, sane and surprisingly well-informed, and if the RAF was vulnerable to the seamen's charge that its navigation was rotten, the seamen were equally vulnerable to the bombs versus battleships argument. Living among grown men who had wide horizons did me a power of good.

At Jess Scott's invitation I joined the family at Mambeg on Garelochside for a couple of weeks holiday, and there fell in love with the girl who eventually became my wife - Isobelle Linck of Portincaple, over the hill on Loch Long.

Back at Cranwell in the middle of September I felt at first very lonely and depressed despite the friendly welcome I received from most of the College Officers. The real problem lay in breaking into the closed society of the new Term to which I was assigned while still living in my old quarters among my former and now senior colleagues whose daily life was henceforth remote from mine. My immediate neighbours, Jo Barnard, George Petre, Goyal, Johnnie Iremonger, Cruikshank and Ronnie Rotheram were kindness itself, but the rest of my entry very quickly drifted away. It took me something like three months to establish myself with the new lot.

Fortunately there was flying: 'Flying is GREAT!' I wrote a few days after my return. I had a new instructor, Flight Sergeant Drake, a nice man. He told me I was "inclined to be split" but let me go solo despite some grim landings on my first day. A few days later I had my first flight in an Audax. This machine was the Army Co-operation version of the Hart. The rear cockpit carried a gunner/bomb-aimer who sat facing aft on a small tipup seat; he was secured to the structure of the machine by a wire strop which clipped onto his parachute harness. When aiming bombs he lay prone with his head beneath the pilot's cockpit, looking through a transparent panel in the bottom of the fuselage.

The Audax was marginally faster than the Hart but did not climb so quickly. I took off on a bright anticyclonic day with a fair amount of haze. The machine seemed very light compared with a Hart, for it was off the ground in no time; but as the throttle was gated to limit the engine to do no more than 2,000 rpm on the level, it climbed rather slowly. Up at 6,000 feet the ground haze formed a brown, perfectly circular horizon with a shallow belt of white knobbly cumulus far to the south. I did a hectic loop (I felt a bit nervous), then another, and

41

another. Seeing a Hart roll a couple of thousand feet below me, I half-heartedly went over onto my side and then came up again: I hadn't the guts to go right round. I stall-turned down a couple of thousand feet and finished with a spin to 2,000.

By that time I was feeling quite delirious, for the Audax was answering wonderfully to the controls. She seemed as light as a feather. I flung a half roll off the top of a loop - I was a bit confused but we got over all right, though I didn't get the stick anything like far enough forward. The next one was much worse: I waggled the stick in all directions before coming out, and a lot of water splashed out of the radiator. The third one was fairly satisfactory. After that I gyrated towards Larch Plantation in a series of stall-turns right onto my back, and had a shot at forced landings. After the screaming dives I had been doing, after all the rush and roar of exhilarating aerobatics, I found it jolly difficult to glide in not too fast, with the result that I floated for miles and had to go round again. The controls of the Audax were wonderfully light on the glide. After a third forced landing I had to return to base, feeling really great. I had not enjoyed myself so much for ages. It was the first time I had tried playing around in a service type; an utterly new and wonderful experience.

Just before my nineteenth birthday I went to London to sit the examinations for the civil Second Class air navigation certificate. The written papers were quite pleasant but I made a mess of the plotting work and I simply could not cope with the Morse flashing - this was ever to be a weakness of mine. While I was away Claude Wright had his second pile-up; he landed an Audax too close to the hangars, braked harshly and nosed over. He was knocked out for about ten seconds.

My next new experience, on 9th November, was a height test. I climbed up to 15,000 feet in 15 minutes in Hart K6445. It was bitterly cold. I had no ill effects other than feeling a bit short of breath and slightly light-headed and lethargic. I put the Hart into a terminal velocity dive down to 7,000 feet, reaching about 280 mph. It seemed a colossal speed; the wires shrieked, my head was nearly blasted off by the slipstream, and the controls went iron-stiff. My ears were only slightly affected.

Flt Lieut Hunter, the Flight Commander, took me up on a navigation test, and I, the so-called King Navigator, couldn't find Castle Bromwich! It was very nice weather at Cranwell, but the further we went the thicker it became until, when I crossed the railway within one and a half miles of Loughborough, I couldn't see the place at all, even though we were down to 800 feet. When I said we were over Atherstone we were actually over Coalville. I never did find Castle Bromwich. Although I found our way back to Cranwell all right, I made a big enough hash of things to fail the test. The King Navigator took no small amount of ribbing after that.

Whenever I flew solo, whatever my briefed task, my immediate desire was to cavort among the clouds. Before aerobatting I would make a steep turn to the right to see that all was clear below me. As the wings tilted steeply down I brought the stick hard back; I was pressed tightly into my seat; and the horizon, a wild chiaroscuro, poured like a waterfall vertically between my centre-section struts. Then I pushed the aircraft level with the nose down. My eye glanced from the airspeed indicator to the little black cloud on which I decided to align a roll, and back again; and when the needle flickered on 140 mph I eased the stick slightly back until the cloud stood between the hoods of the two air intakes. With sybaritic laziness we toppled over to the right.

At first the cloud tried to go to the right, too, because of aileron drag, but I brought it back with a quick jab of bottom rudder. In measure as we slid over, the cloud tried to go off to the left; I followed it with top rudder. Suddenly strife took languor's place; as we passed the vertical I was thrown heavily onto my tight harness, I had to force my feet to stay on the rudder bar, I had to fight the stick forward with all my confused strength as the nose did its best to drop below the inverted horizon.

Grimly I forced the cloud back to its proper position. The engine, starved of fuel, spluttered and died; a plume of pulverised petrol streamed back out of the gravity vent, and hot water from the header outlet splashed onto the windscreen. I pressed the stick harder over to the right and we wallowed round with the speed of an unstable log in a pond. To keep the cloud where it should be I had to kick on full top rudder. The horizon screwed crazily vertical, but I had eyes and confused thought for nothing but that cloud which kept on sliding jerkily away from the hoods of the intakes. Then for a last hectic second we hurtled sideways into the teeth of the wind: I yawed and centralised all the controls, and we were floating down on whistling wings for an instant until the engine caught again. This sort of thing really did blow the stuffiness of College routine out of one's hair.

I was beginning tentatively to form friendships in my 'new' term. Jerry Hayter and I enjoyed long conversations about cabbages and kings and things; he had a well-developed, iconoclastic mind. There was also Michael Savage, our No 1 intellectual. He had the new cult of talking intellectually about sex while really having no apparent sexuality. He and I and Tony Major were persuaded by 'Bass' to undertake the compilation of an anthology of the poetry of flight for publication.

Nigel van Someren, a taciturn man, came to me one evening with the draft of a play about Warren Hastings that he had written, and asked me to give an opinion. I thought it was patchy; it lacked dramatic unity; it lacked feeling; and though the material was there for clashes and climaxes he hadn't developed them sufficiently. Solemnly he said he would fill it out, round off the corners and rewrite the climax. It was the beginning of a fascinating experience in amateur theatricals and a warm friendship with a man of strangely reserved character. He and Tony and I were to form a triumvirate of close friends. Both of them were fated to die young.

Back from Christmas leave I took the first opportunity to do some aerial cavorting in a Hart. While trying a half-roll off a loop I stalled upside down and lost my prop at 2,500 feet. Automatically I got her pointing straight at the ground. I remember asking myself if there was time to turn to gravity feed - I ought to have done it straight away. I moved the throttle. After what seemed like an eternity the engine burst into life. I pulled out at 200 mph at roughly 1,000 feet. If the engine hadn't caught I suppose I would have switched over to gravity and waited till I was practically on the deck: then I would have been in the soup. I would never have had the slightest chance of finding where the

44

wind was and I would have had to park down where the gods put me. This sort of thing was fun indeed!

One day towards the end of January five of us in Harts and Audaxes congregated on Melbourne landing ground, used for practising forced landings, and tried an unauthorised formation take-off. It was pretty appalling. When the five of us got to 3,000 feet we broke off and had a quarter of an hour's hectic dog-fighting. Why nobody collided I don't quite know. It was a great thrill to stall-turn onto an aeroplane and hold him in your sights for a few seconds.

After a while Henderson got on my tail and stayed there. Do what I would, I couldn't shake him off. There were too many aeroplanes about for me to do any aerobatics, but I did all forms of tight turns, figures of eight, diving turns and oblique loops until my right arm was nearly dropping off with the effort of shoving the stick about. Finally I managed to shake him off by doing a fast vertical aileron turn.

My next new experience was night flying. I only did three circuits that night. It was very dark. We were swimming in the blackest depths of the ocean, it seemed, with only the vagueness of something less opaque above, and below us only occasional bright pinpoints shining out of the infinite pit. In a steep turn one looked along the dim line of a wing past the interplane struts, more imagined than seen, into lightless nothing. When I looked back to the aerodrome I could see seven atom-sized holes of light in the shape of a 'T'. As we motored in a wide arc towards the flare path we passed over the camp, a dazzling, unreal glitter of thousands of pinpoints of light.

Our flying training continued in a steady routine of night flying, instrument flying, cross-country trips and, for me at least, lots and lots of aerobatics, and officially at last, formation flying. I went up with the Adjutant, Flt Lieut Stainthorpe. We took off in formation with Flt Lieut Sweeney and Hallifax. At 500 feet we broke out of the haze into dazzling blueness. We climbed to 3,000 feet where I took over control and followed Hallifax. For half an hour I had eyes for nothing but his Hart, a span away from me, sliding and bouncing about. At the end of that time, when I was beginning to feel the strain somewhat, Sweeney signalled me ahead to take the lead.

For the next half hour I cruised gracefully up and down Ermine Street at 3,000 feet and 100 mph in a yellow aeroplane sandwiched between immeasurable slabs of blue and white. Only very dimly through the bleach-white ground fog could we see the odd wisps of ground, dark and indistinct. I sang loudly and drank in the wide austerity of my world, but all too soon it was time to go in and land. We broke formation: the other machine reared up like a shot tiger, fell on one wing, and in a second was far away without motion.

"May I do a couple of rolls before we go down, sir?" I asked.

"All right. Now do a roll to the right."

That done, "Now roll off the top of a loop."

I put the nose down and watched the airspeed indicator - 130, 140, 150, 160 mph. Gently I eased the stick back. As we screamed up in a half loop the blue sky flickered grey for a second. I threw my head back and watched the horizon coming over. Just when it lay along the leading edge of the centre section I moved the control column smoothly forward and across to the right, with a touch of right rudder. The flat horizon did a crazy half cartwheel. So simple, so exhilarating. Then down onto the aerodrome in a soft glide.

On a bright March day curtained by lowish clouds that hung over us in tints of white and yellow and grey, Jerry Hayter and I, solo in Audaxes, flew in a formation of three led by Flt Lieut Hunter. I did my first take off and landing in formation. All the time I was concentrating tensely on Hunter's head and the tailplane of his Hart, while automatically I kept a fluid motion of rudder, stick and throttle. I caught brief glimpses, like stroboscopic flashes, of a glorious background whenever I looked down tilted wings in a turn. The clouds were bright and tufty: hillocks, mushrooms, heads of strange animals. Against this supremely lovely backdrop (which, seen in such fleeting glances, never became a surfeit) one salient thing stood out: the leading aeroplane. The whole scene was made so much more beautiful by the instant visions seen in holes, patches of the small earth 5,000 feet below: white threads that were roads, cluttered with minute dots that went to form towns and villages. When you are on the outside of a turn you seem to be looking down through a tube.

We had by now finished selecting material for our anthology which was to be published as *Icarus* by Macmillan. I had also been pulled onto the Editorial committee of the College Journal. Even more onerous, 'Van' having completed his play *Reward for Service* had set about producing it with me playing the leading part of Warren Hastings. The play was a great success when it was performed on three nights towards the end of term. The other principal roles were played by Phillip Cook, Bobby Morgan, Jerry Hayter and Tony Major. Bobby, whom I already knew well as a fellow member of the fencing team, was a very remarkable junior termer, another of these tall, handsome and gifted people whom the gods love. He, too, was to die young.

I went to Scotland for the Easter break and spent the long weekend with the Lincks of Portincaple before going off by myself to do some serious hill walking in the Braes of Balqhuidder. Isobelle and I were quite deliriously happy and came to an understanding.

At the end of April 1938 I returned to Cranwell and put up my pilot's wings on my tunic. I now had 107 hours in my log book and my proficiency as a Hart pilot was officially 'Average'. We transferred to the Advanced Training Squadron, D Flight, under Flt Lieut White. Here we learned how to drop bombs, take aerial photographs and aim guns.

The first time I flew in the back cockpit of an Audax I very much enjoyed it, though it was damnably uncomfortable lying curled up on the floor with my face poking through the bombing trap into the scorching blast from the radiator. Aitkens was piloting me. Taking off was most intriguing: you looked back and saw the ground at a quite absurd angle. The exercise was to find windspeed and direction at 6,000 feet using the drift-sight, by the three-course and the ninety degree methods.

After I had finished finding WS&D there was just time for Aitkens to try a few aerobatics. I tied myself in and he looped. It was extraordinary. Of course, looking backwards one saw things happening in quite the reverse way. Then he half-rolled off the top twice but that, strangely enough, was quite tame.

The next time I was up with him in an Audax finding wind it was my turn to give him a shaking before we started work. Apart from ordinary rolls I did a terrific rocket loop and also a simply stupendous vertical upward roll. While wind-finding it was marvellous just floating along at 6,000 feet in unlimited visibility. On our last leg of the three-course run we were over Lincoln and I could see Boston, and away beyond Hull. The coast was fringed with a thin roll of cumulus at about 2,000 feet. Up where we were it was perfectly calm, but when I came down to 1,000 feet to join the circuit it was hellishly bumpy.

Actually, at 1,000 feet I didn't believe my altimeter, it seemed so low. We could see all the contours and we seemed only a couple of hundred feet above the church-towers.

Early in May seven Hawker Hectors arrived in the Flight. One morning I flew a Hector and a Fury, each for the first time. The Hector was an advanced development of the Hart for Army Co-operation. Its engine was the 805 HP Napier Dagger IIIMS which gave it a maximum speed of 187 mph. Heavier than the Hart, its centre of gravity was further forward, and to compensate for this the sweep-back characteristic of the other Hart variants was abolished.

The Fury, of course, had the appearance of the Hart family but was slightly smaller and had a Kestrel IIS engine of 525 HP. The standard single-seater fighter of the day, she had a top speed of 207 mph, a ceiling of 28,000 feet, and could climb to 10,000 feet in four and a half minutes. Light and sensitive on the controls and beautifully balanced, she was probably the finest aerobatic biplane ever designed. She was a magnificent little toy, as light as thistledown.

The rudder especially was very sensitive, as I found to my cost during landing and take off, when I kept on over-correcting. I did three landings and had no time but to try some phenomenal zooms and a few very steep turns, on which she handled like a pixie and nearly blacked me out. I longed to get a chance of aerobatting one.

Immediately after this I went up in a Hector, which somehow left more of an impression on me. I used no rudder bias on the first take-off, and she swung dreadfully - the opposite way to an Audax. But her climb was terrific; it seemed even steeper and faster than a Fury's. She was, however, horribly heavy on the controls, and a changeover from a steep turn to starboard to one to port needed every bit of strength I had got. These Hectors cruised at quite a high speed, round about 160 mph, and to fly them round the circuit at the regulation 110 mph necessitated throttling right back. They would not decelerate for love or money and their landing run seemed very long. But being so heavy, when you touched down, even with your wheels alone, they stayed down; so I managed three magnificent landings.

That afternoon Dennis Mitchell had a marvellous escape. He was in a Fury taking off in formation with another Fury and an Audax. Just as the machine became airborne, he somehow swerved into the leader's slipstream and dropped a wing onto the ground, with the result that he cartwheeled a couple of times and finished in a cloud of dust, completely written off. Miraculously he wasn't hurt and he went about quite cheerfully. It was a nasty pile and he was very lucky to get away with it.

A week later Michael Savage provided the next nine-days' wonder. He set off on a night cross-country to Scampton, lost himself, and, after two abortive attempts at landing using his wingtip flares, bailed out. Once his parachute had opened he enjoyed his descent very much. In fact he was in the middle of examining the aesthetics of floating in utter darkness when he hit the deck with a colossal thud with his legs peacefully crossed.

When next I flew a Fury I aerobatted it and found it a marvellously light little toy. Then I went on to do some air-to-ground gunnery in her. It was stupendous (though my results were awful). Those climbing turns off the ground after firing were shattering. Each time I came out right on my back dead over the target at 1,000 feet and had to half-roll level. It was really exhilarating. After my last shoot I held her down at about 50 feet and put her in a tight turn, with the somewhat startling result that I blacked out for a moment or two.

George Petre flew up from Armament Practice Camp at Sutton Bridge one afternoon and I had a long chat with him. He told me that Bobbie Halliwell had made a forced-landing on the mud flats at Sutton bridge and had turned over; Brian Kingcome had piled a Fury in a ploughed field; and Charles Newman had piled an Audax on the aerodrome.

49

My Entry had by now been reduced by a quarter of its original strength, and in the matter of crashes, too, had been pretty hectic: Burt, Claude Wright, Romer, Newman, Payne, Mitchell, Halliwell, Savage, Miley, Murphy, Lambert, Major had each written off one aeroplane.

The Senior Term - my old entry - returned from practice camp feeling very full of themselves, and my corridor came alive again. The last few days of term were lived in an alcoholic haze and the Passing out Parade was carried out, as usual, on automatic pilot. As soon as we were free I high-tailed it to Scotland. When I returned to Cranwell from our Scottish paradise at the end of September it was to find that the world was on the edge of an abyss. On the first night back we had a practice blackout. On September 26th I wrote:

'The world is on the edge of breaking down. This Czechoslovakia business looks like bringing the end of everything. Groundlessly, perhaps, I remain optimistic: one must, in the face of all the pessimists. War! It is unthinkable. And yet hourly people talk about it calmly enough. In this country, people talk of nothing else, and there seems to be a quiet willingness to fight Hitler if he annexes Czechoslovakia.

'We here at Cranwell drift along on our gentle way, comparatively unaffected by all the turmoil, save where we argue hotly in the Mess and avidly listen to the news on the radio. What do we want? Our rational selves hope that the peace will be kept; and yet at the back of our minds something whispers that war would be thrilling, exciting, good fun; it would give us a purpose, it would make our lives full of hectic thought and action and experience. Yes, perhaps lasting peace will never come to mankind until it is as purposeful and as thrilling as war.'

The impossible did happen. War was postponed. I for one thought that the day might yet come when we would wish that we had fought Hitler then.

More Fury flying: I flew without a helmet so that I could be the more in unity with the power of the machine, visually, tactilely and aurally overwhelmed. I went up to 4,000 feet and wrote my exultation in colossal sweeps over the sky. First a lazy loop through 2,000 feet: the dark earth folded itself gently over my head, slid past my eyes and

50

away again. Then a climbing roll, my head thrown right back to watch the dignified revolution of the ground. And a full roll off the top of a loop, followed by a gentle dive out.

I remember the easy feeling of hanging upside down, and feelings of sudden pity for the crawling human beings so far above my head with their dull stability; and seeing a fully upturned aileron sliding past a large wood. After that I did a vertical half-roll and a loop out.

As the earth disappeared from sight I revolved up into the sky only knowing of my revolution by reference to the strange twisting of the skeins of cloud. I threw my head right back and saw the aerodrome just above my right shoulder. When I centralised and eased the stick back, I saw by glancing rapidly at each wing tip that we were coming out crookedly, so I ruddered the nose into the heart of a fast-moving railway station. Then two fast rolls with the nose pointing low under the horizon.

Gliding rolls always seemed to have something of a wild abandon about them; the earth, appearing to be measurably nearer, was always just in front of your head so that you felt you must brush it away with your hand.

At the end of October we sat our final exams; for me, they passed comfortably enough without my having to exert myself. Having expressed a preference for being posted to Flying Boats, General Reconnaissance or Hind day bombers in that order, I was delighted when I was told that I had been selected for Flying Boats. That meant three months at Thorney Island learning navigation, followed by three months conversion at Calshot before ever reaching a squadron.

At the end of the first week of November we trekked to Sutton Bridge, a one-eyed, windy, muddy hutted station on the edge of the Wash, for our final Armament Practice camp. 'It is distinctly below sea-level' I wrote. 'What a dim place.' On the afternoon of our arrival, while we were out on the sea wall having the range layout and signalling systems explained by the Armament Officer, we saw a shocking sight: a Blenheim on fire spinning down over the range. One parachute deployed before the machine hit the ground, cartwheeled and exploded in a colossal burst of flame and smoke at least 200 feet high.

We spent four weeks at Sutton Bridge doing nothing but fly or sit around waiting to fly. Hitherto our fixed front-gun work in Furies and our free-gunnery in Audaxes and Hectors had been carried out with camera guns, and our dummy bombing runs had been assessed by Camera Obscura. Now we were shooting live ammunition and dropping real practice bombs. It was a vivid, busy life. If flying was substituted for fishing or yachting or shooting, it had all the ingredients of a holiday.

One was awakened at 7.30 in the morning by the rumble of aero engines and their brief bursts of power, got up at 8, had breakfast and prepared leisurely to fly. When I was not flying, there was little to do except watch others flying. The tarmac was full of busy people filling aeroplanes, loading bombs and fixing guns. The Despatching Officer walked up and down with his board, and aeroplanes landed and took off with set purpose.

Latterly there was much fog and rain and cold to hamper flying. On a typical day, teamed up with Jack Holmes, I was awakened at 06.30. Looking sleepily out of my window I saw a bruised dawn and a clear atmosphere. I drank foul sweet tea, dressed quickly, and walked with him through the tear-making coldness of the morning to the locker room. My sidcot was clammy. We went to the plotting room and signed things. I collected a parachute and harness on the way to our aeroplane. After I had drop-tested the bombs Jack climbed in and started up the engine. While he warmed it up I checked the bomb sight and the computer and filled in various things on Form 3073. Then Martin Waddington, whose day it was to be Dispatcher, appeared all muffled up in the half-light, giving us thumbs up.

Off we went. As we climbed higher the ground looked queerly grey-brown. I found windspeed and direction and then dropped eight bombs one by one on North Range. Each white practice bomb would fall away in a clear curve of beauty, until in a short time it became a small speck of white moving with increasing apparent speed over the golden-brown sand. Is it going near the target? No, miles away. No, no, quite near...then it would vanish from sight. After a pause a solid puff of smoke would suddenly appear. "About 75 yards SE..." - then to Jack:

"Time and heading please." Hasty scribbling down of data on the Form 3073, and a rough plot of the fall.

It was good fun and the results, however bad, were strangely satisfying. A long curving flight over the serpentine creeks and the wrinkling, shallow sea to the next run-up; looking through the bomb-hatch I saw an infinite void, save when we turned across the rising sun: then there glowed a translucent sheen of wrinkled gold across the sea.

We flew back home in the brightness of the young sun. It was high day and there were many people about and the tarmac was buzzing with activity. Before going off to breakfast I discussed and analysed my results with F/Sgt Oatey. They were not good. After a much-needed meal I washed and changed, cleaned my Lewis gun, and joined the tarmac scorpions in the sun to make caustic remarks upon landing techniques. Then lunch and a couple of hours reading in the ante-room until it was time to leap into the air again, this time piloting. The sun was low behind a bank of clouds which hid it from the dark earth, but up in the air it was bright. I climbed to my bombing height in lazy sweeps; we moved without motion above a strange world wreathed in wisps of ground-mist.

One of Jack's bombs hit the edge of the target. I had a standing bet on with him, who would be the first to land a bomb through the hole in the middle of the target. As the dying light grew more golden, the land and sea became blacker until finally we couldn't see the target. So down I went in steep spirals with the aerodrome in front of my eyes; round in a low, fast circuit, and back to earth in a brisk, swishtail landing. Again we discussed results in the plotting office for nearly an hour. Jack's results were better than mine this time, and over a beer we disputed hotly whether this was because I was a better pilot or he a better bomb-aimer.

I finished with Cranwell on December 16th 1938. We passed out amid a welter of congratulations and advice from all and sundry. I was commissioned as a Pilot Officer the next day and went on leave until the middle of January, when I reported to the School of General Reconnaissance at Thorney Island.

3

Boat Ahoy

ALTHOUGH IT STILL HAD A GRASS AIRFIELD, THORNEY Island was a fine, modern station. Its spacious Officers Mess, nearly a mile from the main part of the station, was situated towards the southern tip of the island, close to the lovely old flint church by the hard on Thorney Creek. Two minutes' walk from the Mess, one was in a different century with nothing but the sound of the wind in the reeds, the lapping of the water and the calls of the marsh birds and waterfowl to disturb the eternal peace.

I was there in excellent company: Jerry Hayter and Jack Holmes were going on with me to flying boats: Hol Porteous, Ian McDonald and Hugh Garbett were going to Coastal landplanes. I enjoyed the practical application of all that I had learned theoretically at Southampton, but I found ground school infinitely boring. In addition to navigation theory and plotting, we studied ship recognition, Naval codes and ciphers, Fleet tactics, anti-submarine and anti-mine measures and weapons, and other such arcane subjects. What was much more fun were our visits to various naval Establishments, ships and submarines at Portsmouth and Portland.

We did about 65 hours flying as navigators, mostly over the sea out of sight of land, in the old Mark I Ansons. I was usually paired with Dick Furseman, a truly delightful character from the Aberdeen Highlands. We alternated as first and second navigator. The first navigator plotted and directed the pilot; the principle duty of the second was to handcrank the retraction and lowering of the undercarriage (a hundred and something turns in each case), but he did otherwise assist by taking drifts with the bombsight and bearings with the Observer's compass. While he sat up in the nose alongside the pilot, the lead navigator was stationed at the chart-table immediately behind the pilot, commanding an expansive view of the port wing and engine nacelle.

One of the great joys of plotting was that we still used the old, beautifully engraved, linen-backed Admiralty Charts. Behind the navigator was the wireless operator (W/Op). The starboard side of the cabin was comparatively open so that the crew could pass up and down in the performance of their several jobs.

The off-duty life of a young Officer was full of delights. We all had our cars. I bought a 14 foot clinker-built sailing dinghy which I kept at the hard and later in one of the creeks at Calshot. Jerry and Jack and I rode regularly on the South Downs at Singleton. Nigel van Someren was flying Hectors at Old Sarum so we often spent weekends together in various delectable places on the south coast, talking about literature and life and half seriously making plans to chuck the Air Force, buy a yacht and spend a couple of years sailing round the world.

On other weekends it was an easy drive to Tony Major's home in Kent where I formed a warm relationship with his bookish parents. Tony, always ready for a mad escapade, was now flying fighters. He pressed me to join him in the Land's End sports car trial at Easter, but Portincaple was a stronger magnet. It was in those days easy to drive up to London for theatre or opera or ballet and supper afterwards, and get back not too late to be fit for duty the next day.

Indeed, on more than one occasion I drove up to King's Cross on a Friday evening, parked my car and caught the Fort William sleeper which dropped me early in the morning at a halt a few hundred yards from Isobelle's home on Loch Long. Catching the night train at Helensburgh on Sunday I would be back in the mess for an early breakfast. That spring and early summer was indeed my Golden Age.

Eden nevertheless had its black holes. In February I learned that Peter Jameson had killed himself flying a Blenheim. He was a good pilot, a striking watercolourist and a grand type. In May I was deeply depressed by the death of Bobby Morgan in a collision in the air near Cranwell. We had been good friends despite the separation of our terms. He was a really fine boy, loved and admired by us all. A natural

56

King among men, 'he left an indelible mark, a faint vibration in the sea of time which will go on and on through ages.'

Worse was yet to come: Nigel van Someren was killed flying at the end of the month. I fled to the solitude of the Western Highlands to come to terms with my grief, for ours was the deepest friendship I had ever known. The last time we had met, we had sat in the sun on the Downs above Studland and made plans for celebrating our two 21st birthdays. I liked him and admired him enormously. 'He was the one person in the world for whom I was prepared to make allowances and hold myself back,' I wrote. He was a deeply sincere man.

Many people thought he was humourless, but I knew his love of fun; I admired his keenness and ability to work hard; I respected his honest dislike of shams, red tape and meanness. He was one of the few people I knew who could relax and enjoy beauty without making banal remarks at great moments. In all these 59 years since the moment of shock when I read of his death, Nigel has never been far from the forefront of my memory.

In the middle of June I reported for duty at Calshot. In addition to Jerry Hayter and Jack Holmes, other friends I had made at Thorney were there: Don Lindsay, Henry Breese, Dick Furseman and, from Cranwell, Horace Porteous and John Armitstead. Calshot was a lovely station, mellow, comfortable and refreshingly free of petty discipline and over-organisation. Happy and relaxed, it nevertheless had a subtle atmosphere of efficiency. There we were in a wholly new world where a 'boat' meant a flying boat and a 'marine craft' meant a boat.

I started off in a Supermarine Scapa with Fursey and Jack doing nothing for a couple of hours but learning to taxi and pick up moorings. As it was blowing almost a gale, it was rather fun and more than ordinarily wet. The next day half a dozen of us got caught and made to help bring the Scapa up the slipway, which wasn't so funny in pouring rain because we hadn't got any weather clothing on. After that, there was a Stranraer to be launched. They couldn't get the oil pump in the starboard engine to work so we wasted an hour and a half just waiting. I clambered all over the boat asking questions while the others all sat in the cabin smoking, playing poker and reading.

My first dual in a flying boat was shared with Jerry and Jack. We did circuits and bumps in a Stranraer. I found it peculiarly exhilarating and satisfying once more to hold under my hand an aeroplane and make it do what I wanted it to do. I was greatly amused by the sight of two bollards always in front of me; I liked the steep gliding angle; in a gliding turn I liked the attitude of the steep earth and blue sea with all its yachts; I liked the sensation of lifting her onto the step at the take-off, and the solid crunch of the water meeting the hull when we alighted; and I liked floating on the dancing, sunlit waves.

After two hours solo on the Stranraers, which I came to like very much, I went on to Short Singapores. At first words failed me. They were enormous, they were clumsy, elephantine, they were hard manual labour; in short, they were impossible. One juggled with four throttles; one heaved one's whole weight to and fro on the control column (and all one's strength on the rudder bar had little effect); and the damned things cruised at 85 knots, glided at 90, and climbed about 600 feet in a minute if you put the throttles through the gate. I did not like Singapores. Flying them was too much like training for a heavy weightlifting championship.

The Supermarine Stranraer, powered by two Pegasus X engines, had a maximum all-up weight of 19,000 lb and cruised at just over 90 knots. In contrast, the Singapore III had an all-up weight of 32,400lb. She was larger all round, with a span of 90 feet, a length overall of 64 feet and a height from keel to top of nearly 24 feet. Powered by two pusher and two tractor Kestrel IX engines each of 675 hp she had the same range and cruising speed as a Stranraer, 1,000 miles with normal tanks.

After a week in which I put in quite a lot of hours, I became reconciled to the heavy unwieldiness of the Singapore. One typical day a runner from the Guardroom awakened me at 06.30. Rain was pelting out of a black sky. Flt Lieut Sinclair drove me down to the Spit whence we embarked on a Singapore shortly after 7, having got completely soaked on the trip in the dinghy despite our oilskins. The crew made ready for getting under way; the riggers and I pulled her up onto the short slip while the fitters primed the engines. By this time I was so wet that I discarded my oilies for ease of working. We were all in that cheerful watery state of mind which accompanies a thorough soaking. When I had done a pilot's check inspection of the cooling system we were ready to set off. "You might as well warm up the engines even if we don't fly" said Sinclair.

"Start starboard front!" I shouted to the fitter. When it was running I pointed to the port front engine, which he started also. I waved at the bowman to slip the mooring, opened the two throttles, and away we went in a cloud of spray. As we cleared the trots the fitter started the two rear engines on my orders. For ten minutes we did some fast taxiing until the fitter signalled that all four engines were warm. We buffeted through heavy spray, the flare of the hull shovelling the water wide on either side. By now the rain had abated slightly. "OK" said Sinclair, "You might as well try a circuit."

Up I popped through the cockpit roof-hatch to have a look-round. Driving rain, grey heaving water and four airscrews idling: all clear. Settling myself into the seat I prepared for take-off. First of all open wide the rear throttles, then the front ones, and screw up the friction nut, watching the revolution indicators as I did so. As the Singapore gathered way I had to push on the control column with all my strength, fight the wheel one way and the other so as to keep her level, and stand hard on the rudder bar to keep her straight. After half a minute she was running high on her step. The push on the control column became a pull, more and more firm until it was a hard pull. She lifted. Very, very slowly she climbed. At 400 feet I throttled back to 2,100 revs and spent the next five minutes trying in vain to synchronise the motors.

Up to 1,000 feet and round in a wide circuit. The whole of space was grey driving rain and sea. Facing once more into wind I shoved the nose down and throttled back. She dropped like a brick.

In the glide my arms were braced straight out in front of me against the push of the control column. I kept her into wind by watching the smoky wind-lanes on the water. At 400 feet I was drifting perceptibly, but that was only because the wind at that height had not the same direction as the surface wind. I was often worried by that at first. The wrinkled sea came closer and with a sudden rush leapt up to me with real tossing waves instead of wrinkles. I broke the glide, held her level. Sweetly she touched, but what a hellish din the water made on the bottom plating. When she began to settle I heaved the stick forward to keep her nose down in the water.

I did several circuits until it was time to go in for breakfast. "Mooring Up!" I shouted back to the crew. Two riggers went into the bow cockpit, one of the fitters to the 'midships hatch to operate the drogues - there was a strong tide running with the wind, so I did not need them. A hundred yards downwind of the buoy I cut the rear engines and came up slowly with the front ones just idling. One bowman caught the loop of the buoy with a boathook while the other slipped a short slip through it and made fast. When he signalled thumbs up I cut the forward motors.

Quickly everyone made ready to leave the boat. The main pendant and the anchor chain were shackled onto the mooring strops; flying controls were locked; swashboards were fitted at the bulkheads and everything closed down. I was beginning to feel extremely cold but was still exceedingly cheerful. Nearly half an hour passed before we were picked up by a dinghy despite our shouting, blowing whistles, semaphoring, shooting off Verey lights and using the Aldis lamp. Those marine craft people were chosen for deafness, dumbness and blindness. After all this came the crowning joy of a hot bath, bacon and eggs and coffee.

The weather, with very little exception, continued to be bad; nevertheless I did a great deal of flying in the Singapore, until I said goodbye to the old girl somewhat reluctantly. Back to flying Stranraers I found them quite light and pleasant, and the thought occurred to me that this was evidence of an awful degeneracy: what sort of a showing would I make on a Fury if I found a Stranraer light? But I liked them very much; they had performance, they were just the right size, for all the world like a cruising launch that could fly.

I found night flying on the Stranraer quite amusing. To begin with, the flare path was almost superfluous because you couldn't see it until you were almost on it; and then the process of flying the boat onto the water was a matter almost entirely of instrument flying. One began to glide at the normal 80 knots until one was at 300 feet and undershooting well; then one brought the nose right up and eased the throttle open until one was motoring along at 60 knots steadily losing height. After that it was a question of keeping the speed constant with throttle and watching the altimeter and rate of descent until you hit the water.

At the beginning of August, together with Jerry, Jack, Henry Breese and Dick Furseman, I joined No. 240 Squadron which was just forming at Calshot. It was equipped with the Saro London Mark II, designed to much the same specification as the Stranraer and much the same size, but in every respect a far more attractive boat. With uprated Pegasus X engines it was faster, cruising at 110 knots, and its overload saddle tank gave it a substantially greater range, 1,740 miles. The wardroom would have graced any yacht.

I was assigned as second Pilot and Navigator to K6929, skippered by Flying Officer - and soon Flt Lieut - H.C. Bailey, affectionately known by everybody as Bill. He was a cheerful, kindly and gentle man who treated me tolerantly, and sometimes quizzically, as an equal. In those days the RAF did not have the one-winged Navigators who later played such a distinguished role. Navigation was the duty of the second pilot. Bill Bailey, however, enjoyed navigating, and unlike most of the other skippers on the squadron shared both the piloting and the navigating with me. I thought the world of him.

The squadron was due to fly to Invergordon for exercises with the Home Fleet a week after I joined. My first flight in K6929 was a 15 minute test flight on 8th August. My next was the flight to Invergordon on the 12th. We flew in two formations of three aircraft via the East coast. After taking off in open formation we closed a bit, made a circuit of Calshot and set off on our direct course for Spurn Head. We climbed to 6,000 feet and flew just below the peak level of some glorious cloud formations as far as Northampton, where we descended to 3,000 feet.

It was rather dirty below the clouds, especially after the lovely glories of softly shaded white and bright blue. Bill handed over the controls to me at 2,000 feet over grey sea out of sight of land, flying in very loose formation. We had tea and biscuits at lunchtime, and a very welcome cigarette (no smoking until the overload tank was dry). The fitter wrote letters, the rigger read, the W/Op, a very young lad fresh from training, fell fast asleep after the first excitement.

After flying for 6 hours 50 minutes we arrived at Invergordon having experienced some pretty filthy rain and low cloud from Macduff onwards. It was a delightful place, mottled sunlight on hill and water, surrounded by big mountains in the distance. One or two Naval ships, including the *Royal Oak*, were in harbour, giving it a warlike air, and yet I perceived it as an utterly peaceful corner of the earth despite naval moorings and targets and the odd flying boat glinting in a shaft of sunlight, all so incongruously scattered on the surface of the Loch. I refuelled our aircraft before going ashore to feed.

Early on the Monday following a rest day we all went on board K6929. Bill and I went over the charts for the exercise, discussing points of procedure and calculating fuel consumption, endurance, range etc., getting ourselves familiar with what was likely to crop up. Meanwhile the crew was busy with masses of technical checks including examining the fuel filters on account of a watered petrol scare.

I liked our little wardroom-chartroom. It was very like a yacht only far more airy and well lit, painted green and cream with dark blue upholstery. Oilskins, Mae Wests, parachute harness and training papers were scattered over the bunks; my mascot 'Jimmy' was sitting above the clock; but most incongruous were the three Lewis guns stowed under the second pilot's seat.

Through the door I could see a slab of green shoreline and the rain-spattered, leaden water flowing past smoothly, rapidly. A dinghy came alongside with orders for me to report to the operations room. This was a very wretched, fuggy shop that had been commandeered for the purposes of the Fleet Exercise.

The Station Commander, Gp Capt Louis Le B. Croke, a large man with the voice of a nautical fog-horn, told me that I, and one of the other second pilots, Bud Lewin, were to be attached to the Operations Staff as coding Officers to instruct the Volunteer Reserve Pilot Officers manning the Operations Room, none of whom had ever heard of the

Naval Aircraft Code or seen the cipher machine. The snag was that the Ops Room had to be operational 24 hours a day, so until the VR types were proficient Bud and I had to work eight hour watches on and off.

Miserably small though it was, the Ops Room was the nerve centre of two Squadrons (No. 209 with Stranraers had joined us). Linked directly to 18 Group HQ at Donibristle and 15 Group HQ at Gosport, in wartime it would play an important role in naval/air strategy in the North Sea. Bud and I found it great fun knocking the place and the people into shape.

Zero Hour for the Exercise was at 06.00 on the Monday. We were part of Redland forces comprising the Home Fleet and 15 and 18 Groups' aircraft. Blueland (notionally Germany) comprised a few Southampton class cruisers and the *Cumberland*, and some submarines and destroyers. The exercise was to start with three boats of 240 Squadron on a ten hour parallel track search to Norway and back. I was on the midnight to 08.00 watch when the pilots, oilskinned, bescarfed and sweatered, came in for final orders. The first three days of the exercise seen from the Ops room were incredibly hectic, and John Barraclough,[1] another of our second pilots, was drafted in to help with deciphering; but gradually the wheels began to run more smoothly as the VR types came to grips with the NAC and the intricacies of encryption.

Whilst I enjoyed it all hugely, I was delighted when my squadron Commander told me on Wednesday evening that I would be flying on the morrow. I was awakened by the Corporal of the Guard at 02.30. Wearing several sweaters I walked down to the Ops room feeling dopey and cold. I didn't really begin to wake up until we were on board the power boat, when the eastern sky was just beginning to pale. Once on board 29 we got away from moorings quickly and taxied to Nigg Bay in growing light. Being busy doing preliminary calculations at the chart table I didn't see much of the growth of dawn on the way to Tarbat Ness, though I caught a glimpse of the North Sutor, big, grey and rather formidable, sliding steadily past the port wingtip float.

There was practically no wind; the sea was calm and misty. We

---

[1] Later, Air Chief Marshal Sir John Barraclough

reached our datum point six minutes early by DR, so I dropped a sea marker and we circled. Ten minutes after leaving datum we sighted a Southampton class cruiser which we reported and shadowed successfully for three hours, each piloting in turn, and had a very welcome breakfast at 08.15. Bill was just finishing his bacon and eggs and sausages when I sighted our relieving aircraft, a Sunderland. At the same instant the cruiser realised that she was being shadowed. She immediately signalled by lamp 'SUNK'.

At that we roared with laughter despite feeling pretty set back, though rather pleased with ourselves for having remained unspotted for so long. Even then it was the Sunderland, not us, who was spotted.

I shot the cruiser up and found she was HMS *Glasgow*, representing one of the German 10,000 ton battleships. In accordance with our orders we then turned back to resume our patrol.

It was a delightful day for flying, plenty of sunlight, brindled by lots of small clouds at 3,000 feet, and a sea almost as smooth as a blue glass mirror, full of small drifters like midges. When my calculations showed we had only four hours of fuel left, I made a signal to Group who recalled us immediately. On our way we dropped an oil bag and fired three or four hundred rounds from the Lewis gun at it which was rather fun.

While up in the bow cockpit I had a new view of the London, foreshortened and tail high, with a hatchet-faced man wearing a field service cap and sun goggles sitting rather grimly in the 'office'. It didn't look at all like the pleasant, helpful Bill Bailey that I knew! Eventually we made our planned landfall near Wick and enjoyed a delightful run along the edge of the red cliffs of Sutherland with a view of its great wilderness of barren and rocky hills. We alighted at noon. After refuelling I reported to the Ops room with track charts and signals. The Group Captain patted us on the back for our shadowing.

The next day we took off before sunrise for another eight and a half hour patrol which brought us to a thrilling landfall at Utsire, whence we ran up the Norwegian coast for a bit; 'I've never seen so many islands and inlets and tortuous fjords, all backed in the distance by enormous mountains too far away to be anything but vague silhouettes,' I wrote.

'Scotland is brown or grey or green, but Norway seems to be just black.'

I spent the following two days on board 29 superintending the crew doing a 60-hour technical inspection of hull, airframe and engines. For much of the time Bill sat up on the tailplane fishing. When we got back to the Squadron Office on Sunday we found quite a flap on; King and Barber in one of the 209 Squadron Stranraers were more than an hour overdue. Two Stranraers and a destroyer were sent off in search that evening. Orders came through to launch a parallel track search with five boats on a north-easterly track of 065 degrees from Rattray head at first light, but Bill and I were out of it because our boat was still unserviceable.

At breakfast there were whispers of a serious international political situation. The VR people had received orders to stay on. Down at the Squadron Office we learned that all our boats were to be flown to Calshot on the morrow to be thoroughly serviced and brought back to Invergordon as soon as possible. Only Sinclair, Pam, Barraclough and I were to remain behind.

Between the flap and the lost Stranraer, the Home Fleet exercise was completely forgotten. Despite thick fog, a search by five boats was maintained all day, and over the next few days with whatever aircraft were available, but with no result.

The Fleet came in on Monday. The whole character of the Firth and of Invergordon was changed dramatically by the presence of *Nelson, Hood, Ark Royal, Edinburgh, Aurora* and about 15 Javelin and 'W' class destroyers. The town was submerged under matelots. We struck our tented camp and abandoned the schoolroom, the Officers moving into the luxury of McLaren's Temperance Hotel.

Late on Wednesday while the Group Captain, Pam, Bailey and Barraclough were sitting over our night-caps, Mrs McLaren called Bill, who was Duty Officer, to the phone. He came back looking both excited and grim and reported to the Group Captain that it was 18 Group wanting to know the number of aircraft available and the state of their serviceability.

They said that the situation was tense and that we were to expect a

Form Green (i.e. an operations order) some time during the night. My heart suddenly began to beat quickly. For a few minutes we talked normally of some trifling matter, then John Barraclough said "God, the balloon is just tottering on the verge!" and we broke up.

I went to the camp to find Jones, our fitter, to see whether our boat was serviceable. Then for about half an hour, while the hills lost all their depth and colour against a cream western sky, Sinclair, Pam, Barra and I talked hilariously of the prospects. At the bottom of my heart, however, there was an awful longing to live and see other dusks as lovely.

I was aware, as I watched the burnished light of the afterglow flash in reflection from the wings of a Skua that was wheeling overhead, of a new picquancy. Life was very precious. I saw what the morrow might bring; Bill and I flying along in bright sunlight making occasional foolish remarks; and our sudden fear as shells from the German fleet began to burst about us. Perhaps we might be lucky enough to get back. Others might not: Jerry or Jack, Barra or Henry Breese; and there would be an aching emptiness in one's life which the stark nightfalls in the hills would only make more painful. I was aware of all this as we jested.

Form Green duly came through, ordering two boats on a search from 05.00hrs on 24th August, to shadow very unobtrusively any German surface vessels. I was on duty in the Ops room until midnight. The two operational boats were scheduled to take off at 02.30, and as Bill and I had the standby boat we didn't go to bed. I recorded 'I shall do my stuff and enjoy doing it if the occasion arises, but God forbid that the balloon should go up.' The whole station was working at full steam. Live bombs were brought from Evanton to be loaded onto scows in readiness. The Fleet quite suddenly disappeared.

I went to bed at 9pm and was up at 01.00 on 25th; we slipped moorings just before 03.00 in a flat calm and darkness like the pit, on our way to Sullom Voe in Shetland. Our first attempt at taking off failed. Bill couldn't get her up on the step. It was rather shattering crashing along at +5lb boost into an impenetrable blanket of darkness, knowing that at any moment we might write ourselves off on one of the navy's huge, unlit mooring buoys. After an age, Bill throttled down and we taxied all the way back to Invergordon for another shot.

Once we had moved some of our freight forward, we did get off, and to be in the air was an enormous relief. We didn't see a thing. I gave a compass course for Tarbat Ness and another one from there to a point offshore of Wick. For as long as I could see Tarbat light I sat with my eyes clamped to the bearing compass, having no intention whatever of letting us come anywhere near the mountains that we couldn't see.

It began to grow light as we left Duncansby Head and I just managed to make out the vague blob that was Copinsay before the ground was masked by low cloud. But fortunately, on our ETA at Sumburgh Head there was a gap through which we went down, and found ourselves bang on the Head.

My first view of Shetland: white water smashing at the foot of low cliffs (was ever a place better named than 'Fitful Head'?), a sea like wet slate in the twilight, and barren hills vividly green in the burgeoning ecclesiastical light of dawn. About half an hour later the weather cleared. We made our landfall within a mile or two of where we should have been, just south of Utvaer. Norway being up-sun we didn't see much of it in the haze.

We had an uneventful trip back to Shetland; our landfall was quite good at the Holm of Helliness after passing Noss Island, which is not a place to hit in bad visibility at zero altitude. We flew up the coast past Lerwick and over a neck of land to Garth's Voe (a small offshoot of Sullom Voe) where we alighted alongside s.s. *Manela*, refuelled and did 'daily inspections' of the boat before going aboard the ship to our luxurious cabins.

Despite an awful lot of fog we did three Norway patrols out of Sullom Voe. I enjoyed myself up there; life aboard *Manela* was 'First class P&O', and despite mobilisation signals and the various orders for bringing the war machine into operation the atmosphere was more peaceful than anywhere I had been for weeks, but the moment we got back to Invergordon on Wednesday 30th we were put hard to work. The character of the place had greatly changed; not only were the two squadrons back in full strength but the place was humming with reservists manning the station up to its war establishment. I was appointed Squadron Armament officer and found myself running round all day in small circles, busy with anti-gas measures, A.R.P, anti-sabotage, and trying to get hold of a couple of empty shops for armouries. Lots of wives came up, and Jerry made arrangements for his Audrey to drive my car up if war broke out so that they could get married.

I wrote 'I am in a strange mixture of outward cheerfulness (which seems to come naturally) and internal nervousness and depression, and I am bloody tired. I have written hundreds of long letters at all odd hours of night and day. The future doesn't hold any hope at all. I would give anything to see some of my friends just now, so that I may pay as it were my final regrets to the old happy life, button things up and get on with the job in a clear conscience. Most especially do I want to see Isobelle. I have written to her parents; they must let her come. My only fear is not of death, but of loneliness. Jerry may not be right over his frantic patch-up wedding, but my God I'd give anything to marry Isobelle right now. For all the friendliness there is here, I feel awfully lonely.'

After two hours sleep I was up at 02.00hrs on 1st September for a patrol. We took off at 03.30 by the light of a full moon high in the velvet sky. Bill was very dopey. The only memorable thing about the patrol was dawn: we were flying over a hill-and-dale cloudscape with the moon high to starboard above a waste of chaste whiteness; but to port we saw the warm glow of the new dawn infecting the clouds with a fleshly warmth. It was a contrast as breathtaking as it was astonishing. About 13.00hrs, after alighting back at Invergordon, while awaiting the refuelling barge we had our radio on. We heard then for the first time of Germany's invasion of Poland that morning. You can imagine how keyed up we were. We came ashore about tea-time, and I was fairly busy with squadron armament business. The Home Office had originated the 'Precautionary Period' signal. Each news bulletin was more depressing. Now that the worst was almost to be taken for granted I was much calmer; a sort of numbness prevented me from having any real feelings or doing any constructive thinking.

On Saturday 2nd September things seemed as though they were at a standstill though mobilisation continued. The next day we were at war with Germany. Yet it was just like other days except for the instructions on the radio. I was frantically busy. It was nearly 23.00hrs before I finished superintending the bombing-up of four Londons, each with two 200lb anti-submarine bombs. Four boats from 240 Squadron were scheduled to take off with four from 209 at 03.30hrs the following day, to search for the German High Seas Fleet, which was at sea. It was thrilling to be on the first patrol of the war; but I was frightened. 'I might not get back. Still, I shall do my damnedest to do my job properly. Here goes! We are on the edge of great things.'

It was a very queer war at first. We had all expected mayhem, but the pace of life slowed down; in the first week Bill and I did only three patrols over a strangely empty North Sea, and a few standbys. The rest of our time was incredibly slack.

Flt Lieut De Gruyther brought a Lerwick up to Invergordon to give familiarisation flights to the Squadron's pilots. It was put about that they were to replace our Londons soon. Bill and I each had an hour's dual on consecutive days. The Lerwick was a high wing monoplane powered by a pair of Hercules engines. She had a deep, narrow hull, and the pilots sat in tandem in a perspex and glass 'greenhouse' on the upper deck high above the waterline. Here I encountered for the first time variable pitch propellers. I enjoyed flying her. Apart from a certain trickiness in juggling with the throttles to prevent swinging on take-off, I had no difficulty. She was a bit of a bitch to handle on the water because of the windage of her high, narrow hull-form, but in the air she was quite sensitive despite noticeable heaviness in the controls. When she was moving fast on the water she shook like a mechanical coal-sifter, but once in the air she displayed a joyous power and liveliness.

Isobelle arrived on 4th September and stayed for a week. Although I saw too little of her until the weekend her presence was a most miraculous tonic. She certainly made a great hit with my fellow officers. We came to an understanding about where we stood with one another; we would not get married, or even engaged, just yet; she refused to be panicked. Seeing her did me all the good I thought it would; after she left, I felt I could face anything with a quiet mind.

A few days later Bill and I, in company with two other Londons, flew down to Mount Batten by way of the Great Glen and the west coast. There we flew a number of convoy escorts, one of which was particularly eventful. I took off at 11.15. We steamed out to pick up a large, straggling convoy under the care of two overworked destroyers. Just before 15.00hrs we noticed a certain amount of confusion among the ships, and very soon afterwards we were called up by a destroyer, who told us to go and have a look at one of the ships at the rear. We found a big cargo boat, the *Teakwood*, lying head down with a very heavy list to starboard. She had been torpedoed on the starboard side just under the bridge, which had been fairly shattered by the explosion. A destroyer was standing by, picking up a boatload of people.

We duly rushed off to hunt for the submarine, but finding nothing we flew a good distance away and reported the incident to group HQ. When we got back to the convoy the destroyer in charge sent us off to search the area astern, but again we found nothing. The destroyer then started to go haywire, careering around the sea like an angry hen. 'Search around me for submarine' she signalled. Excitement rose to fever pitch.

At 18.15, however, we decided to leave the convoy because we were scheduled to alight at Falmouth and we had to get there before dark (there being no night flying facilities). As we passed over the original scene of the torpedoing we saw three destroyers and a Sunderland doing a hunt. Later, to our surprise, we found *Teakwood* escorted by one destroyer making laborious progress towards Falmouth, still down by the head and her pumps going full blast.

It was dark when we got to Falmouth. The whole populace seemed to turn out to see us in, and we certainly gave them a run for their money. We did a tight turn 50 feet above the housetops, sneaked between a couple of cranes, touched down at 75 knots and suddenly saw a ledge of rocks looming ahead. Although we were still on the step, Bill stood on the rudder bar and whirled the wheel over, and we did a perfectly banked turn on the water through 90 degrees, missing the rocks by a matter of 15 yards. It was close, yet very interesting.

70

We did two further eight-hour convoy escorts from Falmouth before returning to Calshot, where we alighted in the dark, unheralded, after a somewhat perilous trip running the gauntlet of all sorts of anti-aircraft defences. Our boat was due for a major technical inspection, so after spending a day unloading all our gear we went on leave for a week. When we reported back to Calshot, we were told that we were to take over K5257, still in the hands of the maintenance flight. I spent my 21st birthday in the hangar watching their work. Gradually she came more under our hands and less under the control of the organisation which had mysteriously taken her to pieces and put her back together again.

The morning came when I started stowing charts and navigation gear aboard, the afternoon in checking guns and ancillary equipment. Standing on the tarmac under the walls of the Castle she looked awfully clumsy, like a great stranded duck. We mercilessly piled all sorts of gear in - refuelling hoses, two rubber dinghies, cooking stove and crockery, Lewis guns, signal cartridges, navigation books, bomb-sight, parachute packs and harnesses, engine covers, oars, boathooks, camera, a foot-pump, life-jackets, sidcots, tool kits, inspection platforms, tinned food, first aid kits, sleeping bags, all our personal gear, bomb racks and so on. Corporal Owen (the W/OP) fixed up a very useful little loudspeaker so that we could listen to sweet music when we are on the water.

The last thing before launching was to swing the compasses on the compass base. On 12th October we launched her down the slipway at 07.00, took her up into the air for an hour's flight test of everything, topped up with fuel and left for Invergordon. The nearer we approached, the colder it got, and when we arrived there we found a heavy swell running straight through the Sutors. Nevertheless Bill got us down safely on his second attempt. From above, the wrinkles on the water were heartless but insignificant, but as we come lower they grew in size, became more menacing.

Could we get her down? This was a cold, unemotional fear, the fear experienced in dangerous action. I was tense, probably a bit pale around the gills. It was our skill against the impersonal enmity of the water. An enormous wave shot past us, striking a cold patch of fear somewhere inside me, a patch which lasted to the end of the ordeal to the exclusion of all else save the vital actions of putting the boat down. And out of the corner of my eye, beyond the waves, I saw the pier, the dirty foreshore and the huddled grey houses - and safety.

We slipped at 07.00hrs next morning with a load of passengers and freight for Sullom Voe, the first of a number of ferry trips during the next few days in advance of 240 Squadron relieving 201 Squadron on the *Manela*. Then, after a day of farewells at Invergordon and a terrific party in the Club, Bill and I left at dawn for a three month stay up there. Apart from the occasional party in a visiting destroyer we settled down to a tough routine of Norway patrols, almost every day and usually in pretty rough weather. There were a number of air raids directed against *Manela*, but we were only present during one (actually refuelling 57 on the water), and each of them was driven off by protective fire from HMS *Coventry*. One of the Londons, however, was sunk by enemy gunfire in Lerwick Harbour.

Then Hooky Sinclair, who had taught me to fly Singapores, went missing. All available boats were sent to search for him the next day in the teeth of a tearing gale and torrential rain. Our airspeed indicator read a steady 40 knots at moorings. Bill and I were detailed to search the western coasts of the Shetlands and it was simply bloody. The turbulence near the cliffs was sometimes terrifying and there was no way of avoiding it with a ceiling of less than 700 feet. Hooky, the most senior Captain, was a great loss to the Squadron. An amusing little man who could be very charming, he had a pleasant whimsy of pretending to be very tough, misanthropic, misogynistic and stony hearted, but his crews thought the world of him. He had a lively, unorthodox mind: he was an excellent pilot and a good seaman.

When Flt Lieut Gandy went down with flu, I was selected to stand in as Captain of his boat, with Dick Furseman as my second pilot. Being the first of all the second pilots to be promoted thus, I was thrilled beyond words and wrote 'I am full of visions of great deeds; we shall capture the *Bremen* single handed, carry out a daring rescue of starving castaways on the high seas, or sink the *Deutschland*....' Dick

72

and I had been good friends since our Thorney Island days, and now thanks to his fine sense of loyalty and discipline we began to work together smoothly and happily. My first patrol in command turned out to be a disappointing fiasco. On 24th November I took off in K5911 on my 28th war patrol. We had been flying for an hour or so when one of the starboard flying wires sheared - these were the wires which transmitted the lift from the upper mainplane to the hull. After much balancing of the pros and cons, I reluctantly decided to return to base rather than hazard the machine in eight hours of turbulent flight. Nobody questioned my decision, but I have always felt in retrospect that I was over-cautious.

Things were quite different on the following day. We cracked off on the usual Norway trip about 08.00hrs. On the way we flew through a very bad snowstorm with some heavy downdraughts which were somewhat alarming while flying on instruments. We saw, when we arrived just south of Stadlandet, a couple of large merchantmen close inshore making southward. On further investigation we identified one of them as a German loaded with iron ore and wearing the Russian flag, and the other a suspected German, for she had neither flag nor neutral markings. We were full of beans at our discovery. On the way back we met several British cruisers carrying out a parallel track search towards the north, presumably looking for the *Deutschland*. We also sighted the British Battle Fleet about 20 miles SW of us.

Almost at the same time I saw away on our port beam a small speck against a snow-cloud. Fursey and I watched it carefully through binoculars.

"It's a Walrus," said Fursey.

"To hell", I replied two or three minutes later. "It's a high-wing monoplane. Coming straight towards us. Fast. Vaguely like a Lerwick. Go and show it to the crew and get the guns manned."

Still watching it, I edged the London into a climb towards a cloud. When the oncoming aircraft was about 4 miles away he swung back onto a reciprocal course and I breathed a great sigh. So off we dashed towards the Fleet to signal to the Admiral information about this aircraft's presence. Making a wide detour to pass behind them, I saw a second aircraft about 15 miles astern, flying very low. This one I was able to identify as a Dornier 18 flying boat.

I found it hard to make up my mind whether to attack or not. We were a reconnaissance squadron, not fighter boys, and the doctrine was to avoid unnecessary combat. The fact that there were two of them, one a Dornier which was about equivalent to a London (having more speed but one gun less), the other something unidentified and quite possibly more formidable, persuaded me that discretion was the better part. Safely back on *Manela* I had serious doubts about the rightness of not pressing them.

Gales kept us weather-bound on *Manela* for the next two days, and at dawn on the third day I was hoicked out of bed and shown a London plunging about some five yards off the shore. It was K5911 - she had dragged her moorings some 150 yards during the night and was in danger of destruction. I collected the crew, and we went out to see what we could do for her. It was blowing great guns and there was a fairly stiff chop running. On boarding her we found that she was badly holed and that the water was over the floorboards in the crew's quarters and the wardroom.

We bailed and pumped solidly and got her dry at about 15.00 hrs, but it needed a lot of pumping just to hold the water at bay. The main keelson was buckled the length of three frames forward of the step and the planing bottom was badly dented. We bunged up as many holes as we could with putty, which materially reduced leaking. Even so, pumping was quite hard, for the auxiliary power unit had packed up. Back on board *Manela* I discussed the situation with the Flight Commander and the decision was made to try and fly her back to Calshot the next day despite a very gloomy weather forecast.

We managed to get into the air without difficulty at dawn, the crew having taken turns at the pumps all night. As soon as we left Sumburgh Head behind us we ran into the promised murk and only just managed to squeeze into Oban. A combination of bad weather and magneto trouble on the starboard engine kept us there for four days.

On the third day the bilge pumps seized solid, so we couldn't pump her dry for take-off. In desperation I off-loaded some fuel and got her into the air in heavy rain and low cloud and whistled around the islands in filthy murk while my noble crew filled the bottom with pitch when the water had drained out. As we alighted after more than two miserable hours in the air, the pitch coating cracked and she leaked worse than before.

'We are all just about at the end of our patience,' I wrote that evening. 'To beach her would be easy, but it would mean writing the hull off. Probably when they see the damage at Calshot they will write it off anyway; but having been commissioned to take the bloody thing there, I suppose I had better deliver it.'

The next day we made it to Calshot. I circled low over the Castle until I could see that the slipway party was ready to receive me, and was lucky enough to make a faultless touchdown in full view of a considerable audience including my Flight Commander and the latest arrival from Cranwell, Jimmy Stack,[2] whose father had known my father. Within half an hour K5911 was safely beached.

We all were given a few days' leave. I went up to Portincaple for a spell of magic with Isobelle and her family. When I returned to reality at Calshot the sad news was that Flt Lieut Pam, an enthusiastic fellow for whom nothing was too much trouble, had been killed in action.

At the end of the year, as a consequence of Bill Bailey's being sent off on an astro navigation course, I was told that I was to take over the Captaincy of K5257 during his absence, but it was another couple of weeks before she was released from the Maintenance Flight. On Monday 8th January we swung the compasses, launched the boat and gave her an air test. She flew very prettily, but there was a lot of play in the throttle linkage. We meant to crack off bright and early to Invergordon the next day but were held up first by finding a leak in the lavatory and then by inability to get the starboard motor running, with the result that we got no further than Pembroke Dock in a pretty murky trip. After two days' delays en route due to fog we reached Sullom Voe on the 13th.

At crack of dawn the next day we took off on a patrol to Ytteroerne with lots of low cloud and rain on the way. We carried the first 'one-

---

[2] Later, Air Chief Marshal Sir Neville Stack

wing' Observer on the Squadron, Sergeant Underwood, very keen but for the first few trips rather shaky and needing a lot of advice from Fursey and me. In fact he turned out to be a very good navigator indeed once he had got the hang of our arcane tricks of the trade.

After mooring up Corporal Smith was foolish enough to bring a loaded Lewis gun inboard; while he was trying to unload it, the thing went off. By the Grace of God there was no damage to person or thing, only Smith jumped so high that he cut his head on a bulkhead.

After that patrol I wrote 'I certainly seem to have more confidence in myself as a Captain now than in the first few days. Much of it is due to the confidence I have in the crew, and I can't let them down. In spite of feeling so easy-minded on patrol, I was conscious when we moored up of a tremendous feeling of relief. And now that I am safely back on board *Manela* I can feel anxiety gnawing away down at the back of my head: because there is tomorrow, and after that interminable tomorrows like never-ending terraces fading into the mist of the future, until one day when there simply will not be a tomorrow. How will that moment show itself? I am scared of being frightened.'

After a filthy trip trying to find a convoy off the Norwegian coast in thick snow, we received a signal from 100 Wing indicating that they were expecting bad weather, so I turned back. Off the Shetlands we could see that all the islands were under a thick pall of snow-clouds, but fortunately there was a narrow alleyway through which I could spot the Out Skerries. It was a race against time but we managed to reach Lunna Ness before it closed in behind us.

Yell Sound was absolutely black, wherefore I looked on the Admiralty chart for a suitable place for a forced landing. Vidlin Voe at the landward end of Lunna Ness seemed to fit the bill; it was sheltered from everything except a heavy NE swell, there was a long clear channel running north and south, and telegraph posts leading to a house at the head of the voe indicated communications.

There was black snow falling on all sides and a glade of light on Vidlin as I flew low up the narrow stretch of water, the shore streaking easily past. I glimpsed submerged rocks on the western side of the voe; telegraph posts and a house; people appeared from nowhere, little black figures of men with a dog striding across the white land.

I made a steep gliding turn onto the water, aware of Fursey by my side sitting rather tensely upright. I got her safely down; we felt our way slowly across the calm water, sounding for an anchorage, and dropped hook at the head of the voe before the snow descended thickly on us. Engines off: and a crisp silence such that we could almost hear the first fine snowflakes falling.

Soon three or four dories manned by fishermen surrounded us, and one of them came alongside with three courteous Shetlanders on board. Although it was hard to understand their rapid, sibilant dialect, I discussed with them technical points concerning wind and swell and tide and bottom before being rowed ashore with Fursey. The house with the telephone was also the local shop where we were met with "cold weather!" and a courteous silence; they did not presume to ask who we were or whence we came, but let me ring up 100 Wing without charge.

We bought masses of food. We invited some of the locals back on board for a cup of tea. I think they were a bit overwhelmed, and seemed slightly frightened of our monstrous home and shy of the guns and bombs, or they expected the petrol to go up in flames perhaps. Simple folk but extremely intelligent. Being seamen the first thing they asked about was the rubber dinghy. When we produced it for them and inflated it, they were awfully tickled.

As they left, it was snowing heavily; you could hear it kiss the water. After eating our meal we all settled down to playing *vingt-et-un* in the wardroom. As usual I lost vast sums of money. The water was lapping metallically on the flare chine and there was a slight motion as she dropped so lazily from one wingtip float to another. The chuff of the water on the hull became louder and more insistent: I put my head out through the coupé top and saw with slight anxiety that the wind had freshened from the north; but the snow had ceased and it had turned out to be a glorious night, a superb composition in pale blue and indigo, snow and water, stars and sky and the dear old silver moon.

More anchor chain was laid out and a couple of cross bearings taken in the moonlight. We slept on board. I didn't know it could be so cold. The morning arrived cloudless. After chipping the ice off the wings, the starboard motor started at the first kick, but I switched it off after warming up. It took us half an hour to start the bloody port one. A sharp turn on the motor and drogue, then the starboard motor was started and we slid down the voe again.

She came off the water without effort; I held her inches above the calm surface; saw the people at the head of the voe scatter as we charged at them; lifted her easily in a climbing turn and saw rolling fields of white hills unfold to my vision, with Foula, majestically remote yet seeming only feet away, chinese white and soft lemon yellow between sky and sea.

Two or three days later I was in my bath after a day's flying when Duck Pirie, the Adjutant, shouted "Johnno, would you like to do the Long Navigation Course?". I answered "Yes, love to. Why?" He said that there was a vacancy and I could have my name put forward for it if I liked, but there was no guarantee that I would come back to 240 squadron. "Give me a minute to think it over," I replied.

I lay in my bath pondering. It meant giving up the Acting rank of Flight Lieutenant. On the other hand I was keen on navigation and this would be a marvellous opportunity to broaden my skill and deepen my knowledge of an interest I had inherited from my Father. So I went along to the Duck's cabin and accepted his offer to have my name put forward, if only because it was an adventure into the unknown.

We continued to suffer snow and severe gales which restricted flying. I made my 46th and last war patrol with 240 Squadron uneventfully on 11th February 1940.

4

Navigation Instructor

IT WAS A DEPRESSING TRANSLATION FROM MY LUXURIOUS cabin with its own bathroom in the *Manela* to a camp bed and a pine-wood dressing table in a misapplied married quarter at St Athan in South Wales. The hutted Officers' Mess, ten minutes fast walk away through seemingly perpetual drizzle, was grossly overcrowded. Among the hundreds of anonymous faces, however, there was a handful of contemporary Cranwellians and, most welcoming of all, Tony Major who was just finishing a short navigation course for fighter pilots.

I joined No. 3 (War) Specialist Navigation Course. Although it took some time to adjust to the safe, slow, unchanging pace of life in a lecture room, I found the syllabus thoroughly interesting. It lasted 14 weeks, during which I did some forty hours of flying as navigator in Ansons, a quarter of it at night. All the air exercises involved astro navigation, using the Mark VIII bubble sextant.

My main private preoccupation was to bombard Isobelle with letters arguing that we should get married as soon as I knew my next posting. It took me about six months to persuade her to say yes.

We became engaged on Wednesday 26th June 1940. Meanwhile the Battle of France had been lost, the Miracle of Dunkirk had come to pass, and the Battle of Britain was just beginning: but all this hardly touched me.

After graduating as a Specialist Navigator I reported to RAF Squire's Gate, Blackpool, on 10th June for duty as a navigation instructor at No. 2 School of General Reconnaissance. It was something of a ragtime station, quite fun; the school was in the old racecourse grandstand on the edge of what was then a grass airfield, and the instructors under the Chief Ground Instructor, Sqn Ldr Moseley, were a decent crowd, several of whom I had met before at Thorney Island. Jack Mould came with me from St Athan, a solid, kindly chap with an extremely glamorous, sophisticated and witty wife Bunty; both of them became lifelong friends. Blackpool itself I hated like poison.

Despite having spent so much time navigating Ansons, I had never actually piloted one. On arrival at Squire's Gate I was plunged straightaway into the lecture room to lecture to a new course, so that it was not until a week later that I was able to get my hands on an aeroplane. A Volunteer Reserve Flying Officer, Eric Starling, who had been Chief Pilot of Aberdeen Airways until being called up, gave me a 45 minute checkout on a Mark II.

She had two Cheetah engines, so incredibly reliable that nobody ever thought of practising single-engine flying; a retractable under-carriage that had to be cranked up and down by hand; and flaps that had to be pumped down but which retracted, when so selected, by the pressure of the air flow. In the air she handled lightly and crisply and, in the configurations in which we flew her, she was nicely stable at a cruising speed of 120 knots.

I soon learned that she was a delightfully agile machine for wing-overs and exaggerated stall turns, though care had to be taken not to overstress her during the pullout from dives, for the elevators, though heavy at high speed, were very powerful. The stall, heralded by slight elevator buffeting, was gentleness itself. She had no vices whatever.

Although she was easy to land, I had some difficulty at first with the shallowness of the gliding angle at her normal 65 knot approach speed - we still glided into the grass field from a circuit at 1,000 feet and used the flaps in the last 50 feet as a sort of air brake, if we used them at all. Lowering the flaps produced only a slight nose-up change of trim which was actually helpful during the hold off; but if one was going round again one needed to beware of a very much sharper nose-down change of trim and loss of height as the flaps 'blew' up.

During the rest of the year I managed barely ten hours a month in the air. I was too busy on the ground. Each intake was assigned to two Officers, one of whom was the Course Commander. Whenever our course was airborne, either I or my Course Commander had to man the operations room to handle the routine position reports coming in from the aeroplanes, and to keep a safety plot. As the navigation instructor I not only delivered the bulk of the course's ground lectures, but had to devise and assess classroom plotting exercises and analyse in detail the navigation logs and plots kept by all my students in the air. Later, when I was more experienced, I became slick enough at this to make much more time available for flying with my students on their air exercises.

Isobelle and I arranged our wedding for Saturday September 7th in Glasgow. I left Squire's Gate on Thursday evening for a long weekend, being due back on duty the following Tuesday. That weekend there was the first serious invasion alert, and I was recalled from leave at 03.00 hrs, but Wing Commander Tom Moseley, my CO, must have sent the telegram to the wrong address, for I never received it.

Tony Major was to have been my Best Man, but he, like everyone else except me, was detained by fear of Herr Hitler. Isobelle and I were married in great style and enjoyed a happy mini-honeymoon at the head of Langdale totally unaware that everyone else was standing by to ward off an invasion of the United Kingdom and that the first nightly blitz of London was taking place.

Half way through November I was told to be ready at the beginning of December to move to Nova Scotia with the School. Precisely at 01.30 on Tuesday 18th December I kissed Isobelle goodbye. My unit arrived at Charlottetown on Prince Edward Island in the mid evening after a very long journey, to be met efficiently by buses for the troops and taxis for the Officers, with seemingly the whole town turned out to clap and welcome us. The brand new RCAF Station, four miles out of town, blazing with lights but almost deserted, was quite small, a hutted camp standing in wet slush on a red clay base. We were an oddity, an RAF unit dumped on an empty RCAF station, and RCAF HQ seemed to have not the slightest idea what a School of General Reconnaissance was for.

The story went around that the ship which was bringing our aircraft and equipment over had been sunk. The RCAF lent us six Ansons in the latter half of February, but because all the Staff Pilots were given priority I was not able to lay my hands on one for another three weeks. The Island, of course, was still under a solid blanket of snow, and that led to a number of minor ground accidents. My course of 24 Australian pilots arrived on the 22nd, a crowd of husky looking toughs with a surprisingly zestful thirst for knowledge. Although a pretty rough crowd they were quite conscientious over their work and I found them infinitely more likeable than most of the Canadians.

In delightful conditions I made my first flight early in March. Flying gently under a blue sky over ice-floes was a new experience: the whole of the Gulf of St Lawrence appeared to be under ice, with only rare patches of water. Unfortunately I had to turn back early as the W/T transmitter packed up. I made the most perfect approach to and landing on the runway that I had ever done. Usually I saw the aerodrome below and after a series of steep turns and sideslips and swishtailings, arrived on it. This time I kissed it lingeringly.

The CO had been talking much about the difficulty of landing on snow and had insisted that all pilots should do 30 minutes of circuits and bumps before carrying pupils - which I hadn't done - so I was careful: flaps down and engines throttled to 75 knots in a gentle powered glide at 500 feet; an easy turn in at 300 feet; and a perfectly judged approach, such that with an even backward pressure on the control column she was exactly in the right attitude at touchdown. It was magnificent and I was astonished. The moment she touched, throttles shut - and there she stayed. Only once had I ever done anything like it: that was when I put K5911 down at Calshot when she had had her bottom stove in.

Most of our training flights were over the Gulf of St Lawrence out of sight of land. One day, flying before breakfast, I had my first glimpse of the Magdalen Islands through persistent snow, a lump of white snow sticking up out of white ice, rather desolate but surprisingly enough full of wooden shacks along the south shore. I also flew over Deadman Island, a small chunk of land shaped like a coffin, about half a mile long and 300 feet high with one lonely shack on it and no vegetation.

The weather was rather lousy. When I was flying blind at 500 feet unable to distinguish the ice below, visibility about 300 yards in snow, the airspeed indicator needle started to fall back. For a few wild moments I thought the airframe was icing up, so I opened the throttles wide. Having stuffed the nose down we lost height rapidly, and when we were dangerously near the ice, which I still couldn't distinguish through the snow-murk, I suddenly realised that it was merely the airspeed indicator that had become iced up. I regained some altitude, but I really was quite panicked for a moment.

Fortunately a few minutes later the snow stopped and we sighted South Cape. Not wishing to fly blind without an ASI for longer than necessary I set course for Cape Stanhope flying as low as I could so that I should always be in sight of the ice. Even so it was tricky in patches when we were flying through thick snow. All the time I was as cold as charity and swearing like a trooper.

On my next trip I flew some of Jack Mould's Canadians on an elementary exercise. Never in my life had I come across such a pitiful show. Their sheer uselessness reduced me to such a condition of temper by the time we got back to base that I wouldn't trust myself to speak to them. In anything less than ten miles visibility they would have been positively dangerous.

Most of the air exercises lasted about a couple of hours. There were roughly three sorts: first, the dead reckoning navigation exercises of increasing difficulty, starting with a simple point to point flight over the sea, followed by triangular tracks out of sight of land, and ending up with a long flight over the sea on random courses selected by the pilot, who would then suddenly ask for a heading for base; then the tactical exercises such as the square, extended Y and creeping line ahead searches, the interception of a ship, or a radius of action problem returning to base at a predetermined time; and finally, visual and photographic reconnaissance, usually of a harbour. As a 'freelance' pilot, moreover, I was called on sometimes to volunteer for transport or ferry flights. There was therefore plenty of variety.

One morning in April I flew with No. 2 Course on a reconnaissance of Chatham, New Brunswick, and had the time of my life. It was a wizard day. The Island was knobbly, like blistered paint with burnished gold shining through. Offshore there was a sparkly sea. The coloured land held undertones of blue and sombre red between the steel blue wrinkled sea and a sky of peerless amethyst. We flew along the coast from Point Escominiac to Kouchibougac Lagoon, as drear and desolate a seashore as I have seen, grey grass and deadwood by the sea, backed by an interminable stretch of forest and swamp. From Kouchibougac we flew only a few feet above the pointing trees, sometimes having to swerve to miss a giant. One almost expected momentarily a vile prehistoric monster to rise up out of the filth and snatch us out of the sky.

It was viciously bumpy. I had to fight to keep control. Twice I hit the roof and my pupils were almost incapacitated. At Chatham eleven aircraft were beating hell out of the place at nought feet. I damned nearly had a head-on collision in the middle of the river, but it was grand fun. After landing back at Charlottetown I disgraced myself by getting my aircraft bogged off the runway.

My Australian pilots departed with quite astonishing quantities of goodwill on both sides after a heavy series of parties, and I was fortunate enough a few days later to be given charge of a second bunch of them for No. 6 Course. They turned out to be a damned good crowd, too, perhaps a bit quieter and more civilised than No. 2 course.

Tommy Thomson and I were asked to ferry some pilots over to Dartmouth, near Halifax. They were going to spend the next fortnight ferrying Oxfords to Winnipeg. We took off and flew there in formation. It was a delightful, cloudless day. Seen from the air the country from Truro to Halifax was delightful: mile after mile of plum-coloured rolling forest studded with amethyst lakes and tiny emerald clearings of cultivated land. Dartmouth was a vast aerodrome hewn out of virgin forest at the water's edge. We saw for the first time the 'Digby'. After inspecting it we were most enthusiastic; it was a wonderful looking aircraft, beautifully fitted out inside with everything arranged for ease of operation and comfort. The view from the pilot's seat was amazingly good.

One day in May we had intelligence of three corvettes on passage from the St Lawrence to Halifax. This information was of the scantiest,

84

merely saying that they would pass Cape Gaspé between noon and 3pm (Atlantic Daylight Saving Time); nevertheless the Chief Instructor decided to put out a search for them and called for volunteers to fly after tea. I went as pilot of one Anson with a couple of pupils navigating, while Jimmy Stack and Spence flew the other two.

After being briefed in the Ops room we took off at 17.40hrs and flew in formation, myself leading, to a dispersal point some 30 miles out to sea. Then we diverged into a search pattern. It was just like old times. Everyone was keyed up to meet the challenge and the weather was foul - low cloud, rain and visibility about three miles. We had tremendous fun barging through the murk and peering at the ocean for signs of our objective. We investigated three or four ships but reached the end of our search off Bonaventure Island without finding the corvettes. My navigator did a wizard job; our final landfall at Tracadie Bay was bang on position and ETA.

On the way back the weather was even more vile, and it was getting dark. My mind flew back to those grand old days when we steamed back from Norway in the dusk with a head-wind, and I remembered how worried and forlorn I used to feel. Now I loved flying in such conditions when the drizzle fell and the clouds and the haze and the sea all merged into a single wash of varying density and all the world was grey and forlorn and timeless. It was nearly dark when I landed at Charlottetown, and just as I touched down the other two aircraft roared overhead in line astern.

We all enjoyed the break from routine enormously although we were frightfully disappointed at missing our objective. It had been assumed that they were heading for the Gut of Canso; but they must have gone north about Cape Breton Island. We might, of course, simply have failed to see them in the poor weather.

On 1st July Jack Mould and I received telephone calls from the shipping agent in Halifax telling us that our wives were on board a ship expected to dock the following day. Just after noon I stood on the quayside watching a dirty old tub with a heavy list to starboard being nudged alongside by a couple of tugs. Of course we had an ecstatic meeting and began two weeks of honeymooning at Pictou Lodge, a magical log-cabin country hotel on a lagoon in northern Nova Scotia. On returning to Charlottetown we took an unfurnished house at the fringe of the city on the road to the aerodrome.

My Australian course (No. 6) departed at the beginning of August after a couple of monumental parties. They worked harder and produced better results than their precursors although they were not so hot in the air. Some of the older ones who came from Western Queensland were men of the highest quality whom I would have followed anywhere. For my next course, No. 12, I was appointed Course Commander. It consisted of Canadian pilots. I found it hard to understand them. We seemed to speak entirely different languages.

I talked to them until I was blue in the face; I instructed them until I lost my voice; but all I got when I asked them to put my words into practice was a blank stare and perhaps "But we've never done this before."

Certainly if I demonstrated things to them very slowly they eventually understood the method; and equally certainly they would never in a month of Sundays grasp so abstract a thing as a principle. I was awfully disappointed in this Brave New World. Perhaps my way of teaching was at fault. I told them, just as I told the Australians and the English, first the principle and then the application of the principle to practice. The Australians and the English reacted. The Canadians didn't know what I was talking about.

Talking with any Canadian airman left me with the impression that he thought I was a complete bloody fool, which wouldn't be so bad if I was not so well aware of his own incompetence.

In the middle of August I learned that Henry Breese was posted missing. He was quite one of the most charming and understanding people whom I was lucky enough to call a friend. Humour, poetic fancy, a graphic pen and a keen appreciation of the loveliness of wild places were things in him that I greatly admired and enjoyed.

Towards the end of the year the Flying Squadron received a bunch of pilots fresh from Canadian Flying Training Schools. Within a month they broke more aircraft than the unit had broken in all the time since it was formed in June 1940. In one day two of them bent aeroplanes: one

86

of them by overshooting on a runway 1,200 yards long and wiping off his undercarriage (he put full brakes on and tried to do a ground loop at 30 knots); the other by getting lost on a map-reading exercise round the Island and forced-landing 20 miles from Summerside.

On a fully moonlit night with unlimited visibility another of them forced landed in Gaspé after getting lost on his way to Chatham, New Brunswick. Another of them fell into the forest near Sherwood. On a further occasion one of the new pilots, having got lost in the dark, found an aerodrome at which to land. It turned out to be Chatham. He took off to return to Charlottetown without bothering to refuel although he had already been in the air for more than two and a half hours. He went missing.

All the next day there was a highly organised but fruitless search system in action. I took part in the final parallel track search sweeping NNE from Northumberland Strait to a depth of 120 miles. It was a grand afternoon, crisp and cloudless, with a 30 knot westerly streaking the sea surface. The sun was setting, and shortly after we had turned at the limit of our search it sank blood-red into a wrinkled sea of gold, and the green sky began to grow dim. Just beyond the tip of the new moon shone Venus. The sea, changing from powder blue to featureless grey behind us, merged indistinguishably into the night mists.

On our port side, we picked out the Magdalen Islands looming greyer than the sea as we raced the night southwestward. Just as we made our landfall at St Peter Bay I picked out the lights of another Anson. I closed into formation with him. There he was, a dim shape against the afterglow; and below us, in the cavernous darkness of the land, the lakes and bays and waterways shone like pearls. Far away to port I could pick out East Point light, and ahead, like a tiny jewel cluster, the lights of the aerodrome. My landing in the dark was like the touch of thistledown, perfect, and I was as pleased as Punch.

One day in mid-January two of the old hands, Johnny Rofe and Calderhead, took off in two aircraft for unauthorised air tests. Over Charlottetown at 6,000 feet they began a dog-fight, during which one aircraft struck the tail of the other. Both aircraft spun in, one exploding on hitting the ground. There were seven people killed. This was quite a

87

nine days' wonder for the people of Charlottetown, for practically everyone in the town seemed to have seen the whole thing.

In 1942, we worked hard and we played hard. The original gang knew that by the end of the year it would be due for repatriation and back to the war, and this lent an additional sharpness to our determination to enjoy with our wives all the pleasures that the Island and neighbouring Canada had to offer: in winter, skiing and skating and cosy Bridge parties and dances; in summer, fishing and sailing and swimming and riding. There were, however, dark days.

In the spring, my father-in-law died in his 64th year. He was an amiable man with an impish sense of humour behind the grave Scottish façade. Immensely respected by the shipping business community in Glasgow, he was one of the most utterly reliable men I have ever met. And then in the summer, in his 24th year, Tony Major was killed in action, flying a Spitfire. It seemed to me a very fitting end for him, for he could never have grown up. I felt honoured by his friendship.

'Beside him I always felt like an oaf, at once cloddish and wise with a complacent, middle class wisdom, for I saw him as an Elizabethan, charming and decorative on the surface, and tough too, tenacious, loyal and vivid. Most of the things he did and the people he did them with didn't interest me. I was always criticising his values and motives. But there was some inexplicable bond and a feeling of confidence between us. I suppose much of the time that vivid hot-head spent in my company was the quietest in his life, and for me, happy.'

The School expanded, courses were shortened, entries came and went through what was now a highly efficient sausage machine. Eventually it split into two. I remained at Charlottetown which served the RAF solely; the others, including Jack Mould and Jimmie Stack, went to open a new school at Summerside to serve the rest of the Commonwealth. Only one entry stood out, because on it was the long, skinny, pop-eyed figure of David Knightly who had been a great buddy of mine during my last two years at school. The complete iconoclast, he had a lightning mind and a tongue of vitriol.

At Charlottetown he was one of an unholy triumvirate who had come through Initial Training and Flying Training together: David and

Donald Kirk (a quiet, grave man) and Bill Fletcher (as ebullient as a front-row Rugby forward). We saw a lot of them in our house during May and June, and I flew with them whenever I could for the sheer pleasure of their lively company. By now the old splitarse glide approaches were verboten; with a single runway in operation and high intensity operations we had to conform and queue up in the circuit for long, shallow engine-on final approaches as much as two miles long, with visual signals from the control tower to give us permission to land.

There was a certain amount of U-boat activity in the Gulf of St Lawrence during the year which lent spice to our routine. On one or two occasions, indeed, we loaded up with bombs and flew serious U-boat searches. We were also called upon occasionally to do convoy escorts. Since all the Staff pilots queued up to fly these quasi-operational missions, I volunteered on several occasions to fly as navigator with them.

By then, the elegant Admiralty Chart had long been superseded for air navigation purposes by the utilitarian Mercator plotting chart, little more than a grid printed on thin paper with a crude coastal outline superimposed, and the combined manipulation of a perspex ruler with a five-inch Douglas Protractor had taken the place of 'Captn Field's Improved' parallel ruler with its brass linkage. There was no longer any feeling of romance in laying off the navigation plot!

I was still, and was to remain for many years yet, addicted to plotting the track and distance made good to derive my DR position, despite the fact that the official doctrine was to lay off courses and air distances flown, and apply a wind vector to the air position so derived. After all, our patrols were along pre-defined search tracks and the whole object of the exercise was to stick to them, easy enough when you always flew within sight of the sea and could measure drift directly, as well as observe on the surface any significant changes of wind velocity.

At the end of January the unit had its first and only incident of a forced landing out on the ice. The aircraft was put down 20 miles north of Sandhills light. Sleeping bags, food and a stove were parachuted down to the crew who spent the night out there before being rescued one by one the next morning by a pilot of Maritime Airways flying a little Finch fitted with skis. The Anson could not be recovered. In those days none of us carried survival gear and many, as I did, flew in service dress with only a service greatcoat for protection against the cold, such was our faith in the Cheetahs powering our machine; but this incident gave us food for thought.

Despite still enjoying pottering about the Gulf in the faithful old Anson, I was by the end of the year stale and bored to tears with the dreary repetitiveness of the classroom. With the turn of the year, postings of the old stagers back to the war accelerated, and in the middle of February I was warned that I should expect my replacement to arrive within two or three weeks, and be ready for repatriation at the end of March. 'For the rest of the day,' I wrote, 'I was as excited as a child promised a visit to the Zoo.'

From then on, although I was working to almost the final day, there was a constant series of farewell parties both at Charlottetown and Summerside, for I was not the only one to be setting course due east. Together with Sqn Ldr Bindloss, I was posted to RAF Ferry Command at Dorval, near Montreal, to fly back to UK as navigator on an aircraft delivery.

And so at 06.00hrs on 25th March 1943 I bade farewell to Isobelle, not knowing when the authorities might call her forward for a return passage to England, and left Charlottetown by train for the 24 hour journey to Montreal.

5

Boats Again

DORVAL – RAF FERRY COMMAND HQ - WAS A FASCINATING amalgam of RAF and Musical Comedy. Not only did you see, as you might expect, every shade of uniform under the sun; but also a million pretty girls dressed in anything from sables to slacks. Every Officer, however humble his station, had a secretary, so the place literally twinkled with young women. In most respects the unit was unorthodox, and apparently chaotic and happy-go-lucky, yet it seemed to deliver the goods.

Bindloss's conservative soul was shaken to the core, but there was something picaresque about the whole thing that appealed to me. We had a cheerful lunch in a cafeteria where Group Captains, Yank non-coms, civilians and aircraftmen rubbed shoulders to help themselves to good food. There we had a brief chat with Jimmy Stack, on his way to Bermuda. We were directed to one Sqn Ldr Franklyn whom, it turned out, we both knew. He fixed us up with what we wanted in no time - Bindloss to go across in a Liberator the following week, and myself to start off for Bermuda to do a short conversion onto Catalinas before going across as Co-pilot/Navigator.

A ten-hour train journey took me to New York. The next day another longish train journey took me south to Cape Charles for the three hour ferry crossing of the mouth of the Delaware River to Norfolk, Virginia. As I stepped off the ferry I was accosted by the Negro driver of a Station Wagon. In it, to my great delight, was Jimmy Stack, who had arrived the previous night. We were driven the odd forty miles through a gloomy pine forest to Elizabeth City, North Carolina, where we arrived about 8pm. The next morning we reported to the Senior RAF Officer who told us to forget everything for three or four days.

On the third day of oppressive heat and greasy Southern food, just when I was beginning to fear that we would be at 'Lizbeth City for the duration, we were told that we would be leaving the next morning as passengers in the first production Coronado flying boat. The resident Press photographer immediately corralled the four of us who were to be passengers, telling us "I guess you'll be news if you don't make it."

Alas, the weather around Bermuda delayed our departure 24 hours, so we spent a morning having a look at the Coronado. It was a young ship, about the same size as a Sunderland, full of complicated and bewildering equipment. Next day, it used up a great deal of ocean to get airborne. There was a thirty knot wind from NW, a lot of well-developed cumulus, the air was very rough and she wallowed about like a barrage balloon. I managed to get a sun position line for the navigator shortly after leaving Cape Hatteras, but after that it was far too rough and too cloudy to use a sextant to any effect. The navigator was an RCAF Pilot Officer, not very brilliant. We would never have found Bermuda had it not been for the W/Op's ability to get D/F bearings.

After coming ashore we were carried to the Belmont Manor Hotel in a truck. I thought it one of the most lovely places I had ever visited. In the evening I met Wing Commander Tubby Vielle, the arch navigation specialist stationed at Washington DC. We sat talking advanced navigation shop for a good three hours: rather, he did the talking and I listened with my mouth agape to his account of trends of development beyond my wildest dreams.

After breakfast a power boat took Jimmy and me over to Darrel's Island for a heavy morning learning about the electrical circuits of the Catalina before returning to the hotel for a quick swim and lunch. Back on Darrel's Island in the afternoon we spent a couple of hours crawling about inside a Catalina to learn where everything was. The amount of gadgetry and ancillary equipment on board seemed to me fantastic.

The next morning we did the radio systems - three receivers and two transmitters- an installation far better than anything I had seen in any British aircraft. I had another three hour session in the evening with

Vielle. He went into a lot of highly secret developments and I was left absolutely staggered by the amazing equipment which was being brought out. My whole conception of the uses of aircraft was shattered and my ideas about navigation underwent revolution.

Jimmy and I started with circuits and bumps under the tutelage of a Canadian ex-bush pilot called Casgrain. It was enormously satisfying to hear the chatter of water on the hull again, and to be gadding about in dinghies and launches. Out in the Sound there was quite a good chop running which made powerless alightings damned tricky. I soon decided that the Catalina was a bitch to handle. She was a very sloppy aircraft to fly, mainly because she had no inherent stability and the controls were very heavy indeed compared with the Anson. I had to develop special Catalina muscles.

As Casgrain said, she was merely an instrument designed to stay in the air for a long time; her rating as either a marine craft or an aircraft was zero. In the air she was utterly unstable, none of the controls co-ordinated, and she was as heavy as treacle; and when you were alighting or taking off, the shape of the hull was entirely against your doing so smoothly unless you were really skilful. If you alighted under power, of course, it was much easier because the high centre of thrust tended to keep the nose from being thrown off the water.

I had a lot to learn. For one thing, apart from a brief acquaintance with the Lerwick this was the first aircraft I had flown with variable pitch propellers. The control of engine revolutions independently of the throttle setting was no problem; but now I had to learn how to feather and close down an engine in flight, and restart it, and a whole new technique of flying on one engine, including engine failure immediately after take-off, and single-engined alightings.

As time went by the Catalina, although slow and heavy, gave me a feeling of solid reliability in the air. On the water, on the other hand, she could be something of a handful. The closeness of both engines to the centreline made directional control difficult whilst taxi-ing slowly, and the cockpit, being very close to the water level, tended to become immersed in heavy spray, particularly during taxi-ing across wind, when the large amount of asymmetric power needed to prevent weathercocking inevitably built up a lot of speed.

While taking off in a heavy chop the Cat seemed more like a submarine than an aircraft as the cockpit became enveloped in solid cascades of green water until she got running on the step. Alighting on really rough water, on the other hand, was a fairly simple piece of cake: you put her into a fully stalled attitude, very steeply tail-down, a few feet above the water so that when she lost flying speed the sternpost of the planing bottom hit first, and then she would smash down with a terrific bang - no skill required - and come almost instantaneously to a full stop.

By April 22nd I had completed sufficient conversion flying to catch a Cat which was being returned to the contractors at Elizabeth City. I passed the time taking sextant shots of the sun while we were cruising at 95 knots in very smooth air at 7,000 feet. I got a series of sun shots at meridian passage which proved to be very accurate. The navigator and I had an unexpressed difference of opinion and I proved the more correct. He was using far too low a groundspeed and was attempting to make use of all the dozens of position lines we obtained, without a foundation of dead reckoning, a dangerous thing to do unless you really are clever. Having made a landfall just north of Cape Hatteras we descended to 2,000 feet, where it was awfully bumpy. As we alighted on the river at Elizabeth City just after 18.00hrs I saw with revulsion that the spray was a dirty dun colour, the water dark and brackish.

After Bermuda, Elizabeth City was horribly dreary. The first thing I did was to send a cable to Isobelle suggesting that she meet me in Montreal. I arrived there to find her already ensconced in the Mount Royal Hotel. Although the two of us had a marvellous time together, I kept my eye on my goal. At Dorval they were extremely vague about my future. By the middle of the second week I began to get irritable about having no work to do while there was a war on. Then a human dynamo shattered the calmness of my days - Jerry Hayter whom we had long thought dead.

The passing of the years had hardened him into an almost insufferable egotist with boundless energy, yet I still found I liked him. As we were both scheduled to do a single delivery trip to UK, we teamed up together, he as Captain, I as Co-pilot/Navigator. We picked up a decent crew: a pleasant young RAF Sergeant pilot to do all the hard work, a dapper civilian wireless operator, a US Army private as his second, and an excellent civilian flight engineer.

Jerry, I discovered, had been a Catalina test pilot at the Marine Aircraft Experimental Establishment after completing an operational tour on them in the UK, so his mastery of the beast was beyond question.

As soon as we arrived at Elizabeth City we discovered they had a Catalina waiting for us. Without delay, we went right through the aircraft. Jerry did a noble job of pulling all the gear out and re-stowing it while I checked out all the navigation equipment. The rest of the crew did likewise in their own departments. After we had done a final check, run the engines, and waited for a storm to pass, we taxied into the water, discarded the beaching gear and flew for a couple of hours.

Jerry handled the Cat as if it were a toy, beautifully, as you would expect with a man of his experience. When he had finished amusing himself, Sgt Davies and I each did a couple of circuits; then we went off to test George and calibrate the D/F loop and compasses. We got back to the Virginia Dare Hotel at 7pm tired, hungry, drenched with sweat but utterly happy. As Jerry put it, the aircraft in the air was full of odd people fiddling with knobs and switches; but once we got away he expected we would shake down efficiently into a crew.

We left Elizabeth City in torrential rain, Jerry flying the aircraft. I navigated the whole trip. We got off the water easily, but 300 feet was the highest the weather would let us climb. It was very rough indeed. For the first half hour Jerry was literally wrestling with the controls, while we inside were being thrown about like pieces of soap in a whisker. Actually the weather cleared much sooner than had been forecast and we did the last 400 miles at 4,000 feet in perfectly smooth air where conditions were ideal for navigation.

I did perfectly normal 'drift' navigation the whole way: that is to say, kept a track plot from drift observations, and checked the wind (for groundspeed) by drift and wind-lanes when we were low, and by multiple drift every hour when we were at 4,000 feet. Soon after leaving the coast I got two D/F loop fixes; around the halfway mark two or three sun position lines; and towards the end I also kept a fairly steady astro check on the magnetic compass which I found to be some four or five degrees in error. We duly sighted Bermuda dead ahead and made our landfall half a minute late on ETA but some five miles north of where I had intended.

It cheered me enormously to find that the methods I had taught did produce results. Bermuda with its sapphire and turquoise sea was as bright and lovely as ever. So we put our white flying boat down on the turquoise, unruffled waters of the Great Sound and taxied slowly to Darrell's Island, I sitting on the top of the front turret smiling in the soft air, feeling very happy.

For two days our boat was in the hands of the technical people undergoing RAF acceptance checks. Then we went back to work. The first thing was a full compass swing on the ground. Next, we put her into the water, and I flew her on the test flight and the compass checks in the air. She handled beautifully, an entirely different thing from the Catalinas I had flown before - or perhaps my Catalina muscles were by then fully developed. Of course, she was a later Mark, special to the RAF. On the water the most obvious difference was the bow gun turret which degraded the pilot's forward vision, particularly when manoeuvring to pick up a buoy. I felt a growing interest in the Cat, amounting almost to enthusiasm.

I was awakened at 04.30 on the Sunday and did not shut my eyes again until 01.00 on Tuesday. At dawn the launch took us to Darrell's Island, where our boat had already been put in the water for us, so we had only to clamber aboard and stow our luggage. At 10.15 GMT we were airborne. We climbed to 6,000 feet, above fairly thick cumulus, on course to Gander. Jerry wanted to navigate, so I flew the aircraft the whole way. After about ten hours flying we made a landfall in Placentia Bay, nicely on track.

I had never seen such a breadth of barren land as Newfoundland. From 6,000 feet it looked like a very wet swamp but in actual fact it is a land of hummocky rock, quite high in parts, covered with a comparatively sparse growth of pines and riddled with lakes and

1. A Audax–Pilot, F/Cadet Aitken
    Passenger, Self

2. Self taxying out for first flight in a Fury

3. My First Command
London K5257 being prepared for me after major servicing at Calshot

4. Self as Captain of London K5257 at Sullom Voe

5.   Anson over the St. Lawrence icepack

6.   The Catalina

7. Brief Encounter, Ottawa, June 1944
between my wife Isobelle (wearing Canadian Women's
Army uniform) and myself

8. A 224 Squadron Liberator Mk VIII

9. Photo Recce Mosquito Mk 34 and Spitfire Mk 19

10. Our Hastings
('The Double-Breasted Gooney-Bird')
Snowbound in the Canadian Arctic–Resolute Bay

11.   Martelsham 'Circus'
Sqn Ldr Frank Alder in Avro Lincoln, Self in Varsity,
Flt Lieut Holden in Devon, Sgt Spittle in Meteor Mk 11
and Flt Lieut Gibson in Meteor Mk 9b

12.   Self, piloting one of my favourites
The Meteor NF Mk 11

13.   The Avro Lincoln

14.   The Short SA4 'Sperrin'

15.   No. 1 Air Navigation School Marathon

16.   No. 1 Air Navigation School Varsity and Vampire Formation

streams, an almost impossible country for communication by land. Map reading to Gander was by no means easy because 90% of the lakes were not represented on the maps, and those which were represented were drawn inaccurately.

We alighted and moored up on Gander Lake, a broad sweep of water among pine-covered hills, stark, empty and impressive. A power boat took us ashore and a station wagon rushed us along an appalling forest road to the airport, an enormous place hacked out of the bush. As we were keen to push on, the weather forecast being unbelievably good, we had to bustle; there was only an hour's daylight left, and night take-offs were not allowed on the lake. We were all pretty tired; making out a very detailed flight plan was an awful business requiring my whole power of concentration.

Within the hour we were back on board. It was fast going. During our absence they had piled a lot more freight on board, but, not having time to stow it neatly, we left it lying about to be stumbled over. Burns, the flight engineer, was a tower of strength with his cheerfulness and efficiency at this time when Jerry and I, although we wouldn't admit it, were both feeling pretty done up. All the parties we had enjoyed in Bermuda had weakened us. We were airborne on the last embers of dusk at midnight GMT.

Once on course and with work to do I bucked up enormously, although at first I found it required a lot of determination to go through the lengthy process of obtaining three-star fixes. Throughout the flight Jerry and I alternated between sitting in the first pilot's seat and doing the navigation, but we left the detailed business of monitoring the autopilot to Davies in the co-pilot's seat.

During the first hour I carefully checked the flight plan and plotted our routes on our charts in case we should get too tired to navigate properly. The rest of the crew slept at their posts for most of the time. With intelligent use of astro navigation and dead reckoning we ultimately made our landfall at Tory Island, about 15 miles south of where we should have been. It was a perfect morning, cloudless, calm and clear. We could have selected no better day for returning home.

As we flew along the coast past Malin Head, past Inishtrahull, approaching Scotland, my excitement rose higher and higher. First we saw Islay to port, then, beyond Rathlin, the Mull of Kintyre. We actually crossed the coast of Scotland at Machrihanish, then flew low to Pladda, above Arran, across to the Cumbraes and made a perfect alighting in Largs Bay.

There was not a cloud in the sky, not even on the peaks of Arran; and although the distances were clear, all the mountains seemed to have a soft blue-green veil of vagueness about them. I cannot begin to suggest the lift of spirit which this scene gave me. Nowhere in the world can there be such beauty as belongs to the west coast of Scotland. It was about 14.00 GMT (4pm local time) when we moored up at Largs, the crossing from Gander having taken thirteen and a half hours.

Air Ministry sent me on a fortnight's leave, much of which I spent at Portincaple, where I received my instructions to go to RAF Limavady in Northern Ireland to fill a navigation specialist post in No. 7 Operational Training Unit for Wellington night torpedo crews. 'I give up,' I wrote. 'Anything at once more damned stupid and more unfair it would be hard to think of. What do I know of the peculiar navigational problems of night torpedo operations? What do I know of the various sorts of ASV (radar designed for anti-submarine search) used nowadays on operations? And surely three years is enough time to have spent instructing? I think this posting is a very dirty trick.'

In fact Limavady was a very pleasant station and once I had got over my initial disappointment I began to enjoy it. There were several people there whom I had known at Squire's Gate or who had been my pupils at Charlottetown, and the Chief Navigation Officer, Sqn Ldr Ellis, was a most charming and sympathetic chap to have as boss. A new synthetic crew trainer was in the process of being built, so he gave it to me. It was a challenge, and as time went on I became quite enthusiastic about its potential, but before I had a chance to do more than a few trial runs on it during the acceptance phase I left the station.

The flying squadron was also happy to give me some quick circuits and bumps on the Wellington and let me fly as an instructor captain with some of the crews. I rather enjoyed flying the 'Wimpey'. Of my first dual sortie, which lasted 20 minutes, I noted 'Too easy!' in my logbook. At 7 OTU they used Mark Ic for conversion and Mark VIII for operational training, both of them Pegasus engined. Although the cockpit was in many ways an ergonomic nightmare, there was something in the positioning of the pilot's seat in relation to the control column and the small windscreen that made me feel immediately in command, almost king of all I surveyed. Whilst it had taken me some time to be skilled in the operation of the wheel brakes in taxi-ing the Anson (you had a ratchet lever which applied brake pressure progressively, but movement of the rudder bar superimposed differential braking), I was immediately at home with the 'spectacle' control incorporated in the aileron hand-wheel of the Wimpey: you squeezed the port spectacle to brake the port wheel, the starboard one for the starboard brake and both together to brake both wheels.

The take-off, using 20 degrees of flap, was straightforward, with only a gentle tendency to swing to starboard which was easily corrected by rudder, and when you were more expert could be prevented by opening the starboard throttle ahead of the port. One pulled the machine off the ground at about 75 knots and climbed away at 110. There was a slight sink and nose-down trim change as the flaps came in.

I found the Wimpey in general delightfully stable both in pitch and in azimuth, but it had an engaging little trick, if you let a wing drop, of dropping the nose too. The most interesting feature of the aeroplane was, however, the flexible 'feel' of the controls when she was flying in turbulent air; one's hands and feet could sense the elements of the machine weaving like a boxer's limbs to counter the onslaught of the gusts.

At the normal cruising speed of about 140 knots the controls were firm, nicely balanced and responsive. Unlike the Cat, the Wimpey was a gentleman's flying machine in this respect. She stalled at about 65 knots clean: one wing would drop fairly quickly, followed by the nose. Coming in to land one would apply 20 degrees of flap on reaching 120 knots on the downwind leg, then, having reduced speed to 105 knots on final approach, apply full flap; in each case there was a slight nose up trim change. One aimed to come in over the runway threshold at 80 knots with power on, and it really was a piece of cake to put her down nicely. A flapless landing was somewhat different; the technique was to make a long, low approach at 95 knots with plenty of power, and the elevator trim wound well back, and to cut the throttles smartly as you crossed the runway threshold. At the weights at which I flew her, there was no problem with single-engined landings, and you could climb away again on one engine at 100 knots even with 20 degrees of flap.

While Isobelle and I had been in Montreal there was still no change in policy over repatriating wives, and from what enquiries we were able to make there seemed no likelihood of any change in the forseeable future. After long discussions we agreed that her best bet was to join the Canadian Women's Army Corps and volunteer for service in Europe. She enlisted in the middle of June, and even as she was on her way to a recruit training depot her name was called forward together with those of all the outstanding wives at Charlottetown, for an immediate passage to UK. But it was too late, for she had already attested. She took this bitter disappointment with characteristic courage. Alone in a foreign land, by sheer force of character she worked her way through the ranks from private soldier, won a commission and two years later came to the UK as a platoon commander.

At the beginning of July 1943 my boss told me that he thought he had managed to secure me a posting to the Catalina Operational Training Unit on Lough Earne. This cheered me up no end, for I had been depressed by a series of unhappy letters from Isobelle, who was finding the coarser elements of recruit training to be particularly distasteful. My promotion to Squadron Leader came through in the middle of July, but my pleasure was somewhat diluted when I learned that I was to go to the Catalina OTU not as a pupil but as the Chief Navigation Instructor. Feeling doomed never to be an operational pilot again, I reported to 131 OTU at Killadeas at the beginning of August.

The station was on a big, heavily wooded estate by the waterside towards the southern end of Lough Erne, and after the wide prospects of Limavady, which had the mountain Binevanagh in the circuit, I felt horribly shut in. Together with Wing Commander Alan Lywood, the Chief Instructor, and all his departmental chiefs, I had an office in station headquarters on the top of the bank close to the boat slipways,

100

but the ground school with all my instructors was two miles away.

My senior instructor was an Australian, Flt Lieut Maund and, like all his excellent team, an Observer. He was a tough guy, a damned good instructor and a far more experienced navigator than I ever would be. His attitude, moreover, made this quite clear at first. What made things even more difficult was the Station Commander's edict desiring his departmental chiefs to be instantly available in their offices at headquarters, so it was difficult to spend very much time down at the ground school two miles away. In any case I soon realised that I had absolutely nothing to contribute there, for Maund ran his side of it extremely efficiently. It took quite a long time for me to win his respect.

One day coming back from Limavady I landed a Martinet on the satellite airstrip at St Angelo in shallow but very dense fog. He asked "Jesus, was that you stooging about in that Martinet? You are a braver man than I thought you were." But the full reconciliation did not come until I had written the report on a practical experimental programme of compass swinging using the camera obscura, for which I did the flying in both Catalinas and Sunderlands while he made the observations on the ground. Having read the draft, he conceded that I really was acceptable as a Specialist Navigator despite my handicap of being a pilot. I remember him with affection. But this was in the future.

For the present, I wanted only to get airborne and establish my credentials as a pilot. A day or two after arriving I persuaded Pete Ruston, who had been a couple of terms behind me at Cranwell and was now one of the Flight Commanders, to check me out in the Cat. The local flying area turned out to be a delightful place. Killadeas was a modest estate near the narrow end of the Lough which here was studded with little wooded islets and bordered by innumerable little bays, one of which contained the OTU moorings and slipway. A buoyed channel twisted northward between the islets to the broad reaches of the main lough where most of the instructional flying was done, though it was possible, with the wind in the right direction, to take off and alight among the islets in the vicinity of Killadeas.

I always loved flying from the water. Even though I said rude

101

things about the Cat when I was in Bermuda I had really developed a sort of nostalgic love for it. Now it was sheer joy to see the layout of the cockpit, the capacious navigation table, the electrical distribution panel and those carbon pile voltage regulators, the blister compartment, to take delight again in sitting up on the sliding roof of the cockpit when taxi-ing towards moorings. The mere actions of wielding a boat-hook, picking up strops and hitching rope-ends around cleats and snubbing posts were poetry.

The Unit had a landing strip near the ground-school for the Martinet target-towing aircraft, and this was my next type. The Martinet was the first single-engined aircraft I had flown since the day I played with a Moth at Portsmouth in 1939. As soon as I opened up the throttle the surge of power from the Mercury was evident. I belted down the runway, admittedly swaying a bit from hands and feet unused to such lightness of control, lifted her off uncertainly at 120 mph and climbed away from the aerodrome fiddling with the unfamiliar throttle, undercarriage, pitch and cowl-gill controls. My course in all three dimensions was a bit erratic. At 2,500 feet I levelled off and began to throw her about gently to get the feel of her. Lord, what fun it was; and Oh, the gentleness of the controls, the sensation of power. I was not in an aeroplane as I knew them but seemed to have been given smooth wings of my own which I dipped in great curves from steep left to steep right; diving, climbing, stall turns - the greatest thrill that any aeroplane had given me for years.

The easy smoothness of those great swinging curves across the sky: that was flying. Then some circuits and landings. The first landing, a trifle uncertain; the second, smooth and perfect on three points; the third rather alarming because I ballooned a bit and as she fell the last five feet the port wing stalled and dropped with a sudden whip. Two more reasonable ones and then I had to call it a day. Henceforth I happily used the Martinet whenever I had to make liaison visits to units on the mainland.

I took up a Canso (the amphibious version of the Cat) for a compass swing. Very, very heavy on the controls, and I thought she was never going to rise from the water. In smooth air I found the slow, solid controls very satisfying, though definitely very heavy; but there was great satisfaction to be had in squaring the shoulders and gritting the teeth to heave her round in a steep turn.

On my return from a couple of weeks' summer leave I found Donald Kirk, who had been one of David Knightly's trio of Musketeers at Charlottetown, doing a Captain's course. I went out for eight hours in a Catalina as his instructor captain, trying to find a convoy out in the Atlantic. On the outward trip, when the visibility was good, the sweep of Donegal Bay presented an impressive picture. We could see all the way down to the three pimples of Inishboffin, Inishark and Inishturk on the horizon. Although our navigation, according to the final landfall, was excellent, a square search and a creeping line ahead failed to find our objective. The weather out there was none too good: cloud at 300 feet and visibility between one and two miles.

I did an hour's navigation myself during the search. Unlike in the London where the navigator had the wardroom to himself in flight, which was very pleasant, in a Cat the navigator, the wireless operator and the radar operator were all crowded together with their equipment in one dark little compartment. The pilot's cockpit, on the other hand, was spacious and comfortable.

Bored by insufficient work in my own field, in October I persuaded the Chief Flying Instructor to take me on as a part-time flying instructor. He put me in the right hand seat and gave me a tough two hour check-flight practising propeller feathering, single engine alightings, stalled alightings with and without engine, and recovering from bounces. I also began to fly a series of trials to determine whether the camera obscura could usefully be used for swinging flying boat compasses. The snag of the current method was that the boat had to be beached and put onto a compass base.

It was an interesting project requiring quite a lot of flying to establish statistically significant results, and I was busy all the time. I flew the aircraft with Flt Lieut Haugen sitting beside me taking readings of the P9 compass at ten second intervals and averaging them; while Manson in the blisters and Allen in the turret were making astro compass observations.

Flying at 2,000 feet we started each swing from a pinpoint south of the camera site, and as soon as we were on course engaged automatics and called up the camera on R/T. I homed visually on the site, sometimes helped by them over the R/T. They gave me 'On target', at which we commenced our readings which lasted for two minutes. At the end of that time I swung onto the reciprocal and went through the same drill, on top of which I passed our average readings to the ground and they passed theirs to us. We repeated the process through all eight points of the compass.

The trials were quite successful. The combination of flying, analysing observations and writing a long report was just my kettle of fish.

Towards the end of October one of our Cats crashed, killing ten. They were practising stalling. It got into a spin, an almost unheard of thing in a Cat, with insufficient height to recover.

In my early days as a flying instructor I was learning all the time - learning perhaps more than my pupils. They had anything from 200 to 400 hours as second pilots in Catalinas against my 90 hours, so that when my general flying experience was weighed against their special knowledge (but not skill in handling) of the Cat the balance was barely perceptibly in my favour. It is not that I could not fly the thing, nor that I could not get them out of their scrapes; but that I was apt to be floored when a pupil asked me detailed questions about boost settings, revs, rates of descent and so on. There is a great gulf between flying an aircraft by instinct and feel as I always did, and giving instruction in terms of what it says in the book.

My first night landing of a Cat, indeed of any flying boat since 1939, promised to be interesting, but I wasn't the least bit worried because it was a glorious night with a full moon rising red and bloated behind the Donegal Mountains. The wind was light southeasterly. I had taken off one afternoon in a very ropey old boat with a skeleton crew to search for an aircraft dinghy. On our way home darkness overtook us. My alighting on Castle Archdale flarepath was not polished. The correct thing to do was to motor in at 70 knots at a rate of descent of 200 feet a minute. I undershot considerably, applied power to hold her at 100 feet until I was level with the downwind green light, and then more or less fell out of the sky at 80 knots and 400 feet a minute. Consequently we hit the water unexpectedly (but nicely level with No. 1 flare) and heavily. We bounced.

Fortunately we hit in a level attitude. The second arrival was as gentle and sweet as you could wish. Taxi-ing home from Archdale was delightful. In the shelter of the islands the water was as smooth as oil. The moon was big, bright, and low, and a gentle, cold spray fell on my face as I peered through the top hatch to pick out the leading lights.

A new course began in January, with David Knightly as one of the Captains under training. It was easy to see that the Great Leveller - the Service - had had its effect on him. He had lost a great deal of his rebellious individualism; he was much the same as any 'decent type' you met around the bar.

I now began to do quite a lot of night flying. The CFI always seemed to want me to do the late session. In the ante-room I was slightly different from the rest. They were drinking but I could not, and I was also the only one still wearing battle dress. On a typical night-flying session, while they were carousing and all the rest of the station was at play in pubs and canteens and lonely lanes, I walked alone through the dark woods to the deserted Headquarters building. The morning concert of birds had not yet begun; only the wind among the trees and the aircraft in the distance made noises. The fire in my office was dead, the electric light harsh on my eyes while I put on flying kit. In his tower the duty Met man spoke to me of a gently rising SW wind and of increasing amounts of high cloud during the night. Down in the flight offices my two pupils were waiting for me, alone.

After I signed Form 700 and the authorisation book we went silently to the pier and stepped aboard the powerboat. There was a new crescent moon dipping in the west. The power boat, leaving behind it a streak of phosphorescence as straight as a die, shot between the islands towards the main lough. The spray hissed on the surface like leaves in the wind, and touched my face. My pupils, as I explained the winking lights, red, green and white marking the buoyed channel, seemed to be bewildered by them.

Rounding Gull Island and heading for the flarepath we ran into a quartering sea which, in the reflected light of the moon, looked a bit ugly and forced us to reduce speed. Here the wind was over 15 knots. The power boat, swinging into wind to come alongside the control pinnace by No.3 Flare, shipped it green and drenched us who were in the well aft. We scrambled onto the big pinnace, which was as steady as a rock. In a few moments an aircraft just waterborne flashed d-d-d on its signalling lamp and the wireless operator on the pinnace told us that it was our aircraft ready to change crews.

There was a fast dinghy hitched astern of us. The driver jumped in. It soon came bobbing alongside and we also jumped in: my two pupils, a flight engineer, a rigger and a W/Op. Off we raced downwind, and came round in a wide curve with showers of spray under the tail of the Cat. It was tricky work going alongside because the aircraft, although its engines were idling, was moving at 4 or 5 knots. Getting aboard first, I went straight to the right-hand pilot's seat. I couldn't see a thing because I was dazzled by an Aldis lamp - and the windows were covered with water anyway.

And so the night wore on with the circuits and bumps: the slow climb away from the flarepath with the airscrews screaming in fine pitch; the lurching passage through the turbulence in the lee of the mountains; the calm of the downwind legs when the revs were brought down to cruising and I could relax for two minutes with a cigarette; the winking light that gave us permission to land; the tension of the long approach to the flarepath - all pupils seemed suicidally minded at this stage and my advice had to be calm and deliberate while my feet and hands were twitching to take over control; and, once we were down, the flurry of spray that enveloped us as we taxied clear of the landing strip; and the bobbing of the aircraft in the waves, and the slap of the water on the planing bottom...

One night while we were thus flying in the dark, a Cat flew into the water after taking off at Archdale. Everybody was killed except one. It was carrying two new instructors who were doing some night flying practice to get their hand in. A sorry affair.

Whilst I enjoyed flying, I never lost that feeling that every hour spent in the air was just so much borrowed time. Knowing how so many people, more experienced and better pilots than I, had come to such sticky ends (or at any rate crashed badly), I could never lose that slight apprehension before flying, nor that feeling of relief after flying. It was this, I suppose, which made flying so zestful. I wonder if most people reacted similarly? I think one of the most important requirements of a successful pilot is humility. The difference between safety and disaster was always a fraction of time.

It having been decided by Higher Authority that 131 OTU was to take on a Sunderland training commitment, Alan Lywood and the CFI brought our first two new boats from Wigg Bay. For reasons unbeknown to me, Lywood put me among the initial select few to fly them and qualify as instructors. It must have been a reward for always being so willing to fly on the least popular late night sessions. Consequently, a few days later he took me and the two Flight Commanders up on a conversion session. We went aboard through the forward entrance door on the port side and climbed straight up the ladder to the flight deck. I was most impressed.

The luxury of a Sunderland, even an operational one, was of course proverbial. By comparison a Catalina was austere to an extreme. Another thing I liked about the Sunderland was the high position of the pilots, well above the water. The next time I flew, we scrambled aboard from the launch through the rear door on the starboard side, and I was immediately struck with the thought that one could almost have put a squash court into the tail section. The only word to describe her was 'massive', and yet she handled far more smoothly and easily than a Catalina both in the air and on the water. She rode the water with more springiness, and in taking off and alighting didn't go through such large and baffling changes of attitude.

The engine controls, of course, were not as easy: there were more of them and they were clumsier. The cockpit lacked the sophistication of the Catalina: most of the auxiliary controls and indicators seemed to be arranged haphazardly, but the enormous bank of twelve large levers on the pedestal between the two pilots - throttles, mixture and propeller pitch controls for each of the four engines - was most impressive, and everything seemed to come nicely to hand.

Flying a circuit in a Sunderland was rather like playing a Mighty Wurlitzer. Take-off was a majestic process. Holding the control column hard back, I opened up the outer engines to take-off power (plus 6.75lb boost and 2,600 rpm). It was easy to keep straight by very slight differential throttle movements until full rudder control was gained.

As the nose rose gently and the spray cleared the inner propellers I followed up on the inner throttles to take-off power. With very little apparent change of attitude she rose onto the step, the choppy water being transmitted to us as a lovely, springy motion on the flight deck, and eventually she swanned gracefully into the air at about 80 knots. With flaps retracted she climbed away nicely at 110 knots.

Later I discovered that the safety speed for shutting down an outer engine was 105 knots, at which I had no problem of directional control.

I was somewhat surprised to be told that the standard practice was to make the landing approach in a power-off glide. In such a configuration the Cat would have behaved like a brick. At 100 knots with two-thirds flap down the Sunderland, on the other hand, was nothing if not gentlemanly, and all one had to do was ease the control column back so as to touch down in a perfectly level attitude at about 75 knots. If you needed power to reduce the gliding angle you applied it on the inner engines rather than the outer. For night landing or when the water was flat calm the technique was a bit different. On the final approach you applied a trickle of power on the outboard engines and maintained a speed about 5 knots below normal gliding until reaching 300 feet, where you eased back on the control column and opened up the inner engines so as to stabilise the speed at 80 knots with a rate of descent of about 200 feet per minute until the step touched the water.

Coming up to moorings was a piece of cake with the inner engines shut down, for the turning moment of the outers running near idling speed provided very delicate manoeuvring control compared with the Cat. In a good breeze you could sail backwards with great precision - just like the old Singapore.

After flying Sunderlands for a few days I returned to Catalinas. What small aeroplanes they now seemed! They were, of course, clumsy

108

aircraft to fly; but they were very handy - I had been known to do a side-slipping turn down to the water and swishtail to kill excess speed just like a Hart! - whereas a Sunderland, being so big, had a large time-lag in everything it did. Nevertheless Lywood treated them much as I did the Anson..

In May the impossible, the magnificent, the glorious, happened. Johnnie Friend and Bob Thompson-Hill marched ceremoniously into my office one morning bearing between them a huge drawing-board whereon was pinned a signal: 'Sqn Ldr Johnston to prepare for posting overseas for Liberator training.' I went almost crazy with delight. 'Overseas' meant Nassau in the Bahamas and obviously I would have a chance to see Isobelle en route.

Thinking it would be a good thing to get some night flying practice on landplanes I organised a programme with an Oxford on the strip at St Angelo. Mike Lawson-Smith gave me some dual. I found it an easy enough aircraft to cope with once I was used to the swing as the tail dropped on landing. Just before packing up I decided to do a solo circuit. Unfortunately I crashed the thing. On landing I held off rather high, and when we bounced, instead of motoring it down onto the ground I decided to open up and go round again.

Forgetting the engines were Cheetahs, not Twin Wasps, I slammed the throttles open. The starboard engine stalled. We swung viciously to starboard, but I managed to throttle back, land it off the runway in pitch darkness, and cut the switches. By vicious use of the brakes I got the thing under control - and then we went bang into a great big ditch at about 25 mph and wiped off the wheels and did sundry fairly serious damage to the airframe.

I was perfectly cool, calm and collected then and for about an hour afterwards: but when I got to bed the reaction set in and I had a very grim half hour before the Doc's pills sent me to sleep.

Apart from feeling very depressed and angry all the next day however, there were no after-effects. But my clean record was broken. I left Killadeas under an official cloud, though everyone there was awfully decent.

6

Liberators

I SAILED FROM LIVERPOOL IN THE *PASTEUR* ON 18TH MAY 1944, arrived in New York on 23rd and caught the night train to Montreal. There I found Isobelle. Her army gave her five days' leave which we enjoyed hugely at a comfortable little hotel in a small paradise up the Gatineau River while, wholly unknown to us, the most momentous event of the war took place - the invasion of Europe.

The journey to New Providence Island, by train via New York to Miami and thence by boat to Nassau, took 48 dreary hours. I found New Providence a small, uninteresting coral island covered mainly with scrub, and Nassau, its only town, a scruffy little place.

The main RAF Base was at Oakes Field. On my first day there, I went up in a Mitchell (B25). She handled nicely in the air, firm and positive on the very well co-ordinated controls. I was rather shaken by the very fast landing with a tremendous screeching of brakes and smell of burning rubber.

The Mitchell was used as a run-in to the Liberator. The idea was that half a dozen hours' dual day and night, and about three hours' solo, would familiarise us with the techniques of nose-wheel aircraft in general and of the flight deck management of these strange American aircraft.

The cockpit layout of the Mitchell, and the management drills, were remarkably similar to those of the much larger Liberator, although the handling characteristics of the two were as different as chalk and cheese. The Mitchell was fast, wonderfully responsive, with an excellent single-engine performance. I have a vivid memory of joyous excitement, flying very low among the little islets and rock outcrops,

111

twisting and turning with the wingtips only a few feet above the sea and feeling totally in control of the machine.

Although she was easy to fly, the multitude of knobs and the drills in these American aircraft seemed at first more than I was made for. I looked back on the Anson's simplicity with real nostalgia. Everything had to be done according to a checklist which was read out by the co-pilot and repeated back by the pilot. Before starting up: pitot head cover removed, nose-wheel towing pin secure, nosewheel door secure and bolt wired, emergency controls for nosewheel and bomb doors stowed, nose-gear pawl to 'off', check emergency brake pressure, bomb door lever to 'closed', heater off, emergency fuel shutoff to 'on', fuel transfer selectors 'off', crossfeed 'off', generator switches on, inverter switches on, invertor selector 'active', fuel transfer switch off, parking brakes on and pressure checked, elevator trim zero, pitch fully fine, mixture at 'idle cut-off', autopilot off, superchargers in low ratio and locked, oil cooler shutters open, carburettor heat 'cold', cowl gills shut, undercarriage safety clip on, rudder and aileron trimmers at zero, emergency air brake wired 'down', emergency hydraulic selector at 'normal', de-icers off, altimeter switched to static, battery disconnect switches 'on', 12 volt supply on, lower turret retracted, fuel levels checked, ignition master switch on, booster pumps on.

That done - and it followed a logical sequence from left to right across the cockpit, then from top to bottom consoles - you started each engine, which required juggling with three switches, the mixture control and the throttle.

When the engine was running you checked oil pressure, opened the cowl gills, switched off the appropriate booster pump, checked suction, hydraulic and brake pressures, uncaged gyros and tested flaps. Before taking off you ran up each engine checking oil pressure and temperature, cylinder head temperature and fuel pressure; you tested propeller constant speed and feathering unit, magnetos, high speed blower, carburettor heater; you checked take off boost, generators and spare inverter. Then you were ready to *prepare* for take off.

With engines idling you prepared for take-off thus: set altimeter and directional gyro; check gyro horizon uncaged; check suction; check oil temperatures and pressures; check cylinder head temperature; check fuel pressure and contents; check brake and hydraulic pressures; set elevator trim for take-off; set pitch fully fine; mixture to full rich and locked; autopilot off; superchargers low and locked; carburettor heat cold and locked; flaps 20 degrees; undercarriage safety clip off; aileron and rudder trimmers to zero; cowl gills one third open. Then you cleared the engines at 50% power.

As soon as you were airborne after take off you raised the undercarriage and held the aircraft down until she was doing 150 mph. At 300 feet, you raised flaps, adjusted boost and revs to 34 inches and 2200, climbing at 165 mph., checking cylinder head temperatures and adjusting cowl gills as necessary. At 800 feet you started turning and adjusted to 30 inches boost and 2000 revs. Levelling out at 1200 feet, you set revs 1800 and boost sufficient to maintain 165 mph, weak mixture, booster pumps off.

Going down wind preparing to land the procedure was: trailing aerial in; de-icers off; retract lower turret; mixture to full rich; superchargers low gear and locked; carburettor heat cold; cowl gills adjusted; revs to 2100; check undercarriage warning horn; put down undercarriage and check down and locked; increase boost as necessary to maintain 165 mph. Then you came round in a semicircular approach to the runway; 15 degrees of flap as you began the turn, reducing speed to 140 mph half way round, and turning onto the runway at 800 feet. You then dropped flaps to 30 degrees and let speed decay to 130 mph. At 300 feet you opened revs to 2400, lowered full flaps, then after a hectic juggle and with any luck you were down. There were, however, still one or two checks to be done: test brakes, open gills, pitch to fully fine, booster pumps off, elevator trim zero and flaps up.

Once I had the Mitchell more or less sewn up we moved to Windsor Field, right out in the bush where it was very hot, sticky and buggy. Here the real hard work, flying the Liberator (B-24), began. She was very heavy and slow on the controls, although they were very well co-ordinated. In the draughtless cockpit, with the sun blazing through the glass by which you were surrounded, the temperature was above 100°F; and if it was at all bumpy your body was braced between rudder bars and the back of your seat to give you the necessary leverage to heave on the wheel, so that the sweat literally poured from your face and body. At the end of a couple of hours, not only did you have a devil of a thirst but you also felt physically worn out, your hands, wrists and forearms quite painfully stiff.

At Windsor Field I met up again with Flt Lieut David Popkin, who now became my lead navigator. He had been on the instructional staff at Killadeas, having completed an operational tour on Catalinas. A young tea-planter in Ceylon before the war, he was a reserved individual who performed his duties efficiently and without fuss; he was the least flappable man in the crew. We picked up the bulk of our green 'first tour' crew members: three wireless/radar operators; a rumbustious, red-headed Irish flight engineer; an Australian second pilot straight from Flying School, Sergeant Smith, at first rather bloody-minded because he wasn't being trained as a Captain (though in the end he became a sound member of the crew and even conceded that he still had a lot to learn); and a Canadian second navigator/bomb-aimer.

This bunch flew with me on every flight from now onwards, and the aim of the course, once I had qualified on the Liberator after some five hours' dual, was to give us, as a crew, collective training in gunnery, bombing and radar homing drills in some 50 hours of flying. The wireless/radar operators and the flight engineer all doubled as air gunners, manning the three twin 0.5 inch machine gun turrets and the two waist gun positions. We were later to pick up two straight air gunners in the UK.

The two pilots sat in great comfort in a well-designed cockpit. In the Mark VI Liberator the navigator and bomb-aimer shared a reasonably spacious compartment in the nose of the aircraft, but the flight engineer, wireless operator and radar operator with their sophisticated equipment occupied a very cramped space around the base of the mid-upper gun turret, immediately behind and below the level of the pilots. Aft of them was the huge bomb bay which had a narrow catwalk leading aft to the beam gun station.

The basic model from which Coastal Command's Libs evolved was the Liberator Mk III which, perhaps, was the most unpleasant to fly.

Most of my flying at Windsor field was done on the Mark V, which did not have a nose turret, and the Mark VI, which did. Almost the first thing you noticed when taxi-ing was the marked pitching movement as you applied brakes, rather like riding a rocking horse. The brakes were applied through toe-operated pedals above the rudder pedals. If, for example, you wished to turn left, your left toes pressed on the brake pedal, but your right heel had to apply a countervailing pressure on the right rudder pedal, and, if a crosswind was gusting hard on the rudders, taxi-ing could be a somewhat acrobatic manoeuvre which required considerable strength.

The operating checklists for the Liberator were not unlike those of the Mitchell, but now the whole crew was involved. As though in a stage cross-talk act their voices cut in on the intercom:

Canadian: "Bomb doors shut, bombs safe, bomb gear checked, nosewheel lock out. Navigator at take-off station."

Australian: "Magnetos on, batteries on, booster pumps on, mixture rich, blowers engaged, controls unlocked, flaps 15."

Irish: "Bomb doors checked, hydraulic booster off, auxiliary power unit off, generators on."

Northumbrian: "Rear turret locked central, hatches shut, deflectors shut, gunners at take-off stations."

On take off you opened the throttles wide against the brakes, having first ensured that the nosewheel was straight; then as you released the brakes you opened up all four engines to maximum permitted power (turbo-superchargers in). When the nosewheel began to pound on the runway you pulled back on the control column until the pounding stopped, and kept the attitude constant with the nosewheel in light contact with the ground. At about 110 knots (varying slightly with Mark and load) you literally heaved her off the ground. She certainly needed a lot of runway.

Raising the undercarriage and the flaps from the take-off position had very little effect on trim as she gradually climbed away at about 120 knots. We generally cruised for maximum range at about 145 knots, at which speed with heavy loads she was reasonably stable.

The initial approach speed before landing was 130 knots, and when committed to landing one would apply full flap and reduce speed to 120 knots. The rate of descent was checked before touchdown with the object of skimming the main wheels on the runway and keeping the nosewheel off as long as possible.

Up we would go to sit suspended among the cloud tops, the wrinkled crawling sea and the dark shapes of the islands far below us. Whatever work we had to do, each one of us sitting before a bank of dials, buttons, switches and cocks, we perceived the crawling sea and the drifting cloud tops only subconsciously.

For me, hour after hour a steady scanning was involved, methodically from left to right across the engine instruments checking pressures, temperatures and power settings; across the flight instruments checking speed, attitude, height; across the sea from ahead to abeam and back; across the sky from ahead to abeam and back; then the cycle began all over again. Rarely, however, at this stage did we have a chance to float majestically about the air watching. There were too many things to practice: twisting and turning in evasion of fighters; the 5,000 feet swoop to carry out a visual attack on a submarine; procedures for coming down through cloud to land in fog.

The onlooking poet might have likened the swoop of attack to the effortless plummeting of an eagle, but it neither was nor felt effortless. From 5,000 feet to 50 in less than a minute was some going; 30 tons of steel at 300 knots required muscular effort; the noise of the airflow was terrific; and in that headlong dive not only must I position the aircraft accurately for the final attack, but also the bombing gear had to be set up and all the engine controls had to be arranged to make the maximum power available for the getaway. When we were attacked by fighters we may have looked like swallows at play, but of the pilot evasive action demanded brute force of shoulder, leg and arm muscles; while the gunners had to develop a skill not only to keep their aim on a high speed target while they themselves were being thrown about, but also to make a lucid and co-ordinated running commentary so that we all knew exactly what the attackers were doing.

At the end of the course we were despatched to a Manning Depot at Moncton, New Brunswick, and travelled by rail from Miami. By arrangement Isobelle, having wangled more leave, was waiting for me in lodgings. We had a happy time waiting for me to be needed. Eventually I and my crew were flown home in the belly of a transport Liberator. While reporting to Air Ministry for instructions I encountered Jack Holmes squiring the lovely Audrey Hayter, from whom I learned that Jerry had gone into Bomber Command after he and I came back from Elizabeth City, and that he had been killed in a major raid over Germany.

Early in October I went to do a course on Leigh Light tactics at Aldergrove. On my 26th birthday, a horribly grey, misty day, I took off for a shakedown trip lasting four hours. My crew got down to things well after their long absence from the job. In the dismal gloom and haze my landing was safe but a bit heavy. The comparative shortness of the runway made me let the speed drop off on the final approach and I cut the throttles too early. Nevertheless I felt distinctly pleased with life. Flying went on intensively, first with day radar homing exercises against shipping targets. One afternoon I did forty low bombing runs in two and a half hours, at the end of which my shoulders were stiff from heaving the Lib over into steep turns.

One dark night my career nearly came to an end. While I was doing Leigh Light attacks on South Rock Lightship, Jerry Haggas was doing similar runs on Skulmartin. Somehow we managed to approach each other on reciprocal courses at 300 feet. I happened to raise my eyes from the instrument panel just in time and saw his port and starboard navigation lights dead ahead. He must have seen me at the same instant, for as I slammed the throttles fully open and heaved the Lib into a steep climbing turn to starboard, I saw his lights suddenly heel over in the opposite direction. It was a close call.

The Leigh Light, designed to illuminate a small surface target, was a searchlight installed in a streamlined housing under the Liberator's starboard wing outboard of No. 4 engine. You usually carried out a night search on your radar while flying at 300 feet. As soon as the radar operator picked up a response which, from its relative motion, was identified as a surface target, you heaved the Liberator into a steep turn to bring it dead ahead. As the target was moving in its own right and the wind was causing the Liberator to drift, the radar response appeared to move away from dead ahead; nevertheless you held the aircraft accurately on a steady heading until you halved the distance at which you had originally brought the response dead ahead. You then noted the angle at which the response was now offset and turned the aircraft towards it, through double the angle, so that the target was now offset an equal amount on the opposite bow.

In theory this angle should now remain constant if you had performed accurately, so the bomb-aimer set this angle on his bomb sight and on the Leigh Light. At two miles the pilot opened the bomb doors, the bomb-aimer selected and fused weapons and set the intervalometer, and the co-pilot set up the camera timing and the flares for the post-strike photographs. At one mile, the pilot switched on the Leigh Light, the narrow beam of which, if all had been done properly, illuminated the target.

The bomb-aimer would then identify the target to the pilot, who could not see it because of the restricted field of view over the front turret and must, in any case, concentrate on accurate instrument flying. The captain would order continuation of the attack if it was a U-boat, or abandonment if it was, for example, a flak ship.

The order 'attack' having been given, the bomb-aimer would con the aircraft visually to the release point established by his low-level bombsight, and drop the weapons. The pilot maintained a steady course until the flares indicated that the post-strike photographs had been taken. If at any time during the attack the contact disappeared, the navigator, having noted the last known relative position of the response, would direct the pilot to the estimated position of the submarine, and a sonobuoy would be dropped there. If it picked up the underwater indications of a submarine's presence, then the navigator would direct the pilot to fly a pattern in which further sonobuoys were dropped to provide tracking information for a blind attack.

Early in November I learned that we were to join No. 224 Squadron at Milltown, near Elgin, for operational experience pending my being given an operational appointment appropriate to my seniority. The Squadron commander, Wing Commander Terry McComb, was away

118

on leave, so I came immediately under the aegis of the remarkable Mick Ensor, 'A' Flight commander, who was acting CO. His slightly shambling, diffident manner disguised a veritable lion of a man with a burning hatred of all Nazis, particularly Nazi submariners, in the pursuit of whom he had already acquired at the age of 23 a DSO and a DFC and bar. He took me straight to the Squadron Mess at Innes House, a baronial mansion belonging to the Tennant family, and gave me a half-share of his own bedroom.

What I found most difficult to adjust myself to, after the rigours of training and being trained, was the free and easy atmosphere of squadron life. When not flying or required for continuation training, one pleased oneself. Within a few days of my arrival the Squadron was taken out of the line for intensive training on its new Liberators Mk VIII. By then I had learned that this was no ordinary squadron, but was Coastal Command's crack Leigh Light Squadron just fresh from highly successful operations covering the invasion of continental Europe. Among its captains was K.O. Moore, credited with sinking two U-boats in separate Leigh Light attacks within the space of twenty minutes. Among all these veterans, despite Mick's personal kindness and friendliness, I suffered an awful feeling of inferiority.

In the Mark VIII Liberator the navigator was relocated from the inaccessible nose to the flight deck. Radar operator and navigator now sat side by side facing aft, so that the Captain could consult either of them without moving from his seat. To achieve this, however, the Wireless Operator was banished to a cabin in the attic just aft of the bomb bay.

The new anti-submarine radar was a much refined version of ASV Mk V. The navigator had Gee, Loran, and ASV Mk II. The wireless equipment was the same: radio compass, three receivers and two transmitters for short range R/T, and long range W/T transmitter and receiver, plus a special receiver for the sonobuoys. One very useful addition was a set of accurate fuel consumption gauges. So far we had had to rely on calculating fuel consumption from graphs of boost and revs settings, because the tank contents gauges were utterly unreliable.

My first flight in the Mk VIII was quite a decent trip with only one or two minor snags due largely to not knowing where various things were. We were bombing a target about 15 miles north of Findochty. It was a calm day: high grey overcast, grey sea, grey light, but the air was as clear as polished glass, and along the western horizon from Ben Wyvis to Cromarty to Morven in Caithness the mountains were like models moulded in matt-white china, very lovely. On our first night flight, three hours of radar/Leigh Light homings, everything went well and the crew coped with minor snags with commendable efficiency. When we took off at 22.30 it was as dark as a deep mine, but very soon the clouds cleared completely and by starlight alone one could pick out the coastline at two miles. We did eight attacks on fishing vessels, three of which were perfect, two very bad and the rest average. Our strike photographs turned out well.

A couple of days before Christmas we carried out an exercise with a submarine fitted with a schnorkel. We picked her up on the surface off Montrose at noon and, after an exchange of greetings on R/T, she submerged to schnorkel depth. Unfortunately after about ten minutes the automatic frequency control on our radar went for a Burton, with the result that we had the greatest difficulty in keeping the set tuned. That, added to the inexperience of my operators, made the exercise abortive except as far as it showed the whole crew what a damned difficult thing the schnorkel is to pick up either visually or by radar.

I let Sgt Smith do all the flying to and from the exercise area so that I could enjoy pottering about the interior of the aircraft. I exercised the tail and mid-upper turrets; had a chat with Woodward in the wireless cabin; crawled up into the nose and had a general goof at the equipment there; and on the flight deck played with the drift-meter and the radar. I wanted very much to do both the radar operator's and the bomb-aimer's jobs in a Leigh Light attack but so far I hadn't dared go very far away from the cockpit because Smith's night flying was apt to be rather a menace (Popkin agreed with me).

I felt a sort of proprietary air about my aircraft and liked wandering about watching the other chaps at their jobs. Whenever I left the cockpit I always announced on intercom "Captain leaving intercom". Usually when I reached another station, for example a turret, I plugged in again.

When Smith was in charge up front, intercom discipline relaxed somewhat and it was fun to listen to them all being matey (I insisted on rigid drill usually - "Captain to Rear Gunner" style instead of "I say, Ted").

My crew having been checked out by the Squadron Bombing Leader, Radar Leader and Gunnery Leader on sundry exercises, we flew what was technically our first 'ops' trip on 29th December, though in fact it was principally a fuel consumption test. The whole thing was chaos.

We were supposed to take off at 12.00hrs to fly to Lossiemouth for refuelling to full load because our long runway at Milltown was temporarily out of use. First snag was trouble with the ammunition boosters in the rear turret; and then, when they said the aircraft was ready, I found the top surface of the wings was covered with rough ice. So we were about two hours late taking off.

At Lossiemouth they filled the tanks up and we took off at 15.30 at 64,000lb all up. She came easily unstuck in about 1,600 yards with no wind. The power settings they gave us for the consumption test were good; we battered around the patrol at about 145 knots on the average. Shortly after setting course we noticed a big discrepancy between the P10 magnetic compass and the fluxgate compasses; I decided to stick by the P10, but this brought us the wrong side first of Fair Isle and then of Sumburgh. Ford, who was navigating, sorted it out and decided it was the P10 that was at fault. North East of Muckle Flugga we turned for the northern end of the Faeroes and in a very short time ran into cloud.

Although we tried everything from 1,000 to 5,000 feet we were in cloud for the rest of the trip until about 15 minutes before reaching base.

The Loran wasn't giving very satisfactory results. We picked up the Faeroes on radar, flew down to the southern tip, and set course thence to Sumburgh. After that everything seemed to go haywire.

On a very dubious ETA we altered course for base, having failed to pick up either Shetland or Orkney on the radar. About half an hour later Popkin picked up a doubtful Loran fix which put us well out in the

North Sea. I altered course to the southwest and asked Rose to get a M/F D/F fix. In this he failed, but Popkin got a second Loran fix confirming the first, and Rose got a QDM (magnetic course to steer) from base.

The radar meanwhile had packed up altogether; we got no indication of land at all until we saw Lossiemouth aerodrome beacon dead ahead through a break in the clouds. When we called base on R/T they told us to land at Lossiemouth because of ice on our runways. I put her down very nicely, but I was thoroughly fed up with the crew's performance.

In the middle of January we learned that the CO had been posted and that Mick Ensor was going to take command of the Squadron. We were all delighted, for he was not only an ace in his field, but also immensely popular. A few days later, I was made Senior Flight Commander in his place. I was as pleased as Punch although it was a hard act to follow, and indeed it was a long time before the Veterans gave me their complete trust. Almost immediately I had my first lesson in a Flight Commander's responsibility.

I had scheduled myself as No. 1 on the Ops roster. When I got up at 03.15 to be briefed, it was snowing hard. The Met man gave a very gloomy picture of the day's weather. He said, to end his tale of woe, that it would be extremely doubtful whether base would be open for our return, and that it was quite certain that nowhere else in the UK would be. I discussed things with the Controller at Group. He suggested rather off-handedly that we might get down in Iceland. In the end he put the onus on me to scrub the trip. Which, with much heart-searching, I did. When daylight came I was able to see just how bad the local weather was, with continuous moderate snow and low cloud. At about 09.30 Group released all crews until midnight.

I always loathed having to make such a decision concerning my own flying. When I was rostered to fly I felt morally bound to get airborne whatever the conditions, and I felt that, however the conditions justified it, a strong line against flying displayed lack of courage or keenness.

With effect from 01.00hrs on 10th February 224 Squadron became fully operational on Lib Mk VIIIs. Four sorties the first day, five the next. There was considerable activity in our area, resulting in three positive schnorkel sightings and attacks by aircraft. Everybody was pleased and delighted to be back in the war again. The only snag as far as I was concerned, however, was that the CO expressed a strong wish that I should not fly on ops until the squadron had settled into the new routine. Naturally both I and my crew were disappointed, but with the other Flight Commander, John Downey,[1] away on leave things were definitely apt to get a bit chaotic when I was absent for any length of time. John Downey had just been awarded the DFC for a 'perfect model Leigh Light attack.'

As Flight Commander I was responsible for the operational efficiency and deployment of 15 crews each of 11 men. I also alternated with the CO and 'B' Flight Commander as Duty Commander in charge of all flying operations on the aerodrome. The squadron was tasked to provide a fixed number of aircraft and crews daily for operations, month in and month out, and it was the Flight Commander's job to ensure that his crews were operationally proficient, to roster them, to assign them to the tasks which came into the station Operations Room from Group HQ, and to allocate aeroplanes to them.

Each crew, once it had been trained up to operational fitness, worked through a continuous three-day cycle until it went on scheduled leave. 24 hours operational readiness starting at 08.00hrs was followed by 24 hours of stand-down after flying on operations. On the third day the crew would be available for intensive continuation training on the ground and in the air. On these training days most crews flew at least once, and when they were not flying they split up for ground training under the specialist Leaders - Navigation, Bombing, Radar and Gunnery. The ground indoctrination of pilots was, apart from Link Trainer exercises, carried out by their Flight Commander.

If I was not flying with my own crew on our training day, I had to fly from time to time with a new Captain and crew to assess them. My crew, of course, was rostered normally like anybody else, but I myself was rarely able to stand down as they were. Unless we were flying

---

[1] Later, Air Vice Marshal J.C.T. Downey

123

ourselves, both John and I made a point of being down at dispersals to see our crews off on ops trips, and of welcoming them back on landing.

At 22.05hrs on 25th February I stood at the dispersal to see 'D' take off. As Flt Lieut Ponting, the skipper, opened up the engines to taxi away he flicked on his landing lamp and lit me up. I waved to him, and saw his arm, white-gloved, wave back at me. He was leaving for an anti-submarine patrol in the Kattegat. Being Duty Commander I decided to spend the night in the Ops room until Ponting and Downey were due to come off patrol. At about midnight, however, I was told that nine Halifaxes belonging to Stornaway had been diverted to us and would arrive between 01.30 and 03.00, so I went down to flying control.

The first Halifax due was piloted by Ron Frazer, who was with me at Charlottetown. He never arrived and was posted as missing. There was complete silence from Ponting and Downey, as one would expect unless they made a submarine contact, so at about 04.30 when they should have been well out of the patrol area and all the Halifaxes bar Frazer's had landed and been debriefed, fed and accommodated, I went to bed.

'D' never came back: Ponting and his crew vanished in silence. When I was in the adjutant's office in the afternoon I saw copies of the telegrams – 'Regret to inform you...' - and so, although life went on at Milltown exactly the same as before, the sun had utterly gone out of the lives of the wives and mothers of these people.

It was fairly certainly established later that they were shot down in flames by flak from a convoy in the Kattegat. In about the right place at the right time one of Leuchars' aircraft saw an aeroplane so destroyed. Subsequently the body of one of the crew was washed up on the Swedish coast.

A few days later I got airborne at 15.50hrs on a lovely afternoon, mild and sunny with a strong westerly wind. We had been briefed to hunt, with two other aircraft, the area in which there had been a U-boat contact the night before. This area, at its eastern end, was within 50 miles of Lister, the German night fighter base on the Norwegian coast. When I saw the area marked on the wall chart in the Ops Room, I felt afraid; but as soon as I was airborne I was far too absorbed in the job to have any feeling but enjoyment.

Very shortly after last light we got a good radar contact on which, after making a speed check, we homed. It disappeared at a range of 2 miles and was never picked up again. Over the estimated position of the contact we dropped a marker flare which, alas, we lost in the very rough sea that was running (there was a 50 knot westerly wind at 1,000 feet). We assessed it as a positive U-boat contact and reported it by W/T, and subsequently received instructions to make homing transmissions on W/T, which we did for two hours while flying a 15 mile square round the estimated position.

It was a lovely night, the moon was full with broken stratus at two or three thousand feet. Nothing else happened. At midnight we came off patrol. After a long slog against the wind we landed at base at 02.45, gave all the gen to the intelligence Officer and retired to bed around 05.00. The crew had done their job well.

After a full day's work (though not a very heavy one, I must admit) I took off at 20.45hrs one night for my first patrol in the eastern Skagerrack. I was elated, never frightened; and the crew was excited. It turned out to be an extremely interesting and pleasant trip. The weather in transit outbound was pretty poor; we were flying in cloud and continuous rain from Peterhead to within 30 miles of the Norwegian coast. Very shortly after picking up Lindesnes on the radar we broke out of the weather, and in our patrol area we had a smooth sea, very light wind, and good moonlight diffused by patches of high cloud. Having fixed ourselves off Lindesnes we flew at 300 feet close up the coast past Christiansand. It was well lit up and I couldn't help feeling that it was rather like driving down Piccadilly in a dim-out. Off Arendal we picked up a number of contacts. Two which we investigated were MTBs (we identified them in the moon-path), and others were merchantmen.

At midnight we began our patrol proper, which was a box between a point east of Langesund and Skagen Horn in Denmark. We floated gently twice round this box, and it was just like doing a box in, say, the Moray Firth, with the added excitement of expecting flak every time

125

one investigated a radar contact. Visibility was wizard, and the air was as smooth as the sea.

Flying a white Liberator on a moonlit night within four miles of an enemy-held coastline I felt vaguely that we were sticking our necks out, without exactly experiencing fear. Sometimes I felt like an adventurous mouse, sometimes like a cautious cat expecting a nasty shock. Alas, we found no U-boats. We were stalking ships by moonlight. All that we found in the area were two neutral merchantmen, a tug towing a barge, and a minesweeper in company with what looked like a landing craft. We homed to within a mile of the minesweeper before we identified it; and as soon as Gordon Arkley, who was acting as bombardier while Ford was sick, said over the intercom "It's a minesweeper or destroyer" I turned steeply away and quite coolly braced myself for the flak which, to my intense surprise, never came. How they could miss seeing us, big and white, half a mile away at 200 feet, I cannot imagine.

When we came off patrol at 02.45 we flew back along the coast past Arendal and Kristiansand and picked up several aircraft contacts, but none bothered us. Then we ran into the bad weather again. This lasted for half an hour, after which we had a simply wizard trip back to base. Day was breaking as we arrived in the circuit. By the time we stopped engines in dispersal it was daylight, and the smell of rain on the grass was delightful.

On my next Skagerrack/Kattegat job there was no moon, so the prospect was rather alarming because one would have no idea, until it was too late, whether one was attacking a flak-ship or worse. However, as soon as I was airborne I was again too absorbed in the job to worry. It was very dark. All the way across the North Sea we were in cloud as low as 400 feet, but it cleared to a cloudless, calm night just as we entered the Skagerrak. We were on patrol between Denmark and Sweden for three hours without any success. A large number of surface vessels was in the area; these had all to be illuminated by Leigh Light and checked, which made time pass quickly. It was another long stooge home against the inevitable headwinds, so we didn't land until after 09.00.

After this trip it was our turn to have a fortnight's leave. When I got

126

back to the Squadron I learned that it had been working hard, flying masses of hours in a month which had been Coastal Command's record, and having some interesting results. Most notable was Paddy Graham's attack on a schnorkel sub. The photographs showed the depth charges exploding smack at the apex of the wake.

We did a night training flight and I found that everyone was useless after such long abstinence. The next day we did another in the afternoon and again at night, by the end of which we had all regained our skills and more, so I went to bed early in the anticipation of taking off on ops in the small hours. After precisely two hours in bed I was hauled out for briefing. We took off at 02.15 on a job between the Faeroes and Iceland. All went smoothly and comfortably until 09.00, when suddenly the guns in the front turret began firing.

I called up the front gunner and got no reply. He wasn't on intercom. Ford, the bombardier at the time, cottoned on, checked the jack-box outside the turret and switched it over to intercom. "Front gunner to Captain: we have just passed over a fully surfaced submarine three miles back!" I was quite flabbergasted. We were flying at 2,000 feet in the skirts of 10/10ths stratocumulus, and nobody else had seen anything.

While alerting and checking with the rest of the crew, I was throwing the Lib round in a steep diving turn for a visual attack. I couldn't really believe it, though later I realised there was no doubt about it. By now the wretched thing had completely disappeared. We began laying a sonobuoy search pattern; but the first two buoys failed to function properly and the third fouled the aircraft, preventing the deployment of any more of them. We searched round for half an hour with no result. By then we were well past the prudent limit of endurance, so I set course for base. Dallas's failure to check that he was switched to intercom before entering the turret thus lost us an attack on a fully surfaced U-boat. I was at first absolutely wild with anger, and then exceedingly cut up.

The next day Johnnie Barling carried out a very promising attack north of Shetland. Then Broadhurst also made a most promising one about ten miles north of Banff, and was followed up by Graham. Bob

Rayner was sent out to cover the spot. He homed an escort group, saw tremendous quantities of oil and generally concluded that the thing was on its last legs.

Apprehension is a peculiar thing. During the moon-season I usually put myself among the last two on the Ops roster, knowing that if there was a Skagerrak trip to be done it would be I who would do it. Such trips appealed to me. Yet, as soon as I heard there was a Skag job definitely laid on for me, the cold worms of fear began gnawing away in the old belly, and I found myself comforting myself by considering all sorts of wild, remote possibilities, such as 'there won't be enough serviceable aircraft', 'the weather will be too bad', 'I will have a big mag. drop on run-up', etc. So it came about that at the end of another full day's work I took off at 20.35hrs bound for the Kategat.

On the outward trip, having handed over to Smith, I slept for a couple of hours before entering the patrol area. The weather was not exactly what we wanted; the moonlight was diffused by a lot of high cloud. In addition we were somewhat foxed by the exceedingly large number of illuminated fishing vessels right in our area. We patrolled at 250 feet for about three hours, during which time we saw to the south of us a great deal of medium flak thrown, no doubt, at the anti-shipping Halifaxes.

Just as we were about to set course off patrol we got a radar contact ahead and I decided, since it wasn't showing any lights, that we would go in and drop our bomb load. We homed on the contact and at one mile range illuminated a small cargo boat (about 1,000 tons) which immediately began shooting at us. Dallas in the front turret gave back in good measure and Popkin duly dropped his bombs - but rather overshot, I think. I was too busy flying the aircraft (we attacked at 150 feet) to see anything, but the crew tell me that there was lots of tracer. They were thrilled to the core.

The days whizzed past. I seemed to have little time to realise the great events that were happening in Europe until the night of 4th May when the news of the surrender of German forces in Denmark, Holland and North West Germany came through. Group immediately laid on a big daylight effort in the Kattegat. I had only just landed from a 12 hours plus sortie between the Faeroes and Norway so I couldn't go. John Downey attacked a fully surfaced U-boat but unfortunately overshot; Mick Ensor also attacked and straddled one. I took off at 16.30hrs the next day bound for the Kattegat via Aalborg.

The North Sea was so calm that we were getting radar returns off shoals of fish. We flew very low over Denmark. It was a strange sensation to be flying all alone in daylight in waters which 48 hours before had been heavily guarded enemy territory. I landed at 03.15.

When I got up for lunch the news was flying about that Norway had packed it in. Much pleasure was shown on people's faces. Later in the afternoon it became a fair certainty that the war in Europe was over, so a party began to develop in the bar. We were all pretty jubilant in a quiet way. At midnight I went down to the flights to have a natter with the NCOs before going to see the crews being briefed for jobs in the North Sea, and got to bed at 02.30.

Tuesday, 8th May, was 'Victory in Europe' day. The war ended officially at midnight. After two days of great revelry everybody reverted to normal routine with a will. We had aircraft out photographing and escorting surrendered U-boats which were beginning to pop up all over the place. On Friday I got up at 03.15 for briefing, took off at 05.45, flew to North Rona and patrolled a line from there to Loch Eriboll, thence north around the Fair Isle and down the middle of the North Sea to the latitude of Middlesborough, then all the way back. We spotted our first U-boat going into Loch Eriboll under surface escort. The second we picked up about 50 miles northeast steaming along on the surface showing the black flag of surrender: an ugly looking brute with masses of anti-aircraft armament aft of the conning tower and several dejected-looking Huns on the bridge. In reply to our demand she flashed her number, U 802. Thereafter we had an extremely dull trip, seeing nothing until we got back to Loch Eriboll which U 802 was just entering wearing the White Ensign.

I was exhausted when I landed. In the following two weeks the squadron did more flying even than when we set up the landplane record for Coastal Command. But it was on the whole very dull flying. We covered the Norwegian coast from Oslo to Statlandet and the

Faeroes-Shetland channel, and on my next two trips I had to do the latter, as dull a stooge as could be imagined. The blokes niggled a bit about these jobs; nevertheless they did them with a will and put on an extraordinarily good show at a thankless task.

At the beginning of June, Mick went on leave, leaving me in charge of the Squadron. I was too busy to fly anything, except for one quickie in the Station Oxford, which had me all at sixes and sevens because it was so light and toy-like compared with the Lib. Then I myself went on leave, first to London to chase up the Canadian authorities to see if they could do anything to get Isobelle back to the UK, and then up to Portincaple for a much needed rest. It was there that I received a cable from her saying that she had been warned to stand by for a draft to England. I immediately returned to Milltown so as to have some leave in hand for her arrival, probably in the middle of July.

I found that all the Canadians and Australians had left the squadron, and life had become comparatively easy; nevertheless I had to get down to re-forming the crews and bringing them up to operational standard. I acquired a decent young lad as second pilot, but missed my Sgt 'Smudge' Smith who had developed into a very competent and reliable second dickey.

The squadron was now re-equipping with a highly sophisticated automatic radar bomb sight - LAB - which proved to be a tricky gadget to use and demanded an intensive flying training programme. Then Mick got married, and I took a Liberator-load of wedding guests down to a deserted airfield in Suffolk and back for the great occasion. As a supreme act of friendship I let all his old cronies drink to their hearts' content, satisfying myself with one half glass of champagne for the bridal toast, so that I should be fit to drag the Lib off the 1,000 yard strip (I paced every inch of it beforehand). While he was on honeymoon leave I got word that the squadron was to move to St Eval in Cornwall seven days hence. John Downey and I decided not to disturb the bridal pair, and despite a hundred impediments, many farewell parties and much chaos we met the deadline.

When I received a signal from Isobelle saying that she was on board a ship awaiting disembarkation in the Clyde, Mick insisted that I should take some leave. Isobelle and I met in London, where she was to be based, and immediately went off to Portincaple to have a marvellous but all too short spell of Paradise. Mick then sent a Liberator up to Turnberry to bring me back to St Eval and I took Isobelle with me. While waiting for the Lib to be refuelled we learned the astonishing news of Japan's surrender.

There was a carpet of sea-fog over the Western Approaches and dusk was falling when we arrived over base, so I did a controlled descent and broke cloud at 400 feet on final approach. That evening there was a dance in the Mess; worn out as we were, we just had to attend it to celebrate the wonderful news. All my friends in 224 seemed to be delighted to meet Isobelle. Mick offered us the use of his flat in St Mawgan, and at about 2am drove us there dangerously. A day later Isobelle returned to duty.

Events crowded too fast on me. When Japan formally accepted the surrender terms the station was given three days' holiday and there was much good-natured and well-behaved merrymaking, but Mick and I spent the first morning of this new Era of Peace working up detailed plans for moving the entire squadron to the Middle East in the event of a show of force being suddenly required there. The next day I took off on a nine hour stooge to provide close escort to the *Queen Mary* outward bound with General Eisenhower on board. Circling at 2 or 3 miles for nearly seven hours I was held spellbound by her sleek, sturdy beauty as she slid across the sea at a good 29 knots, her nose aggressively down to the swell. We left her at last light.

A couple of weeks later I flew out to the Azores to inspect the detached flight which we had set up there for air-sea rescue duties. When I got back to St Eval, we took delivery of three Mark III Transport Libs fitted with bench seats in the bomb bays. Our first job, on which I flew one of them myself in vile weather, was to move in several lifts the ground personnel and equipment of a Mosquito squadron from North Devon to Norfolk. In the middle of September David Popkin left to be demobbed in order to go up to Cambridge. The whole crew gave him a delightful farewell party. I was sorry to see him go. I had made him deputy captain, fully in charge of the crew on the ground because of my commitments as Flight Commander, and he had proved to be an indispensable go-between twixt my rather severe and single-minded self and the rest of the crew whom I liked and admired but could not easily mix with.

Towards the end of September Mick announced that I was posted to become Chief Instructor of 111 Operational Training Unit, just arriving at Lossiemouth from New Providence Island. This meant promotion to Wing Commander. He and Pat had me to a farewell dinner. In his cups he said many nice things. I want to record now my immense admiration for him. Lion-hearted ace that he was, he had the greatness to hand over his Flight to me and, as my Squadron Commander, leave me alone to get on without interference; but at the same time he was ever ready, when asked (as he so often was), to give wise counsel.

He was great fun to work for. The most modest of men, he was a fine, natural leader who expected the highest professional standards and commanded the unquestioned devotion of his squadron. To a man we would have followed him anywhere. His manner was the essence of informality, but woe betide a transgressor, for his tongue had the lash of a cattle-whip.

My crew gave me a farewell party in the local pub in St Columb. I was very touched, and it was a wrench to leave those men with whom I had shared the fears, hopes, triumphs and disappointments of operational flying, for they had been very good friends of mine. I flew up to Lossiemouth on 2nd October. It was a delight to be back in that part of the world again, where the heart lifted every time eyes beheld the blue silhouette of the mountains across the firth. It was a good station with a comfortable Mess, I knew many of the people there and I was fortunate, now that Isobelle was back in the UK, to be guaranteed some respite from a posting overseas. But the job itself, though not arduous, was not one that appealed to me.

The OTU, with its Liberators but minus its Mitchells, had just been dumped there less than a month before and was still trying to find its feet. Coastal Command had decreed that Wellingtons should replace the Mitchells, and I very soon came to the conclusion that this was a

132

complete nonsense. Nevertheless I had great pleasure refreshing myself on the Martinet and Wellington. Throughout my eight months at Lossie I was pretty well my own master, for I went through three Station Commanders who were too ignorant of Liberator operations to dare interfere, and for the last six weeks was myself Station Commander until I handed 'Lossie' over to the Royal Navy.

At the beginning of November we received two Spitfire XVIs for fighter affiliation work. As we had no Spitfire-qualified pilot on the station I decided one morning to try to fly one. I experienced the most hectic half hour of my life. The cockpit was minute. The most disconcerting thing was a darned great gyro-gunsight right in front of your face. If you peered round or through it, all you saw was acres of long cowling in front of you. Forward vision on the ground was nil. This made keeping straight on take-off and on landing tricky. My first take-off was pandemonium.

The big mistake I made was to put on full starboard rudder trim, which applied to the Mark XI and earlier types, but not to the Mark XVI. Second, I had the elevator trim neutral instead of slightly nose heavy. Third I opened the throttle too quickly. Consequently I zigzagged erratically across the runway, leapt into the air in a horrible attitude, and staggered and skidded all over the sky. Under the terrific urge of the Merlin 66 the acceleration of this tiny aircraft had me completely flummoxed.

When I properly came to my senses and caught up with the aeroplane it was at 2,000 feet doing nearly 300 mph. I thought 'Gosh, I've taken on something more fierce than I can cope with. How the hell am I going to get it on the ground again?'

The controls were fantastically light; so light that I, being used to heavies, had absolutely no 'feel'. At speed they were pleasantly firm, but when you dropped down to about 150 mph in the circuit she seemed to waffle and the nose-up attitude at low speeds was rather disconcerting. My first landing was about as much out of control as my first take-off. She bounced once, then settled: and caught me napping with a vicious swing to starboard which I only just managed to control with full opposite rudder and a heavy burst of engine (which nearly got me airborne again, of course). We snaked violently up the runway to a standstill.

My next take-off wasn't too bad, but I still hadn't got the rudder trim right, and again, disconcerted by the long nose, I staggered off the ground with the tail well down. Off the second approach I did about seven landings, but I did manage to keep straight. During all this flying my control of the aircraft was very precarious. Nevertheless I was thrilled to the core and wore a wide, child-like grin for many hours afterwards. I resolved to get the little blighter weighed up. There was nothing difficult or vicious about her; all that defeated me was the combination of terrific acceleration with extremely sensitive controls. Over the next week or so I came to terms with her. Of all the 22 types of aircraft I had flown up till then, none gave me so much sheer delight as the Spitfire.

Isobelle was demobbed in time for us to spend Christmas together at Portincaple as a prelude to living 'happily ever after'. On 24th April she presented me with Rosalind, the first of two very beloved and talented daughters.

January was a desperate month for 111 OTU; we were fighting a constant battle to keep going as airmen, particularly in the technical trades, came up for demobilisation. No. 1674 HCU had been disbanded and was re-formed as the Halifax Flight of my OTU. In the middle of the month one of the Liberators flew into a mountain in Norway, killing all on board.

I was not particularly inspired to convert to the Halifax. It took off rather like an oversized Wellington, in a very short space compared with a Lib. There was a tendency to swing to starboard when you opened up. In the air the controls were stiff, but positive in their action. On three engines, even with the outer feathered, the rudder trim held her nicely and she seemed to have plenty of reserve power. Application of flap, as well as lowering undercarriage, and their opposites, caused appreciable changes of fore-and-aft trim. The pilot being about twice as high off the ground as he was in a Liberator, I found the height at which hold-off was commenced somewhat disturbing. The change of attitude from the approach to touchdown and the amount of control column movement that went with it took a lot of getting used to.

At the end of March, while acting as Station Commander I was told in confidence that the Navy was likely to be given Lossie in June. To console myself I fitted my Spitfire about me. It was a heavenly day: cloudless with unlimited visibility so that the snow-covered mountains of Sutherland, the Cairngorms and the Monadhliaths seemed near enough to touch. In this wine-clear, smooth air I climbed to 6,000 feet above the aerodrome. I resolved to try looping. Not having been upside down for years, I was a bit wary. With the modern equivalent of a prayer on my lips, I dived the Spit to 300 mph, trimmed her tail heavy, then relaxed the forward pressure on the stick.

I blacked out at about 45 degrees of climb, but kept her going round by feel and regained my vision as she fell slightly askew off the top of the loop with about 180 on the clock. I twisted her straight with ailerons and came out of the dive with my knees knocking together. For the second loop I started trimmed neutral in level flight and eased her round in such a way that I was on the edge of blacking out all the time. At the top she juddered horribly and fell out askew; I had to do an aileron turn in the vertical part of the dive to come out straight.

The third loop wasn't so bad. I was able to fly all the way round, though there was still a bit of buffeting at the top. I got an enormous thrill out of the vertical part of the climb and out of seeing the horizon come sliding down from above me. This aeronautical interlude in a week of insoluble administrative problems was very refreshing.

No. 111 OTU officially ceased to exist on May 21st. I was left in command of a station with neither aeroplanes nor flying personnel. On 3rd July 1946 sadly and formally I handed Lossiemouth over to the Royal Navy at a short ceremony. I high-tailed it as fast as I could to Kinloss which I had been ordered to take command of pending the arrival of its proper Group Captain. Before leaving, however, I was given the news that my next posting was to break new ground as Chief Instructor of the Photographic Reconnaissance OTU at Benson in Oxfordshire.

The first thing I did at Kinloss was to start flying the Mosquito in anticipation of my new job. I was rather disappointed with my first hour's dual on a T Mk III; there was nothing like the thrill that the Spifire had given me. The take-off needed watching; you had to open the throttles carefully and guard against a strong tendency to swing. She needed a very long take-off run, and when airborne her acceleration to safety speed was poor. The ailerons were extremely light but, surprisingly, comparatively slow to take effect.

I was astonished by the single-engined performance with flaps and wheels up; we did steep turns with and against the live engine without any difficulty whatever. Operation of the flaps had a very pronounced effect on the fore-and-aft trim. On the approach to landing the amount of power required to keep the approach flat was considerable. I made three landings, all of which were safe and reasonably smooth, apart from my tendency to hold off too high.

7

Photo Recce Types

ON THE FOURTEENTH OF JULY 1946 I FLEW A LANCASTER from Kinloss to my new job with No. 8 OTU. I was met by a tall, thin, gentle-voiced lad who introduced himself as Arnold Cussons, the Chief Flying Instructor. We clicked immediately, and it was largely due to his friendly sponsorship that I won entrée to the delightful PR Union, an elite band of outstanding individualists who had inherited the traditions of the pre-war Photographic Reconnaissance Unit (PRU) created by the amazing Sydney Cotton.

8 OTU had only recently been dumped in Chalgrove, an empty satellite of Benson's, without any preparation: there were no cooks, no labourers, no services, no communications, nothing but the training staff, the technical personnel, the pupils and aeroplanes.

For nearly a year the unit had conspicuously failed to achieve its targets, and poor training had led to a high Mosquito accident rate in the squadrons. They now expected further training problems with the new Spitfire Mark 19 and Mosquito Mark 34. My job was to turn Chalgrove into a fully functional outfit, to improve training standards and to meet deadlines.

Although it was impossible to fly immediately because we had no communications, safety facilities or tower personnel, I quickly concluded that I could rely totally on Arnold Cussons to organise the flying side. A distinguished Mosquito PR pilot who had won a DFC for getting the first photographs of the capsized *Tirpitz* in Tromso Fjord, he was also an A1 rated Flying Instructor who, having only recently completed the advanced course at the Empire Flying School, had all the right ideas about training task management. I therefore set myself single-mindedly to bully Benson and Group HQ so that I could put Chalgrove on its feet as a functioning domestic organisation.

Nevertheless I resolved to get to grips with the aeroplanes and the training syllabus just as soon as possible. The next few months proved to be a period of hard work and unending frustration, surprisingly happy however, for I had a good team of instructors, most of whom had flown on operations in the PR squadrons. Arnold Cussons, a great man for parties and a good friend, made sure that I joined in all the fun that was to be going with the rest of the PR Union types at Benson.

No. 106 (PR) Group consisted of two squadrons at Benson, No. 540 with Mosquitos and No. 541 with Spitfires; No. 82 Squadron flying Lancasters in various parts of Africa; No. 8 OTU; the Central Interpretation Unit; and sundry other minor outfits here and there. In addition to its strategic reconnaissance mission, the Group had a very large commitment of air survey flying for the Ordnance Survey, the Ministry of Town and Country Planning, and the Colonial Office. My function was to provide trained Spitfire and Mosquito pilots and navigators for the Benson squadrons and a third PR squadron in the Far East. To this end I had two Mosquito Mk IIIs for dual, one Mosquito Mk 34 and two Mark 16s (due to be replaced by 34s); a Master for single-engined dual; 4 Spitfire PR XIs and one Mark IX (all five to be replaced by the Griffon-engined PR XIX). Cussons told me that the Mosquito 34 was considerably more difficult to handle than any of the other marks.

As soon as I could, I went up for an hour's dual in a Mosquito TIII and, having had no trouble, signed myself up (with reservations) as 'qualified on type'. Later I went up for a short flip in a Spitfire Mk IX, which, if possible, was pleasanter to handle than my pet XVI. While I was orbiting Chalgrove I saw a Mosquito Mk 16 crack up on the airfield: it bounced, burst a tyre, swung and broke its undercarriage. The pilot was one of the new intakes straight from a single-engined Service Flying Training School. As it was a clear case of mishandling the controls through inexperience, I made something of a song and dance about it in order to back up my representations that the syllabus would have to be radically altered to cope with such pupils. A couple of

138

days later, another of our pupils dived a Spitfire into the ground at very high speed from a very great height, and there wasn't much left. He crashed about 15 minutes after setting out on a cross-country flight at 30,000 feet. We suspected that his oxygen lead must have come adrift, simply causing him to pass out.

As a tonic to administrative frustration I took a Spitfire XI up for an hour's cruise around the countryside at an easy 280 knots (indicated) at 10,000 feet, and came down a changed and happy man. The Spit XI with full wing tanks (total 200 gallons) handled rather more sluggishly on ailerons than the other marks, but in my heavy hands this was just right. I found her delightful.

A couple of days later I made my first trip in a Mosquito 34, a high-flying test. There had been so much talk about the swinging tendencies of the Mark 34 at take-off that Johnston, determined at all costs not to swing on his first one, opened the throttles so carefully and so slowly that he took the whole length of the runway to get flying speed. His passenger was just a little anxious! But with so much care, of course, I had no trouble at all.

The air was gloriously smooth and the aircraft handled beautifully, climbing at over 2,000 feet a minute at plus 8 boost and 2650 rpm. High blower came in at about 25,000 feet. It was my first flight using oxygen and I found that it made a very noticeable difference above 10,000 feet. At 26,000 feet I felt perfectly normal except for a slightly distended sensation in my tummy.

One feature that I did not like was the very heavy load on the elevators during a turn; she became nose heavy in proportion to the steepness of the bank. It was more noticeable than on any other type I had flown, and made accurate height-keeping difficult at first.

While I was on leave in September, Cussons rang me up to tell me that a couple of pupils had been killed in a Mosquito. The aircraft was seen diving, and when it pulled out one of the wings fell off.

At the beginning of October Air Commodore Nicholetts, a dour but go-ahead man, took over the Group. I immediately submitted a memorandum to him pointing out what enormous economies could be achieved if 8 OTU were reduced to the status of a Training Flight based at Benson. Being a man of action rather than the Empire Builder that his predecessor was, he immediately wrote to Coastal HQ with an ultimatum: decide to man Chalgrove up to its establishment, or move 8 OTU either to Benson or into the Training Group (No. 18). This caused much fluttering in the dovecotes. The immediate compromise was to transfer all the flying to Benson and leave the ground school and the domestic accommodation at Chalgrove.

When the Examining Squadron of the Empire Flying School arrived for its annual check of the flying instructors I decided that I would try to get an instructor's rating. While they were giving a night flying check to Thompson and Farlow, Arnold Cussons suggested that I might combine night familiarisation on the Mosquito with getting some experience of flying in the right hand seat. I took him up on that.

Whereas in the Catalina and the Liberator the pilots sat unencumbered in style on two thrones separated by a broad gangway, in the Mosquito T III they sat in their parachute harness and other clutter huddled tightly together in a tiny cockpit. Merely getting into the seats required a degree of athletic agility. Manipulation of the two throttles from the right hand seat was a bit difficult, and of course you could not reach either the propeller controls or the elevator trimmer. It was a little tricky, but fortunately the night was clear and starlit, so that one way and another I thoroughly enjoyed myself despite the intense concentration which was required. Next morning I set out to try to persuade my Examiner that I was just worthy of a 'C' Category.

On my demonstration take-off I forgot to brake the wheels. I climbed to 6,000 feet to demonstrate stalling. My patter was fine, but I was so keen to give a thorough demonstration that I stalled the aircraft far too severely. My demonstration of a recovery with minimum loss of height from a stall with wheels and flaps down was pretty grim because (a) I stalled with too much power on, (b) I allowed the stall to develop too far, and (c) I opened up the engines unevenly, got a yaw, dropped a wing and applied - at the stall - full opposite aileron. The recovery was therefore pretty wild and horrible.

Next I gave a demonstration of single-engined flight which was pretty sound until I came to the overshoot on one. I started to go round again at 135 mph and lost 800 feet trying to build up safety speed. We were to have finished with a single-engine landing, but undercarriage trouble developed. The starboard leg refused to come up after my overshoot, and then refused to indicate that it was locked down after selection. My Examiner and I agreed therefore that we would be sticking our necks out to try a landing on one engine with a suspect undercarriage, which was a good thing because I had never landed a Mosquito on one.

With only one main wheel indicating locked down he put the aircraft down very gently. Nothing untoward happened. There was nothing wrong with the down-locks after all, only an indicator fault.

When, worn out and perspiring, I had climbed out of the aircraft, my Examiner told me that he would have no hesitation in recommending me for a 'B' Category, I was extremely surprised. It cannot have been my flying; it must have been the drinks I gave him when the team came along to our Quarters the night before.

On the last day of October I spent a distinctly hair-raising morning watching pupils doing their first solos on Mosquito 34s. At one stage, when one of them disappeared behind distant trees after take-off, I was bracing myself for a mushroom cloud of black smoke. Indeed only a couple of days later one of our pupils had a very lucky escape. He was returning in a Mosquito 34 with one engine dead. He made too close a circuit, overshot hopelessly, put down full flap and then decided to go round again. He was lucky: his critical speed at full power on one engine was 180 mph, low for a Mark 34, and he only just made it. He lost 800 feet getting his wheels and flaps up and building up speed, and when he disappeared behind the houses of the village we onlookers in flying control gave up hope.

It took him about six circuits to gain 1200 feet. On some of these 34s the safety speed was about 200 mph, at which speed they could barely climb on one engine. In our training syllabus very heavy emphasis was put on single-engined performance and techniques. It was axiomatic that you never tried to go round again in a 34 once you had lowered full flap on final approach.

This unit taught me a great deal about applied flying which never

141

really came into the handling of heavy, under-powered aircraft. The Mosquito, which at first seemed a simple aircraft to fly, in fact required a considerable amount of skill to be flown properly and safely. Its engine handling was an art in itself. Most of what I learned I picked up from Arnold Cussons whose knowledge of the Mosquito and of principles of flight as applied to it was matched only by his penetrating mind.

My first pupil in a Mosquito III was young Pilot Officer Salmond. He was greatly troubled by the fierce wind blowing across the runway. I wasn't at all impressed by his performance. At the marshalling point by the downwind end of the runway, while he was doing his pre take-off checks (hatches and harness secure, trimmers adjusted, supercharger in M gear, pitch fine, flaps up, fuel selected from outer tanks, gills open and gyros synchronised), I told him to take off, do a circuit and land, to give us an idea of the effect of the crosswind before going on with single-engined landings.

"Remember when you are taking off in a crosswind to hold her down until you can lift her cleanly and finally off the ground. If you come off prematurely you might come back to earth with lots of drift on, which isn't good for the landing gear."

His first take-off wasn't too bad. The air was extremely bumpy. His circuit was lousy. Turning onto the downwind leg he let the aircraft go too far away from the airfield, so that he had to fly the downwind leg converging at 30 degrees to the runway. His turn onto the funnels was too steep, which made him approach the runway slantwise. He let his speed drop to 115 mph on the approach, landed with drift on and bounced for several hundred yards down the runway, then started correcting imaginary swings with fierce use of brake instead of with his rudder.

I taxied the aircraft round to the marshalling point while pointing out his mistakes to him and explaining what he should do to correct them. He must plan his circuit; his rate of turn at each end of the circuit should be even and similar; half the battle was to come into the funnels at the right height, tracking accurately along the line of the runway.

While landing in a gusty crosswind his speed should be slightly higher than usual; he should attempt to do a wheel landing rather than the normal three-pointer so that he could be sure of having full aileron control right down to the ground to correct drift. If he took action to prevent swings early enough he should be able to rely entirely on rudder.

Off we went for a second circuit. Turning from the downwind leg into the funnels he didn't slacken his rate of turn sufficiently to get in line with the runway, so again we came in slantwise. This time I made him go round again. He made it seem awfully hard and took a long time to get his flaps up. The third approach was straight but far too low - too slow, too. To get into the airfield he had to apply a colossal burst of power. Consequently the landing was rough.

Then I made him put on the blue goggles for instrument flying, and did the take-off myself, handing over to him at 200 feet when the wheels were up. I gave him 15 minutes instrument flying, feathering the airscrew on him in the middle. He coped fairly reasonably. We were just going to do a practice overshoot on one engine before having a go at a single-engined landing when the intercom went dead on us, so I shouted to him to do a normal landing instead.

This time he did a good circuit and approach, and a decent touchdown, but he rather spoiled the effect by hasty application of the brakes every time the aircraft seemed to be starting a swing. I taxied back to dispersal going over his faults on the way. In the crew-room afterwards I recapitulated. He was very inexperienced and therefore rather rough. My final impression of him was that he was unjustifiably overconfident.

Towards the end of November while I was examining one of our Masters which had just landed on its belly on the runway, I was called 'urgently' to the telephone. It was only the Group Personnel Officer to tell me that Air Ministry, wanting an experienced navigation specialist to be Chief Navigation Staff Officer at Transport Command HQ, had picked on me of all people. I was furious. I did not want to go back to navigation, I did not want to give up flying, I hated the idea of a Staff job and I was very gloomy at the thought of leaving 8 OTU which I was enjoying so much.

Wing Commander Mitchell, an earnest ex Pathfinder Navigator with a DSO and DFC whom I was to succeed, gave me half a day's briefing before disappearing. The Senior Personnel Staff Officer seemed visibly shaken by my lack of qualifications for the job, but leapt into action more cheerfully when I insisted that I must do the navigation specialists' refresher course at the Empire Air Navigation School just as soon as he could fix it. The course was good value, especially the opportunities for technical reading and for meeting people who had been and were active at the sharp end of research and development in the navigation world. It was encouraging to discover that even the Empire Air Navigation School shared with 8 OTU the manning problems which made it almost impossible to provide serviceable aeroplanes on time to meet the training task.

None of my scheduled long distance trips as a Halifax navigator came to pass; I had to make do with two shortish sorties in Wellingtons. On the first occasion I had some difficulty in catching up with the aeroplane until it slowed down to enter the circuit; on the second I managed to settle down to making a good job of navigating a four-hour trip to Lorient and back.

I returned to my job at HQTC at the end of January 1947. I knew nobody at HQ. There was no HQ Mess, only a canteen, and everybody dispersed to civilian lodgings at night. The pace of staff work in a Command HQ seemed snail-like. I felt both lonely and lost.

In planning to come to grips with my responsibilities for operations on the trunk route to the Far East, I had two options: either to travel as all the other Staff Officers did, formally on a passenger service and step out at each staging post to do an inspection of its flight information and navigation services; or to fly as supernumerary navigator on a freighter York and work my way incognito through the system. The latter appealed to me, and that is what I did, but it was April before I was able to get airborne.

En route I was able to use the staging post facilities, navigate the aircraft whenever we were out of sight of land, and sit in the co-pilot's seat the rest of the time. This way, the workers talked to me and I learned quickly. In Egypt, India and Singapore I stopped over to make my formal Staff visits to the Air HQs.

At 06.30hrs GMT on 10th April I was airborne out of Lyneham in a freighting York bound for Fayid in Egypt via Castel Benito, just outside Tripoli. The view from the cockpit was outstandingly good. Indeed, the whole flight deck layout, spacious, uncluttered, balanced and methodical seemed to me to be quite exceptional by normal British standards. Each pilot had the full blind flying instrument panel squarely in front of him; between them were the engine instruments and a console containing feathering buttons and various system switches; and the throttles, mixture and airscrew pitch controls were, as on the Catalina, suspended from the cockpit roof between the pilots.

The navigation station, on the starboard side of the aircraft immediately behind the second pilot, was ideally, and again spaciously, laid out; I had a large observation window at my side with the periscopic drift sight mounted just below it, and the astro dome above my head. The wireless cubicle was to port at a lower level. Cruising at 150 knots indicated at 10,000 feet we made a nice landfall on the African coast near Cape Bon before altering course for Castel Benito. In the co-pilot's seat I followed the landing with close interest. Flt Lieut Stenner made the final part of the approach, flaps down, at 115 knots and I was surprised at how little change of attitude was required to touch down on three points: vastly different from the Halifax or Lancaster.

We flew the next leg in complete darkness. I handed over to the regular navigator over Tobruk and then sat in the co-pilot's seat watching Jupiter and the rising of Antares and the moon dead ahead. After five hours without a sign of life below, a great blaze of lights ahead denoted Cairo. I was quite overcome by the brilliance of this jewel set in the night.

My first sight of the Nile was to see it in the moon-track. We landed at Fayid at 23.00hrs GMT. Almost at the moment our propellers stopped rotating the aircraft was engulfed by a swarm of airmen, for it was scheduled to go onto Shaibah within the hour with a fresh crew.

After spending a day at Command HQ doing my Staff duties, I caught the next eastbound freighter in the middle of the night. Again it was a black night; the moon, when it rose, was too weak to illuminate the ground. Daylight came when I was working hard at the navigation; it came very suddenly and took me by surprise. After breakfast at Shaibah we pushed on at 08.15hrs local time. I navigated the leg to Sharja straight down the middle of the Persian Gulf out of sight of land all the way. The desert around Shaibah was a very pale fawn; but near Sharja it was so dazzling that when I first saw it I thought it was the sky and that the dark rock walls of the mountains were some sort of mirage. Having flown at 9,000 feet all the way I found it difficult to get any idea of the scale of the mountains and hills, especially as the high sun threw such short shadows.

From Jask to Pasni we flew close to the coast, as arid and vast a wilderness of sand and baked mud as I can ever expect to see. From time to time we passed over conglomerations of jagged, stratified mountains fantastically eroded. We landed at Mauripur (Karachi) at 17.05hrs local (11.35 GMT). The next day we staggered into the air at 14.00hrs local time with whirling dervishes dancing all over the place and a temperature around 108F, quite agonisingly hot. About half an hour en route for Jodhpur, No. 1 engine cut out due to a fuel pump failure, so Stenner turned back to Mauripur.

The next afternoon we had a false start because of supercharger trouble during the run-up of No. 3 engine at the end of the runway. When we got back to dispersal, and after an electrical check, I pulled rank on Stenner and persuaded him to take off with the high speed blower on No. 3 unserviceable. We landed at Palam, Delhi, after three hours in the air. There, as I climbed out of the York, grimy with oil and sweat, wearing a crumpled, soiled shirt and slacks, I was met by Sir Frederick Tymms, my former Guardian. He whisked me off to stay with him and his wife Millie for four hectic days of lunch parties, cocktail parties and dinner parties among the good and the great of senior Delhi society. I was given barely sufficient time to do my business with my opposite number at Air HQ.

Back at Mauripur I joined the crew of a southbound York: its schedule was seven and a half hours to Negombo in Ceylon; a twelve hour rest before departure at 04.00hrs local time; and a nine hour flight to Singapore via Sabang at the northern tip of Sumatra. As one of the objects of my trip was to obtain experience of the LORBA beam installed at Butterworth to provide a track guide for the long sea crossing on which the unpredictable behaviour of the intertropical front had created some navigational difficulties, I navigated most of the sea crossing to Sumatra and the final stretch down the Malacca Straits from Diamond Point.

There followed three hectic days and nights before I joined a crew to go straight back to Lyneham, for I had a date with the weekly Dakota schedule to Warsaw. Although I navigated the latter part of the crossing to Ceylon - this time the LORBA didn't work - for most of the journey home I sat in the right hand seat managing the autopilot while the Captain slept. This westbound schedule going with the sun seemed to be less of a strain than the eastbound. On the last day of April, England greeted us with snow showers and low cloud. It was damnably cold without being invigorating as we stepped out of the aeroplane.

I was half inclined to postpone my trip to Warsaw to get my breath back, but one day in the office was enough to persuade me to get out of it again immediately. The four hour journey to Berlin in the Dakota was very dull, as was the flight to Warsaw and back the next day, just over two hours each way. I was shocked and sickened by the mess we had made of Berlin: the miles of empty shells of former houses and the awful shabbiness of the people and their pathetic attempts to do trade and barter.

As soon as I returned to HQ I resolved that at least once a week I would visit a Transport Command Unit, flying a Proctor from the Communications Flight at Hendon. I had handled the type before, at Lossiemouth, and now for want of anything better I became quite fond of it; she was comfortable, easy to handle and her Gypsy Queen engine was remarkably reliable.

One of the odd characteristics was that if you wanted the flaps down you moved the flap selector lever up. Unlike most aeroplanes, lowering flaps produced a nose-down trim change, and vice versa. The undercarriage, of course, was fixed. Cruising at about 100 knots she could keep going safely for about four hours.

147

It was quite easy to spin her if you persisted with the stall with flaps up: a slight vibration of the stick warned you, then the wing dropped smartly at about 50 knots and if you did not immediately apply opposite rudder and move the stick forward she spun quite pleasantly.

In July I visited the Transport Command Development Unit at Brize Norton, commanded by Colin Scragg, who had tested me for my first solo at Cranwell. He offered me some dual in a Sikorsky R4 helicopter, quite one of the most alarming experiences I can remember. The co-ordination of the controls was entirely different from that of an orthodox aircraft and was at first very difficult. The controls themselves were rather heavy. My attempts at hovering were pathetic. Scragg showed me all the usual tricks - flying forwards, backwards, sideways, hovering, climbing vertically, but by far the most interesting and exciting thing was his demonstration of an engine-off landing.

At 600 feet he throttled the engine right down in level flight at 40 mph. Both the engine rpm and the rotor rpm fell from normal to idling: from 2300 and 230 to about 800 and 80 respectively, so that there was nothing to keep us airborne.

We fell out of the sky in a most alarming manner.

As speed built up, however, the windmilling rotors ran faster and faster, the pitch having been put into fully fine, until they were at normal rpm, when they began to produce lift by autorotation. The aircraft was then in its equivalent to a steep, fast glide under control. As we rocketed towards the ground, pitch was increased and a landing hold-off was made as for an orthodox aeroplane. Properly timed this worked out quite satisfactorily because the inertia of the rotors was enough to provide sufficient lift for a controlled landing.

In the middle of July I went to Buckeburg in Germany as navigator of a Dakota to make an assessment of the Beam Approach Beacon System (BABS) installation which had been causing some controversy because of distortions allegedly induced by the surrounding hills. Within a few days of returning, I left Lyneham in a VIP York as a member of the Staff accompanying the AOC-in-C on a formal tour of inspection of the trunk route. Sir Ralph Cochrane's main aim was to get something positive done to solve the problem of navigating through the

148

intertropical front on the sea-crossing between Ceylon and Sumatra. It was a rather pompous and dreary voyage.

Most of my time in the air was spent writing stupid inspection reports. The only 'real' part of the whole journey was when I was navigating: and this I did on the outward flight between Habbaniya and Mauripur, and on the homeward between Mauripur and Shaibah. Apart from the pleasing drill of navigation and manipulating sextant, dividers, rulers and protractors, I remember many little incidents: the ice-cold orangeade served on the flight deck immediately after take-off; eating a cold lunch while keeping an eye on progress; the slight vibration of the chart table which made the plotting instruments slide slowly to the edge; the pilot's head silhouetted against the sky; the wireless operator's right arm jigging incessantly as he plied his morse key; and the satisfying feeling of communion with other members of a very competent and highly skilled crew.

Early in September Air Ministry told me that they were going to have to reduce me to my substantive rank of Squadron Leader, but I was elated when they posted me back to Benson as Chief Navigation Officer of the Central Photographic Establishment (the new name of the old PR Group). I drove to HQ Coastal for discussions with the Command Navigation Staff. At a very jovial lunchtime session we were joined by Jimmy Stack, whom I had last seen at Castle Archdale flying Sunderlands.

I saw my new job as comprising four tasks: first, development of single-seater navigation both to the target area at long range and on photographic runs at great height; second, a programme of intensive navigation flying for all the squadrons during the winter months; third, the proper organising of a flight planning section; and fourth, dealing with the problems of navigation training in the Training Unit.

I soon discovered that in all aspects navigation at Benson was haphazard; ignorance was rife. The immediate cause of my being selected to become the first Navigation Staff Officer at HQ C.Ph.E. was that a formation of Mosquitoes from 540 Squadron had got lost in fair weather en route to Gibraltar and had made a forced landing on a Spanish aerodrome a long way wide of their destination. The AOC was

149

understandably anxious to initiate a navigation training programme.

The other squadrons in the group were No. 58, flying Ansons equipped with the Decca Navigator system for precision survey flying, No. 82 flying Lancasters equipped with the Gee-H precision bombing system for high altitude Colonial Survey tasks, and No. 541 flying Spitfires.

I flew a Proctor up to Shawbury for a meeting of the High Speed Single Seater Pilot Navigation Panel., which had been set up by the Air Ministry at the instigation of C.Ph.E. to make recommendations on the development of equipment and techniques for pilot-navigation in future long range high speed aircraft. I was their representative on it, alongside members from the Empire Air Navigation School, the Central Fighter Establishment and the Empire Flying School. There were many old acquaintances there, chief among them John Downey who was representing the Empire Flying School.

For travelling to the next meeting of the Panel I joyfully renewed my acquaintance with the Spitfire, this time a Mark 19 with a Griffon 66 engine. Apart from the very considerable extra power and the firm but steady tendency to swing to starboard on take-off it was very little different from the Merlin marks. Alterations of throttle setting had appreciably more effect on rudder and elevator trim than on, say, the Mark 16. Not having flown anything faster than a Proctor for a year, I found that things happened rather rapidly. Cruising at an indicated 300 knots at 2,000 feet I overshot Shawbury and had to slow down a lot and take my time to find the aerodrome.

Coming back the next day was a bit hectic, too. The ground was obscured by a layer of thick industrial haze which brought the visibility below a mile in most places. The Spit, even slowed down for flying in poor visibility, was too fast for my standard of map-reading, so that after leaving Shawbury I hadn't an idea of my position and had to rely on Benson's D/F homer. I saw no recognisable piece of ground until I flashed over the sodium lights at Benson in the dusk. I was glad to get down; it was altogether too exciting in an unfamiliar and fast aeroplane.

Next I renewed my acquaintance with the powerful and slightly menacing Mosquito 34. In many ways a deceptively easy aeroplane, it was in fact quite a handful. I intensely disliked the long, low haul at full power after take-off until she reached single-engine safety speed: you scraped rapidly over tree tops for too many miles, knowing that if one engine stopped, you had had it in a big way.

The end of the year saw me settled in a job which I liked and which had great possibilities. Apart from working with pleasant people in an Establishment which was doing a fascinating job, I foresaw plenty of opportunity for flying interesting high performance aircraft. To dress up in flying gear for the purpose of manipulating an aerial machine gave me a pleasure which, even if it was childish, was profoundly satisfying.

Subconsciously I still looked upon flying as something dashing. Certainly it was character-forming. The longer I served in the RAF the more I saw the abyss that existed between the large-handedness of the Air Staff people who had flown aeroplanes and the niggling obsession with detail of those who hadn't. I did not have the right qualities for a good pilot, of course, being timid, slapdash, slow in my reactions and altogether too 'approximate'; but never mind, it was fun.

I celebrated the beginning of 1948 by taking Stan Hyland, who shared an office with me in HQ, up in a Mosquito III to initiate him into the mysteries of the type. There was a strong crosswind component on the long runway, 10/10ths cloud at 1,000 feet lowering to 800 in patches, and occasional drizzle. I did the first take-off, rather uncertainly as I hadn't flown a Mosquito from the right hand seat for over a year. After letting Stan get the feel of the machine - he was obviously taken aback by the enormous increase in drag caused by undercarriage and flaps when he tried flying with them down - I demonstrated a landing. It went very well until, towards the end of the run, I used a bit of brake to counteract a weathercock swing, overcorrected and went weaving wildly down the runway with too much braking just like my old pupils at Chalgrove.

After that Stan took off well enough except that he was caught unawares by a swing to port as the tail came up and had to make some violent throttle movements to correct it. His approach, although a bit slow, and landing, were satisfactory as they ought to be, since he got his Air Force Cross for a long tour of instruction on Beauforts.

151

Anyway, as we rolled to a standstill we were both laughing loud with mock relief at having made the grade.

I decided to take a Spitfire 19 up to 30,000 feet for the first time, and planned a short cross-country flight Benson-Boulogne-Harwich-Benson, about an hour long. As usual I was airborne and climbing fast long before I had gathered my wits, and it took me only 12 minutes to reach 30,000 feet climbing at 180 knots indicated. I levelled out above 10/10ths altostratus, brought the revs back to 2200 (which gave me plus 2lb boost in S gear) and cruised along at 210 knots indicated, which worked out at about 350 knots true airspeed. With full main and wing tanks I found her slightly unstable laterally at that height.

By the time I estimated I was over Boulogne the heavy ache which I had been experiencing in my right arm had become extremely painful - nitrogen bubbles in the bloodstream, of course. When I dropped down to 22,000 feet it soon faded away and did not recur when I returned to 30,000 feet.

There was a big break in the cloud over the Thames Estuary through which I could see all the coast from North Foreland to Harwich. I arrived over Benson on time and came down in sweeping semi-stalled turns and dives. The airfield was covered by stratocumulus, and on breaking cloud at 3,000 feet I found the change of scale of the landscape astonishing. The canopy and windscreen now became quickly coated with rime ice; by dint of rubbing I cleared it sufficiently for landing. Feeling faintly sick and extremely cold I managed to put the aircraft down safely enough if not very smoothly.

Flying my pet Spitfire PS851 to Hullavington and back for a meeting of the High Speed Navigation Panel, I did some aerobatics for the first time for years. I tried a loop first. The fact that this and all the ensuing aerobatics were remarkably smooth was due not to my magnificent piloting but to the perfection of the Spitfire 19; it was a jewel of an aircraft. After the loop, a half roll to the right off the top of a loop, then one to the left. No trouble at all. Starting from 6,000 feet I dived to 330 knots, went round on the edge of a dim-out with plus 12 lb of boost on the climb and found I still had about 180 to 190 knots at the top; a touch of aileron with corrective rudder, and round we came to level flight again having gained a net 1,000 feet. On the way back I did some rolls. Except for the first one, keeping straight was dead easy.

At the end of January, despite a dubious weather forecast, I set out in a Spitfire to do a high level trip to Kinloss to have lunch with Jimmy Stack. Cruising at 30,000 feet I saw nothing until a break appeared over Fife. I landed at Kinloss after flying for one hour and twenty minutes. When I came to start up for the return flight I used up all my Koffman starter cartridges through overpriming the engine. Kinloss had no spares. By the time some could be borrowed from Lossiemouth it was too late to take off.

In the morning, after a pleasant night among friends, I learned that Benson was at the centre of a fierce little depression. The forecaster assured me, however, that at St Eval I would find cloud which, if not broken, would be thin, so I decided to go there and see if I could get through to Benson later in the day. Very soon after leaving Kinloss, flying at 25,000 feet, I found myself over a solid carpet of cloud. I was quite unable to get any sort of navigational assistance until, after an hour and ten minutes of flying, I got a bearing from St Eval which necessitated altering course fifty degrees to port. At about the same time I saw a break in the clouds so, thinking I must be close to St Eval, I spiralled through it to 1,000 feet and found myself over inhospitable sea. I was then too low to make any R/T contact.

Not having checked the single bearing, I was a little unhappy about it. Furthermore, as time went on I began to feel unpleasantly worried about flying low down over the sea on one engine, without any sort of safety equipment should I have to ditch. After an interminable ten minutes I raised St Eval again; and to my huge relief they confirmed the original bearing. Then I flew for yet another quarter of an hour before sighting Hartland Point.

At St Eval they seemed to think I might scrape through to Benson under the weather, so I refuelled and took off again, following the coast towards Avonmouth. The weather quickly deteriorated, and while doing a steep turn to round Hartland Point at 400 feet I ran into solid cloud. A few hectic seconds occurred while I transferred to instruments, straightened out and rocketed up to a safe height. I decided that this wasn't good enough, and returned to St Eval firmly minded to stay there until there should be a radical improvement. The next morning I got home with no adventures at all.

The Colonial Survey task of the Central Photographic Establishment was being carried out by No. 82 Squadron with specially equipped Lancasters and a couple of Dakotas for logistic support. When one of the Dakotas returned to Benson in February for major servicing, I persuaded my AOC to let me fly back to Nairobi as its navigator, and stay out there to familiarise myself with the squadron's work and problems.

In the middle of March things began to take shape. I prepared my maps and charts and made my outline flight plan, Benson - Istres - Malta - El Adem - Fayid - Wadi Halfa - Khartoum - Juba - Kisumu - Nairobi (Eastleigh). We discussed the feasibility of flying direct from El Adem to Wadi Halfa along the string of oases (Farafla, Dakhla and Kharga) which bound the east side of the Libyan Desert - on my maps an empty space save for the symbols representing seif dunes, barchans and hypothetical wadis - but unfortunately we had to decide on the prosaic Nile route because of the problem of accommodation for our 18 passengers at Wadi Halfa.

After an early rise on Monday 17th we got away. In the peculiar manner of the RAF the Captain, whose word was law in the aircraft, was a Flying Officer; the second pilot was a Wing Commander (David Torrens) and I, the navigator, was a Squadron Leader. In the air the skipper called me 'Johnnie'; but on the ground he religiously stuck to 'Sir'. The leg to Istres went very rapidly. I saw very little from my chart table. Once we had passed over the last ridge of the Cevennes I guided Cooke down through the murk in a controlled descent using Rebecca/Eureka. Although he was an excellent Captain of aircraft, all his landings were rough.

After a stodgy lunch in the French Air Force Mess we pushed on to Luqa, Malta, where it was a sight chillier than it had been at Benson. The next morning I hit off El Adem perfectly, though I found it difficult to keep going in the heavy turbulence. Alka Seltzer was all I wanted for lunch. The Nile Delta was an astonishing sight, its beetle-wing green,

154

intensive cultivation lying across a vast, surrounding area of desert that stretched from the Atlantic to the Jumna.

Fayid was even chillier than Malta. At Wadi Halfa it was still cold when we landed to refuel the next morning. There was a primitive wooden control tower beside the lonely landing strip, one or two huts, the red and yellow Shell bowser, and nothing else except the flat-topped jebels standing like sawn-off tree trunks on the skyline. At Khartoum we had only four hours in bed because we wanted to avoid the turbulence over the Mau Ridge by arriving at Nairobi before midday. We took off there at 03.00hrs local time on a pitch black night without any sort of horizon. Having forgotten to bring some sextant batteries I was rather restricted in the amount of navigating I could do. However, all went well: when day broke after two and a half hours of flying I pinpointed us north of Malakal on the White Nile, bang on track and on schedule.

The strip at Juba was very primitive: before a landing you almost had to beat the place up to get the Dinkas out of the way. Huge rake-thin naked black men, they spent their lives hacking the bush back at the edges of the strip. After breakfasting we forged on, cruising at 8,000 feet until, over Soroti, we began to climb slowly to 13,500 with very heavy cumulus in sight ahead. Over the two ridges that lie between Lake Victoria and Nairobi we encountered little cloud, but the turbulence was severe. While we were in the circuit at Eastleigh we could see very faintly the enormous mass of Mount Kenya filling the sky to the northeast.

82 Squadron was nearing the end of the current season's programme of photographic survey work in Kenya, Uganda and Tanganyika. Theirs was a five-year programme in most of Colonial Africa, one year of which they had now completed. They moved about the continent with the dry weather, operating in small detachments in all sorts of out-of-the-way places between Bechuanaland and Gambia, quite isolated from the normal run of the RAF. They were therefore a group of strong individualists with fierce and outspoken views on anything and anyone: by orthodox judgement a bunch of insolent young puppies. Withal they had a tremendous corporate spirit as a squadron.

155

Once I had demonstrated that I was serious about flying with them, and had not come to tell them how to do their work, they welcomed me into their circle.

Gee-H Beacons were the devices they employed for accurately controlling the flight tracks of their Lancasters. A Gee radar set in the aeroplane transmitted a signal which was received and re-transmitted back by a ground beacon, the time lapse between transmission and reception enabling the navigator to measure his distance from the beacon, and thus plot his position very accurately.

For air survey purposes, where it was possible to establish ground triangulation, a single beacon was used merely as an aid to tracking in order to obtain the desired lateral overlap of photographic strips.

The navigator set up the appropriate Gee co-ordinate corresponding to the radius of each arc that the surveyors wished him to fly; he could then guide the pilot to fly the aircraft along an accurately defined circular path (of many tens of miles radius, the beacon being sited in relation to the survey area so as to provide a manageable curvature). The navigator established the longitudinal overlap of the photographs by feeding his groundspeed into an intervalometer which automatically fired each exposure at the correct instant. A warning light gave the pilot a few seconds notice to establish the aircraft absolutely straight and level following any manoeuvre he had made as a result of the navigator's instructions.

For example, immediately after an exposure the navigator might order 'left 50 yards, next heading 063 degrees'. The pilot would aim to do the corrective S turn and be steady for the next exposure before the warning light was activated by the intervalometer.

The pilots and navigators of 82 Squadron had developed a remarkably high degree of skilful co-ordination, as I discovered when I did the navigator's job later on. Their corrections were smooth, barely noticeable but mine resulted not in one smooth correction between camera exposures but two or three of increasing violence!

The Gee-H beacons, which were transported from site to site by the Dakotas, were accurately located by Army surveyors. The surveyors called for the flying tasks and computed the tracking co-ordinates, processed and made the initial assessment of the photographs and decided whether gap-filling was required. When I arrived they were mainly engaged on doing gap-filling.

During the next five days I made five trips, each six or seven hours long, gap-filling over Kenya and Uganda at heights from 19,000 to 23,000 feet. It was a fascinating experience, for the physical geography of that part of Africa is a complex mixture of vulcanism, denudation, cleavage, uplift and sedimentation on a vast scale. Kilimanjaro seen from afar on a clear morning was a bewitching sight, for its truncated cone, snow-covered, was cream-coloured through the blue haze.

By the 30th March the season's task was finished; the rains were expected on 1st April (but actually turned up some ten days later). The two Dakotas were put to picking up the beacons and their parties at Soroti, Masindi and Nakuru. As the Eastleigh beacon remained operational for a few more days I was able to put in a couple of training sorties as Gee-H set-operator. Then I volunteered to co-pilot the Dakota carrying beacon equipment and people to Salisbury, Bulawayo and Blantyre. The trip south was rather exhausting: drinking, flying, loading and unloading freight and trying, with the worst possible communications, to organise things.

Chileka, near Blantyre in the south of Nyasaland, was the climax of the whole voyage out from England. 'Scraping round the base of a 2,000 foot sugarloaf,' I wrote, 'we dropped into the small, green grass airfield about midday. It is ringed by high mountains. The sky was full of a magnificent architecture of clouds among which the shafts of the bright sun's light moved with breathtaking effect. Showers of rain, dove-grey like gigantic skirts of chiffon, swept across the faces of the mountains, and the light and the rain gave the distances such exquisite colour as would surpass the most subtle dreams of a master of pastels. And it wasn't beauty seen idly; the three of us had work to do: a gang of Africans to be organised and to be supervised in the unloading of two tons of technical equipment from the Dakota. In the middle of it the heavens not merely opened, but seemed to force under pressure a solid stream of water down upon us, churning the baked red earth into ankle-deep mud. Then an hour's bone-shaking drive over a road carved out of the rocks, up the hillside to our hotel in Blantyre. Weary and hot and filthy, how we relished a bath, clean clothes and a bottle of Groot Constanzia with dinner.'

When we arrived back in Nairobi I expected to catch the next day's York back to UK, but because of a fuel shortage in the Sudan they were being restricted to three passengers so that they could uplift enough petrol at Eastleigh to get them through to Fayid. This gave me the opportunity to make a couple more flights as co-pilot of the Dakota, one to Mbeya, another to Tabora. Cooke let me fly the Dakota back from Tabora, my first effort on the controls despite so many hours flying in them. She seemed very tail-heavy on the take-off run, and in fact I leapt into the air with my tail well down long before I expected to. 'The landing was dead easy,' I wrote, 'and even though I say it, much better than many I have seen Cooke do'.

The co-pilot of the next scheduled northbound York passing through Eastleigh was none other than Mick Ensor, now a Flight Lieutenant gaining route experience before becoming a passenger-qualified captain. We duly celebrated not only in Nairobi but also in Malta. I was met at Lyneham by a Proctor from Benson and was back in my office catching up with a mountain of paper almost before my hangover developed.

A couple of days later Arnold Cussons flew over for lunch from the Central Flying School in a Prentice, the new basic trainer. He let me fly it for 20 minutes or so. It had side-by-side dual seating with all the gadgets of a modern aeroplane except for a retractable undercarriage. The all round view from its roomy cockpit was exceptional. In the air, however, its performance compared unfavourably with that of the Proctor, apart from the stall which was very gentle indeed. It was comparatively heavy on the controls and it lost speed rapidly when you brought the nose up. The flaps had no apparent effect on the trim. I was not much impressed. Stodgy was the word that occurred to me.

When I did my first take-off and landing on a Lancaster, having already handled the Lanc in the air quite a lot, I knew the feel of the controls: rather stiff but well co-ordinated, giving one a feeling of solid security like a prosperous Victorian mansion. My take-off was perfectly straighforward. When I came in to land, Benson was lying under a rain-storm, so I did an overshoot from 200 feet because the rain on the windscreen made it impossible to see anything. She seemed to have plenty of power in hand even with wheels and flaps down.

After the rain had cleared I made a fairly good approach despite a strongish crosswind, but crossed the downwind boundary about 15 knots too fast, checked the descent rather late and ballooned. Although I got her onto the ground easily enough, I failed altogether to get the tail down. The result was that I used every inch of the runway despite full use of brakes after the tail settled down.

On one Lancaster sortie I nearly came to a sticky end. We were going off to do a calibration test of the Solar Navigator. The pre-flight run-up was perfectly satisfactory, so, having lined up on the runway, I opened the throttles to take-off power. When we were rolling at about 80 knots a slight swing to port developed which I checked with rudder. As soon as we were airborne, however, it worsened until I could no longer hold her straight. By this time the runway was well astern and our speed was 105 knots.

What in retrospect worried me was the appalling slowness of my reactions.

As we roared low over Wallingford and speed was beginning to pick up I called out on intercom that the port engines were not giving full power. The engineer reported that temperatures and pressures were OK and the second pilot reported that the fire warning lights were not showing. Then I saw that the rev counter of the port outer was only showing 2200 rpm, so I looked at the engine and saw that it was throwing out black smoke.

By this time we had reached 300 feet and safety speed (120 knots) and I had throttled back the starboard outer and was starting a turn to starboard to avoid high ground. I gave the order to feather and shut down the port outer. After that there was no trouble. But if it hadn't been a Lancaster I would have bought it. My only excuse is that lack of familiarity was a contributary factor. I thought at the time that the initial swing was a characteristic of a crosswind take-off. It all showed how doddery and out of flying practice I really was. The cause of it, I learned later, was a broken rocker arm that jammed an inlet valve open, causing a fire which blew out the flame trap. The engine had to be replaced.

This was a borrowed Lancaster Mk III which the AOC had obtained so that I could take it to East Africa to evaluate the Canadian solar compass as an aid to air survey in that region. Its value for air survey was already well established in the high magnetic latitudes of Canada. After my little adventure the AOC wisely decreed that we should also borrow an experienced Lancaster captain from Coastal Command for the trip.

The success of my programme involved teamwork by a pilot who understood the needs of air photography, a meticulous calibrator and operator of the Solar Navigator, and a navigator who could operate the recording and survey cameras and maintain statistical data in flight. Unfortunately the borrowed pilot was ignorant and the navigator was stupid, and I suppose I was clumsy. It was my intention to use the outward flight to drill the crew in the trial procedures. Between Benson and Istres it was a shambles, but the run to Sicily was quite satisfactory and we landed at El Adem after nine hours flying. I was happy to stick to our planned schedule of a direct flight from El Adem to Khartoum.

Owing to the operating limitations of the Solar Navigator we could not take off until shortly before noon. By the time we intersected the Nile after flying for three hours over the unbelievably desolate sand-sea of the Libyan Desert the team was quite proficient, though any results were inconclusive because there was nothing on the ground to photograph as our control. We were, however, not too happy about our aeroplane. There were bad oil and coolant leaks and strange noises in the starboard inner engine. After the technical people had inspected her and discussed things with me, I decided that it would not be prudent to take the Lanc on to Nairobi.

As we were carrying half a dozen passengers in the back, bound for 82 Squadron, I signalled Nairobi to send the Dakota to pick them up. In the knowledge that it would be at least a week before the Lanc was ready to fly back to UK, I went south with the Dakota. Most of the flying personnel of the squadron were away on detachments. By good

160

fortune the Dakota was due to leave on a re-supply mission to some of them, so off I went as volunteer co-pilot/navigator to Tabora, NDola, Kumalo, and as far south as Mahalapye in Bechuanaland. We came back via Salisbury, Fort Johnston, Mbeya and Tabora.

I was pretty tired by the time we arrived at Eastleigh; in four days we had flown 3,000 miles and made ten landings and take-offs. Nevertheless the next day I flew up to Khartoum to hasten the departure of the Lanc to UK. I took the orthodox route to Malta overflying Wadi Halfa and El Adem. By avoiding the sand sea we would see more identifiable features for checking the behaviour of the Solar Navigator. We reached home the next day without further event. Although our trial had to be curtailed I had enough material to conclude that in normal magnetic latitudes the Solar Navigator offered no significant gain as a heading reference over the Lancaster's standard distant-reading gyro-magnetic compass.

Life at Benson continued to be very busy and immensely enjoyable, and my happy home-life culminated in the birth of our second lovely and talented daughter, Caroline Anne, on February 2nd 1949. My job was full of variety and I continued to have all the opportunities I wanted to fly the Mosquitos of 540 Squadron, the Spitfires of 541, the Ansons of 58 and even, occasionally, the odd Lancaster of 82 requiring air tests after major servicing. The Ansons, equipped with the Decca Navigator for tracking control, were being used for large scale survey photography; this demanded a very high degree of accuracy both in tracking and in flying.

I did a number of photographic missions in the Spitfire 19, including a sortie at 40,000 feet. The rate of climb fell off considerably above 30,000 feet and at 36,000 she was wallowing. It took careful handling to win the last 4,000 feet. At 2,500 rpm I could get zero boost and 140 knots indicated, but the slightest mishandling of the controls, which were very light and waffly up there, caused a loss of height. In a carefully flown rate 2 turn through 180 degrees I lost 600 feet. Flying over Benson I could see the Isle of Wight, the Solent and Southampton Water almost in plan view. I found it quite comfortable at that height with a cabin pressure equivalent to 34,000 feet, but it did seem a long way from the ground and I felt desperately lonely, so I was glad when the setting sun gave me a moral excuse to start coming down.

Towards the end of March, the AOC took me aside and told me that I was to be posted to the Air Ministry Directorate of Operational Requirements with the acting rank of Wing Commander. So in May 1949 I left Benson and one of the most enjoyable jobs I have ever had.

8

Desk Pilot

WHEN I TOOK OVER THE JOB OF OR7 IN THE DECAYED splendour of Lily Langtry's old Richmond Terrace I was not entirely ignorant of the world of Operational Requirements.

At the Central Photographic Establishment I had formulated and, against some opposition, I had won acceptance of the operational requirement for installing a remote reading gyro-magnetic compass in the Ansons to improve the success rate of large scale aerial survey photography, and had overseen the trial installation and acceptance tests. I had been involved in the trial installation of Gee-H Mark II in the Lancaster, and had participated in its flight trials. I had also been called in to advise on the navigator's requirements and the installation of Gee-H Mark II in the mock-up of the PR version of what was to become the Canberra and I had been largely responsible for drafting the Report of the High Speed Pilot Navigation Panel which made a number of recommendations to the Director of Operational Requirements for navigation equipment in future fighter types.

I had already acquired working relationships with departments of the Royal Aircraft Establishment (RAE), the Telecommunications Research Establishment (TRE) and A & AEE handling navigation research and development. This sort of work was to occupy me full time for the next three years.

Life in Air Ministry in Whitehall, however, was a far, far cry from the happy little Headquarters on the edge of the airfield at Benson. The job, right at the forefront of development, was highly interesting, but also intensive and fatiguing. It was true I got out and about a lot. In my first fortnight, for example, I visited Vickers at Weybridge twice for mock-up conferences concerning the B9/44, which became the Valiant, and the Varsity crew trainer. I went to RAE at Farnborough in connection with sonobuoy tactical trials in a Sunderland; and I visited the Admiralty Compass Observatory where the senior RAF Officer was Wg Cdr John Selby, an old friend. Nevertheless, I found that the office routine was really tough and the long and frequent conferences and meetings distinctly wearing. Despite the very real pleasures of the Galleries and restaurants that London had to offer, I hated to the bottom of my being the noisy streets, the anonymous people and the crowded transport systems of the metropolis.

We Staff Officers could disport ourselves at the Communications Flight at Hendon and a Reserve Flying School at Fairoaks. At the earliest opportunity I checked out on the Communications Flight Proctors and then went to Fairoaks to get to know their Tiger Moths. The Tiger Moth was by no means easy to aerobat: one had to fly it all the time. Whereas rolling or half-rolling off the top in a Spitfire was simply a question of pushing the stick over at the right time, the same manoeuvres in a Moth demanded considerable rudder and elevator movement as well, carefully co-ordinated at all stages of the evolution. A Moth's aileron control at the beginning of a roll was surprisingly stiff. Again, because one's flying speed was so low, the time and airspace occupied in a manoeuvre were very small compared with a Spitfire. A loop or a half roll off the top seemed to have taken place even before you finished starting to think about it.

I was much happier aerobatting a Spit, but unfortunately my arrangement with 541 Squadron came to an end when I borrowed a Spitfire and pranged the thing landing at Lindholme into the low sun in heavy haze. Dazzled, I held off too high. Although I knew I was too high, I did absolutely nothing about it. The aircraft dropped in from about ten feet, bounced horribly, and stalled. The port wing dropped viciously, hit the ground with a horrid grinding noise, and a couple of seconds later the port oleo leg collapsed. The aircraft then slewed through 90 degrees and travelled sideways onto the grass. At this stage I came out of my trance sufficiently to switch off fuel and ignition. The poor old Spit looked terribly sorry for itself: the propeller broken, the port wheel twisted under the belly and the wingtip smashed.

When my new Deputy Director arrived, the irrepressible Tubby Vielle whom I had first met long ago in Bermuda, he immediately turned the whole of his staff into human dynamos. While commanding the Empire Air Navigation School he had built up a strong team which was undertaking a wide ranging investigation into the fundamentals of navigation and control of aircraft. I had made several visits to them to help them with the requirements of PR and Air Survey, and I conceded that it was a remarkably imaginative project for EANS to undertake. Tubby was now determined to move the whole visual display and his 'Brains Trust' to the War Room in Whitehall, so, in between flying visits to A.V. Roe at Woodford to inspect the Shackleton (a perfect example of a last war aircraft!) and the mock-up of their Delta-winged version of the B35 (later, Vulcan), and then to De Havillands to see the mock-up of their version of the F4 (later the Javelin), I flew up to Shawbury in a Proctor to evaluate the whole thing. I had my doubts about its suitability as an Air Ministry tool and didn't trust Tubby's judgement.

He was terrific on grandiose, global ideas and was a genius at picking little men's ideas and synthesising great projects from them; but he left all the nuts and bolts to others. Being the only Wing Commander on his staff, I gradually found myself being used as his deputy to handle the half dozen Squadron Leaders who were responsible for a wide range of subjects, indeed anything that didn't fall easily into the category of airframes, engines, armament, navigation, or radio.

My Section, OR 7, was responsible for stating the Air Staff's requirements for research and development for navigation instruments other than radio; for the navigation layout in all aircraft; and for advice to the radio branches on navigational radio and radar requirements. Vielle immediately began to fight to acquire full control of all responsibility for navigation requirements, both radio and non-radio, with me as his Deputy having executive responsibility.

As time went on I did in fact assume an increasing responsibility in this respect. Vielle as DDOR4 was responsible to the Director of

Operational Requirements, then Air Commodore Geoffrey Tuttle,[1] who in turn answered to the Vice Chief of Air Staff (VCAS) through the Assistant Chief of Air Staff (Technical Requirements). ACAS(TR) was Air Vice Marshal Claude Pelley, a small, quiet, worried looking little man, very accessible and pleasant. I thought he was quite brainy.

Tuttle was something of a hero because as a Wing Commander in 1940 he was the first regular RAF Commanding Officer of the original Photographic Reconnaissance Unit. He had a massive jaw, an incisive, almost explosive manner and a very merry eye. His mind was as quick as light, almost beating you to the end of your sentence. Most of his decisions seemed to be intuitive, and if they were wrong at least they were firm and clear; I always felt I knew where I stood with him. I thought he was very sound because he combined fearlessness and leadership with an excellent technical brain and an impish sense of humour.

At the end of June, by arrangement with Stan Hyland, I went to Benson to fly a Spitfire on the annual Air Defence Exercise. I was briefed for a low level sortie. I took off just after 3pm. For the first few moments I had very little control. When I raised the undercarriage I caused the Spit to lurch horribly and everything seemed to be happening far too quickly, but by the time I reached 2,000 feet I had settled down so that the aeroplane became more or less a part of me. One of the pleasures of a Spit when you got used to it was that it fitted you like a glove.

I headed towards Rotterdam at 3,000 feet to fly out of RDF cover. Just short of the English coast the stratocumulus disappeared, and apart from patches of sea fog there was nothing in the sky to the east. I was not too happy to be flying over the sea on one engine. The Griffon always sounded horribly rough. At first, definitely worried, I kept saying over and over to myself the drill I would adopt if the engine stopped. I even went so far as to take off my collar and tie, switch on my microphone and select the VHF distress channel. Although I was expecting my port wing tank to run dry at 15.55, I was horribly frightened when the engine suddenly spluttered from lack of fuel at

---

[1] Later, Air Chief Marshal Sir Geoffrey Tuttle

15.54. I was glad, therefore, when one of the islands just north of Flushing hove into view.

In the bright sunlight the Dutch countryside looked delightfully clean. So, too, did Rotterdam. There was none of the industrial murk so typical of Newcastle or Liverpool. Just northeast of Rotterdam I turned onto a heading for Felixstowe and, as I crossed the coast outbound, muttered a prayer, selected main tanks and reduced height to 200 feet. If the gods had decreed an early death by drowning for me, there was nothing I could do about it, but I didn't exactly enjoy the next half hour: it seemed very long, the sea looked far from inviting and the engine seemed (although it ran perfectly) to be making all sorts of horrid noises.

In the end, however, after flying under a great deal of sea fog at 150 feet, I made a landfall at Orfordness, turned southwards along the coast and ran in to take my pictures between Felixstowe and Ipswich. Just after I turned onto my next course towards the next target at Dover I happened to look back, and there was a Meteor sitting comfortably on my tail at 200 yards.

Feeling every inch like a cautious Staff Officer flying a Proctor, I flew on straight and level regardless. I completed my photography at Dover, climbed up to 7,000 feet and returned to Benson via Bedford so as to avoid the London Control Zone. At Benson, to finish an enjoyable trip, I managed to do a perfect three-point landing as a result of concentrating heavily on maintaining the right approach speed.

To maintain sanity and reasonable flying practice I determined to do all my visits outside London by air. A couple of weeks later I borrowed a Spitfire from 541 Squadron and pranged it at Lindholme, as I have already related, just to add to the gloom. What an oaf I felt! Thereafter I used the Proctors for my visits.

For the next twelve months I was far too busy to do any serious flying, being appointed as Secretary of a high powered working party reviewing the whole field of research and development for navigation and blind bombing, and making presentations of its findings at high level. In July 1950, however, I flew for the first time the new Chipmunk trainer which had replaced the Tiger Moth. It was a delightful little aeroplane. In the air it handled with all the sweetness of a Spitfire, with neither noise nor vibration, and appeared to have no vices whatever.

A couple of months later I had my first jet flight in a Meteor 7 with Wg Cdr Ruffel Smith at the Institute of Aviation Medicine, to evaluate a new turn and slip indicator. The absence of noise and vibration, the sense of colossal power, the sheer speed and rate of climb made a tremendous impression on me. Never before had I sensed such smooth passage through the air. From take-off we got to 20,000 feet in something like three minutes.

In the following month I spent two days at Manby flying in the Meteor 7 to see how difficult it was to identify targets at adequate range for visual bombing from 36,000 feet. It gave me a tremendous lift to find that I could cope up there without any physical distress, and it was enormous fun. My co-pilot was Major Lillard, a USAF Officer on secondment. We walked across the tarmac at Strubby and dumped our helmets, parachutes and target maps by the side of a Meteor that was being refuelled, savouring the sharp smell of kerosene.

Overhead there was about three eighths of fair weather cumulus, but to the north there were signs of a medium overcast. After signing the authorisation book and Form 700 in the flight hut we wandered hatless in the sun to our Meteor and clambered in, the airmen having already placed our parachutes in the seats and laid out the harness. When I wriggled down into my place, the rigger handed me first the parachute straps which I secured, then the seat straps. Before plugging in the R/T and oxygen leads, I switched on the oxygen controller and held the delivery tube to my cheek to check the puffs coming from the economiser. My old tropical pattern helmet was beginning to get a bit tight, and my oxygen mask a bit loose. When I had them all buttoned on I switched on the VHF set and checked intercom with Lillard in the rear cockpit.

We closed the massive canopy. After he had pressed the port engine lighting button there was a barely perceptible whine, then a scarcely-to-be-heard, momentary roar as the kerosene ignited; apart from that, the only sign that the turbine was running was the slow movement of the tachometer needle round the gauge to 8,000rpm. As soon as both engines were lit, and without any preliminary run up, he waved the chocks away and taxied smartly down the perimeter track with 10,000 rpm set on the clocks, for all the world like some well-sprung American limousine upon a boulevard. Seen from the cockpit, the wings of a Meteor are absurdly short, which added to the impression that you were driving some peculiar sort of car.

At the take-off marshalling point Lillard called for take-off clearance. It came back tersely "Meteor 648 cleared take-off, out." At 14,000 rpm he released the brakes. She rolled forward, gathering speed slowly at first and as silently as a Studebaker. Halfway down the runway, when the nosewheel was banging slightly like the bows of a boat in a slight popple, I became aware of an increasingly powerful thrust in the back. At 100 knots Lillard brought the nosewheel off the ground, and at 120 knots we were airborne with 500 yards of runway still left and the nose right up. The wheels retracted with three rapid thuds, the pressure in my back continued, and trees, hedges and farmhouses flashed past as the speed built up to 240 knots.

As he eased the trim-wheel back, the rate of climb indicator shot up against the stops, the altimeter needle started to race round the clock, and up we went like a rocket with my ears cracking every few seconds.

It was wonderfully exhilarating. In no time at all we penetrated the cumulus layer at 3,500 feet; in about three minutes we were at 20,000 feet where I was switching the oxygen control to full flow. By then, having moved several miles north, we were above a dazzling layer of altostratus and climbing towards thin cirrus at 28,000 feet. At 33,000 feet I began to feel a bit chilly. When we levelled out at 36,000 feet I felt perfectly fit but found difficulty in working up enough lung pressure to speak above a whisper.

The medium cloud broke up just south of Middlesbrough, showing the minutely patterned earth seemingly an infinitely remote distance away. Below us to the north were patches of thin cirrus at 28,000 feet and, like shreds of towelling left on a man's rough face, broken fair weather cumulus seemed to snuggle against the earth's surface.

From Middlesbrough I could see the Tyne quite clearly, but

Newcastle was obscured by cloud-shadow which, in combination with the cirrus and the brightness of the sunlit cloud, completely obscured the detail. We were quite unable to identify the target from that height because of the combination of cloud and cloud shadow.

My oxygen controller indicated that supplies were getting low, so Lillard put out the dive brakes, eased the stick forward and brought the revs down to 10,500. We went down like an arrow, my ears popping wildly. At 26,000 feet, having levelled out, we turned towards the target. Being now below the cirrus I was able to pick out the details of the target factory from 6 miles away.

The fuel gauges were getting ever lower, so we turned for home at 250 knots indicated. On the way Lillard let her have her head, working up to 0.78 Mach where there was slight buffeting but no noticeable snaking. When the VHF Homer brought us overhead at 22,000 feet he asked for a controlled let-down but decided to abandon it when they asked us to orbit for four minutes, which didn't appeal to us as the fuel gauges seemed to be moving ever more rapidly towards the zero mark.

Choosing a hole in the clouds, Lillard put out the dive brakes again; the deceleration threw me heavily against my shoulder straps; down we went at a fantastic angle with 250 knots on the clock, 10,500 rpm set, and the altimeter needles whirling round from 22,000 to 1,500 feet in rather less than a couple of minutes. I thought the altimeter had a lousy presentation for this sort of thing. Except on a steady course, this descent was not a manoeuvre that I would have liked to do in cloud.

As we levelled out on the downwind leg, ice began forming rapidly on the canopy. At 160 knots, wheels down, then flaps; 120 knots on final, nose well up over the hedge and a nice touchdown followed by a long run that ended with a heavy application of brakes. It seemed incredibly easy compared with a Spitfire.

Ah, the fresh scented air when the canopy was opened, and the slightly dazed feeling with which I clambered down onto the ground which only four minutes ago had been four miles beneath us. And the first refreshing puff of a cigarette as I controlled my post-flight excitement into a seeming nonchalance about it all!

Tubby Vielle was so successful in selling 'his' new, revolutionary bombing system that had emerged from the studies in which I had been closely involved, that it was agreed between Air Ministry and Ministry of Supply that he should be seconded to RAE to run his own project team. Moreover, he interested the USAF in it so far as to have them lend him a B29 equipped with Doppler navigation gear and 20 controlled bombs for trials in UK.

I was involved in the job of finding a new Deputy Director, and was glad to get S.W.R. Hughes [2] moved over from supervising all weather flying in the Directorate of Flying Training towards the end of 1950. I had long liked and admired him as a colleague, but I never expected that he would do the job with anything like Tubby's broad and imaginative approach. I expected to sink back from my privileged position with fingers in very many large pies to the slough of my precise terms of reference in the good book.

In March 1951 I was made Chairman of a Panel of Experts to determine the need for pressure suits in future bomber and fighter types. In this I worked hand in glove with the Institute of Aviation Medicine at Farnborough, where I first flew in a partial pressure suit in the back of a Meteor 7.

We shot up to 10,000 feet and levelled out for me to do a trial inflation. All being well, we went on to 40,000 feet. It was a gloriously clear day: I could see the whole of the English coastline from Portland to Beachy as well as the Cherbourg Peninsula and the Channel Islands. Having had a quick lunch I was full of wind which forced itself to my notice at 36,000 feet. As soon as I had inflated myself my tummy ceased to bother me.

I was inflated for about ten minutes at 40,000 feet. The only unpleasant symptom was the swelling and discoloration of my hands; otherwise the suit and helmet, although somewhat restricting my movements, gave me a noticeable feeling of confidence.

Coming down much faster than the proverbial bat out of hell my ears gave me a lot of trouble, so we levelled out at 19,000 feet where the pain was so intense that I had to remove the pressure helmet to blow my nose. It is of interest that I had the helmet off in a matter of seconds,

---

[2] Later, Air Marshal Sir Rochford Hughes

171

cleared my ears and fitted it on again for normal oxygen breathing before I was aware of any symptoms of anoxia.

Tubby Vielle, now holding a special appointment at R.A.E., had arranged for me to join the crew of the B29 at Boscombe Down for an eight hour trip involving calibration of the N-1 Gyro and the first air tests of the moving map driven by the Doppler drift and groundspeed equipment (APN66-XA1). This was something of an honour. At 8am on a peerless, windless, cloudless June morning I reported to the 'flight line'. The B29 supplied by the USAF was flown by a Marham crew commanded by Sqn Ldr Owen. They had an interesting affectation: the use of American methods of operating the aircraft and of American flying jargon. They even wore the American aircrew jockey caps.

In front of the B29 a long canvas mat was spread, and on this the safety equipment of the whole crew was set out. Dressing, the crew stood on the side of the mat away from the B29. As soon as each man was fully clad he moved across to the side of the mat nearest to the aircraft; and so a line was formed. The Captain then briefed his crew. Finally on the command 'Down locks away' the Engineer moved to take the down locks off the landing gear and the rest of the crew filed into the aircraft.

I enjoyed the flight, sitting on a stool between the two pilots, just behind the bombardier. The noise level was very low indeed, and there was no more than a faint tremor to indicate that the engines were pistoned, not jets. One could converse quite normally; and indeed while on a long straight leg due north to calibrate the gyro, with the C-1 autopilot engaged, Owen and I held a detailed discussion about bombing tactics, our feet up and the sun beating pleasantly on us. As usual I derived a great deal of pleasure from flying in a big aircraft with a large and efficient crew working in harmony.

After about two and a half hours airborne, cruising at 12,000 feet, the Engineer reported falling oil pressure on the port outer engine, and a few minutes later, rising temperature. Owen therefore feathered it and turned back for base.

Having had my pleasure curtailed, I got in touch with Hugh Garbett at lunchtime and arranged with him to do some helicoptering, first in the Mark III Sycamore. I was surprised to find the feel of the Sycamore was very much like that of an orthodox aeroplane. At first the changes of attitude were quite astonishing: for a vertical take-off the nose came up very high, but as you gained forward speed it fell very low; and as you came in for landing it again pitched alarmingly high as the speed dropped.

Later, by way of contrast, he gave me half an hour in the old Dragonfly (S51). Although the changes of attitude were very much less violent (same with the trim changes) the controls felt quite different, markedly heavier and less positive. Even in smooth level flight the stick juddered considerably. She was much more unstable. The lag on azimuthal control was such that it was quite easy to get into an uncontrollable porpoising of increasing amplitude. The Sycamore was vastly superior.

Hugh demonstrated some of the problems of slow flight: the significance of ground cushion effect, the transition to translational flight etc.; they certainly needed an entirely different flying technique. It was all good clean fun.

Almost two years to the day since pranging the Spitfire 19 I jumped a small psychological hurdle by flying my Air Marshal's personal Spitfire 16 which he kept at Hendon and made available to anyone on the staff qualified on the type. I had forgotten that a Spitfire packed so much punch, so I found the take-off somewhat startling; I had forgotten, too, that the Merlin was so incredibly smooth. Compared with the Griffon it was like a sewing machine. To get my eye in for landings I flew over to Bovingdon to use their 2000 yard runway, as opposed to the 950 yards I had taken off from at Hendon. She was a firm, quickly responsive little beast. By dint of calm deliberation and intense concentration I got back into Hendon with plenty of room to spare, having come in perfectly over the railway embankment between 80 and 85 knots at just the right height. I was very relieved, for flying my Air Marshal's personal aircraft was no mean responsibility.

Thereafter I used her extensively for Staff visits. She gave me intense pleasure and not a few hair-raising incidents, not the least of which was getting her over the railway embankment down onto the

173

short runway at Hendon. As Guy Gibson said: you needed to be lucky in this flying game. The professional navigators with whom I dealt often tended to look down upon me as an ignorant amateur, so it was, for me, a satisfying bit of one-upmanship to fly a Spitfire to a meeting of navigators, and never more so than in my capacity as Chairman of the Navigator's Station Committee.

I was once given an opportunity to fly a Buckmaster which my immediate boss, Hughie, habitually used for travelling round the country. At first handling I quite liked it. It was interesting to operate, in that the cockpit was full of gadgets, instruments and knobs to play with. But the directional trim was very sensitive to power settings and speed, and the controls were not well co-ordinated. The rudder, which had spring tabs, had a flabby 'feel'; while the ailerons were fairly heavy and the elevator, particularly at high speeds, was stiff but very sensitive. Towards the end of 1951 I staggered to Farnborough in the gloom of a weeping morning, having volunteered to navigate it to Warton despite the miserable navigation station isolated in the former bomb bay. Met gave cloud solid from 500 to 7,000 feet, breaking towards Liverpool. Hughie decided to go IFR direct. By the time I had sorted out the maps and charts in the aeroplane and made a flight plan it was 9am and our Director, Air Cdre Spreckley, arrived. Once we were airborne the weather was not as bad as had been predicted.

Hughie had a tendency to badger his crew, particularly the navigator, but I was firm with him from the start, with the result that I had none of the trouble which my Assistant, Sqn Ldr Alan Hollingsworth, so often complained of. If you gave him an alteration of course or ETA, or made a slip in calculation and corrected it, he tended to hold a detailed inquest on the spot, which was most irritating. At 200 knots, when you were a bit slow in your processes through lack of practice, life was too short for that sort of thing anyway. The first time he tried it I politely but firmly told him that I was switching off the intercom so as to have my concentration free of disturbance. "If you want me particularly, call me on the buzzer".

The undercast broke near Crewe, where we let down in visual contact to 1,500 feet. At Warton the haze was bad, with patchy thin stratus at 500 feet, and during the day the weather clamped. On the return trip we took-off in 1500 yards visibility and went into solid cloud at 400 feet and were still in it at our cruising height of 7,500 feet. As usual Farnborough control and radar talk-down were spot on.

Until he flew with us on that day Spreckley obviously had never flown in an aircraft equipped and operated to modern standards. He seemed to be tickled pink by it all, particularly the radio compass and the IFR procedures through the Control Zones and Farnborough's CRDF and radar. It seemed to me quite fantastic that the Director responsible for future operational requirements for navigation equipment, airborne radio and radar and flight instruments should be so crassly ignorant of the methods and practical problems of current aviation.[3]

We spent a useful morning at English Electric with Page, the Chief Designer, and his senior minions on the New Look Canberra which was my pet project. The main question was: NBC/VSA[4] or some combination of elements of the Vielle bombing system package? I had arranged the meeting primarily to get Page and ACAS(OR) together to discuss the issue, but as Tuttle couldn't spare the time Spreckley was the next best. Page was strongly and coherently opposed to putting NBC/VSA into the Canberra Development for precisely the reasons that Hughie and I held; he was keen on the Vielle scheme because it was a step towards a viable long range high altitude bombing system. He was most persuasive and Spreckley was at last brought onto our wavelength.

Having been selected for No. 3 Course at the RAF Flying College at Manby at the end of my Air Ministry tour, I took a week off during my last month to do some intensive instrument flying at Farnborough in their Harvard. I teamed up with Wg Cdr Rod Harmon who also had been selected for Manby. On our first day the Harvard was un-serviceable, but they lent us the communications Dominie for a couple of hours - the old biplane with two Gypsy engines. For its size it was a

---

[3] But he had had a very distinguished career as an Armament Specialist and ended up as Controller of Engineering in the rank of Air Marshal
[4] Navigation & Bombing Computer with Visual Sighting Attachment

bit solid on the controls, but very stable and quite pleasant to handle.

It was an amusing experience to be flying an ancient biplane again.

The Harvard was new to me. Apart from a rather vicious tendency to swing on landing (easily held on brakes) it also was a pleasantly stable aircraft to fly. Rod and I took it in turns, the one of us in the front cockpit doing the landing and take-off and acting as captain and safety pilot, the one in the rear flying various exercises on instruments under the hood.

After that delightful but hardworking week, my last four weeks at my Whitehall desk were torture. It was, I think, the happiest day of my life when I walked out of the Air Ministry for the last time on 15th April 1952.

9

Flying College

TOWARDS THE END OF THE 1940s THE MIDDLE RANKS of the RAF were, in the operational sense, mainly specialists: once a Fighter Boy, always a Fighter Boy; and apart from a few Fighter Squadrons their experience was based entirely on piston-engined aircraft. The RAF Flying College was an imaginative but short-lived attempt to remedy this situation.

It took in selected Wing Commanders and senior Squadron Leaders who were pilots and navigators and taught them to operate fighters, bombers and transport aircraft in the air, and on the ground provided the means to study the technical and tactical problems of operating future jet aircraft in all the roles of the Air Force. When I joined No. 3 Course the syllabus was still both unconventional and experimental. My colleagues were men of wartime distinction; I got in only because it was convenient for the authorities, who were finding it difficult to fill the places allotted to navigators; consequently I not only did the full pilots' flying course but additionally performed the full navigator's part of the flying syllabus.

Because the runways at Manby were rather short, the Meteors and Vampires were based at the satellite, Strubby, some three or four miles away. Here I started with a full conversion course onto the Meteor under the very congenial tuition of Squadron Leader John Lawrence,[1] my syndicate leader. He was a quietly humorous man of great intelligence who was both a wholly unflappable pilot and an excellent instructor. In the conversion phase we made four sorties a day, each one packed with high speed, concentrated activity, and I

---

[1] Later, Air Vice Marshal J.E.T. Lawrence

found the going tough. On each of No. 1 and No. 2 courses a Wing Commander had been killed in a flying accident; the victim on the second course had been Don Steventon, a veteran PR pilot who had been a friend and colleague at Benson, whom all and sundry regarded as a potential Chief of Air Staff; and there were times when I suspected that it was I who was destined to be No. 3 Course's victim.

The pupil pilot's position in the dual Meteor 7 was excellent; one immediately felt fully in control of the thing because of the unobstructed view forwards and downwards. Lawrence took off and handed over to me as soon as the wheels and flaps were up, telling me to climb at 13,500 rpm and 230 knots to 10,000 feet. There I discovered the stall, both clean and in the landing configuration. Severe buffeting gave plenty of warning, and at the stall the aircraft sank at a very high rate with no change of attitude.

In general flying below 300 knots indicated airspeed she handled very sweetly indeed, the ailerons being particularly light and the rate of roll very high. Power changes and the air brakes both affected the longitudinal trim markedly. After that little exercise we dived back into the circuit and did three roller landings. I had no trouble at all, but I did tend to hold off rather than to fly onto the runway at the correct speed. By then, after some 45 minutes flying, the fuel gauges were moving rapidly towards zero, so we packed up for lunch.

Afterwards we went up again for another 45 minutes. I found her a bit soggy immediately after getting airborne. As the speed built up rapidly after undercarriage and flap retraction, the trim changed considerably to nose-down, so that if you didn't anticipate it on the tail trimmer you found yourself edging very smartly towards the ground. We did some asymmetric flying. Clean, she handled easily on one engine. I made two single-engine landings. With wheels down and one third flap at 150 knots in the circuit, the foot loads even with full rudder trim were rather heavy; nevertheless I managed the two approaches and landings without difficulty, so Lawrence sent me off solo.

I climbed straight up to 10,000 feet, above the haze. In the smooth air the quietness and lack of vibration were so remarkable that I had to look twice at the rpm and airspeed indicators to reassure myself that everything was in fact working as it should. I worked her up to Mach 0.68, noting the increasing heaviness of the controls, and then extended the airbrakes; they slowed her down very sharply, pushing me firmly against the straps.

At this juncture I noticed that the red light on the nosewheel indicator was on, so I descended at slow airspeed into the circuit. When I selected wheels down, the starboard green light failed to come on and I did a low fly-past. Flying control said that it looked as though the undercarriage was locked down, so I came in and closed the day's flying with a perfect approach and landing. I went home in a dream, savouring the pleasure of the power and the smoothness, the lightness of control and the effortlessness of jet flying.

The jet being essentially a high altitude machine that drank fuel at a prohibitive rate at low altitude, it was essential to have a slick method of bringing it down accurately through cloud into the circuit for landing. My next exercise with John Lawrence was, therefore, to master Strubby's complicated high level controlled letdown into GCA.[2]

We used the Manby VHF D/F to home to Manby, and a 'cut' with Manby SBA beam to establish 'overhead Manby' at 20,000 feet. Having got clearance from Manby to let down, we then screamed down a let-down lane at 250 knots indicated, dive brakes out and throttles closed (rate of descent about 8,000 feet per minute), meanwhile changing frequency to Strubby Approach Control and tuning in to Strubby SBA. At about 12,000 feet we called 'markers' to Strubby so that they knew roughly where we were.

At about 5,000 feet we began a 'procedure turn' at the end of which we hoped to be straight and level at 3,000 feet and lined up on the Strubby beam. Strubby then took us under control either with GCA or VHF D/F to lead us into the GCA final approach and talk-down. From 20,000 feet to touchdown occupied about seven minutes. I found the rapid letdown pattern very much easier than I had

---

[2] 'Ground Control Approach' – a radar system for bad weather approach to the runway

expected. The Meteor was delightful to handle on instruments, being far more stable than the Spitfire was.

When I had my first crack at a single-seater Meteor Mk 4 I found it differed from the Mk 7 only in details of the layout of its smaller cockpit. It was a bit more lively (particularly on ailerons) and noisier. While I was doing about 0.76 Mach, accelerating up to 0.82, five Canadian F86's overtook me at considerable speed. Diving from 35,000 feet to 20,000 feet I worked it up to Mach 0.84 and got no more than mild buffeting and a heavy nose-up change of trim - a good aircraft, I was told later. Afterwards I rolled her: very smooth and simple.

After four years of absence from night flying I took to it (as John Lawrence remarked) like a duck to water, though it needed a great deal of concentration. With John in the back of the Meteor 7 I took off at dusk, climbed up through a desolating overcast and popped out into gorgeous saffron sunlight on the cloud-tops. When later we penetrated the nether-world it was dark: not pitch-dark but a milky dark caused by the diffusion of weak moonlight in the haze. Flying at 250 knots at 1,500 feet I had a strong, almost worrying impression of being too close to the dimly perceived ground. Both normal and asymmetric approaches went smoothly. The Meteor, if you tackled it carefully, was an easy aircraft to fly because it was stable.

Compared with the Meteor, the lack of acceleration of the Vampire - and of deceleration with the dive brakes out - was most noticeable; but the delightful lightness, smoothness and co-ordination of the controls were definitely out of the De Havilland stable. At take-off the acceleration on the runway was negligible, and after getting airborne she took hours to work up to the 260 knots at which you were advised to climb. In the Meteor, on the other hand, as soon as you released the brakes and opened the taps you got a kick in the small of your back. Speed built up quickly and crisply to 290 knots after wheels and flaps retracted, then you literally rocketed heavenwards.

Whether in a Meteor or a Vampire, I was a close fit in the cockpit. As I taxied out with a scream of Nenes or a banshee wail of

180

a Goblin, men working by the side of the perimeter track paused to watch me going by, seeing only my anonymous head encased in helmet, oxygen mask and tinted spectacles. At the end of the runway I began my journey into loneliness, a long, rocket-like acceleration off the ground and over the ground and upward through dark clouds to smoothness and sunlight above. There I was frightened and alone in charge of a machine which, too quickly and too easily, could outrun my ability to control it. In my ears loud, distorted R/T chatter was mixed with the signals from the beam from which I tried to keep tally of my position. The eagle-swoop through the heavy clouds to the ground was an ordeal of concentration: on interpreting the distorted voices of the controllers who were directing me; on the flight instruments; and always on the problem of maintaining control while manoeuvring blind. I was glad when I was on the ground again, and I could hear the scream or the banshee wail as I taxied back to the dispersal.

Aerobatics in the Meteor were my next tribulation. They engraved the plan view of Skegness permanently on my memory. The rolls, both slow and barrel, were simple and pleasing, but I didn't like the loops one little bit. They took up an awful lot of sky. Going up and over the top was all right though it took quite a time; but coming down was terrifying because the centrifugal force was fierce and it took ages to pull out while the altimeter wound down at a fantastic rate and the speed built up very quickly indeed. One seemed to be held poised, aiming directly at the heart of Skegness for an eternity. If I tried to hurry the pull-up I would immediately black out (which always frightened me). I did six loops in a row, after which I had just about had enough.

Aerobatics in a Vampire were rather more gentlemanly. The stick forces on the elevator being so feather-light, one enjoyed an effortless confidence during manoeuvres in the looping plane. She handled very sweetly. In rolling her, however, I found that unless one forced the nose apparently very high in the inverted position she came out with a horrible slither which couldn't be controlled by top rudder alone. Three rolls, two loops and a half roll off the top of

181

another were quite enough for the first time: my heart was pounding and my knees knocking.

On the morning of Friday, 16th May 1952, the Flying College Jinx struck for the third time. One of our Naval pilots, Commander Leckie, and Flt Lieut Woods, were killed in a Meteor 7. They got low and slow on a single-engined approach, put on too much power on the live engine and flicked over and went 'whoomph' practically on the runway threshold.

That night was a perfect night, cloudless, windless, moonless; so that in the air the starry sky gave us a perfect horizon while the ground below was as black as the pit. I could not but admire John Lawrence's insouciance as he sat in the back of a Meteor 7 and made me do a series of single-engined overshoots and landings. Because the ground was so dark my landings were a bit rough. Nevertheless he sent me solo in a Meteor 4, followed by a rather rough one in a Vampire.

I then took a Vampire to 35,000 feet and a Meteor to 42,000 feet to test their handling qualities at these extremes of altitude. Their controls became heavy, the response sluggish. One felt balanced upon a knife-edge above an abyss. The earth was a very long way away and I was obsessed with a fear of falling and a sense of loneliness. I was glad when I could descend to the more homely level around 20,000 feet.

At last light on the final day of the jet conversion phase I took off in a Meteor 4 and climbed to 25,000 feet. Up in the sky it was still sufficiently light to read my kneepad; the northwest horizon was a vivid gash of saffron, but the land below was a featureless grey shadow sharply contrasted with the black sea. After enjoying the scene awhile I homed to Manby and began the rapid controlled let-down into the pit of the night for a GCA approach into Strubby. The approach and runway lights were brilliantly defined points in an inky darkness, but now that I was in the cockpit of the aircraft a quiet confidence in my own competence had taken the place of the day's apprehensions.

The next sortie was in a Vampire. From 25,000 feet the lights of

182

Grimsby and Hull were like miniature diamanté brooches of exquisite workmanship. There was still a thin line of light on the northern horizon. As I climbed up in a Meteor for my last sortie of the night just after 01.00hrs I saw over the hills to the west the menacing shadow of low cloud. The illumined horizon had now moved towards the northeast. At 30,000 feet it was just light enough to read the dial of my wristwatch, but when I came in on my third GCA the runway surface was still invisible in the darkness of the earth.

After that session we began the eight week course on Lincolns and Valettas. I started with four hours of dual in the Lincoln at Manby. For most of the time low fracto-stratus and drizzle made circuits quite difficult. My first impression was that the Lincoln handled more like a Liberator than a Lancaster, although it gave one a greater feeling of power than either. The take-off was quite lively. The controls, particularly the elevator, were surprisingly light; the aileron response, however, was rather slow. I had some difficulty in landing, bouncing every time, but she was very forgiving. In the light wind the 1,200 yard runway at Manby seemed awfully short (although in fact it was adequate).

The clean stall was innocuous: after a slight buffeting about 5 knots above the stall the nose dropped very slowly at about 90 knots, and with the stick held hard back the aircraft simply mushed down. With wheels and flaps down there was a slight tendency to drop a wing at about 70 knots. At cruising power a steep turn had to be ridiculously steep with the speed quite low before you could force a pre-stall judder. Recovery was immediate.

The performance on three engines at landing weights (ie about 60,000-65,000lb) was excellent; I had no trouble with either an overshoot from 400 feet or a landing. With two engines out on one side a slight overbalance of rudders was noticeable. I could maintain height but could not climb at any worthwhile rate.

After the Meteor I found instrument flying at Lincoln speeds to be a piece of cake, and did three GCAs with the greatest of ease. So, although at that stage I still could not do accurate instrument flying on a jet for love or money, my experience at Meteor and Vampire speeds had at least had a terrifically beneficial effect on my piston-engined IF.

My first Lincoln night flying took place on a filthy night: as dark as a cow's innards, with drizzle falling out of a cloud-base varying between 600 and 1,000 feet. Strangely enough it didn't worry me in the least. Flt Lieut Merriman gave me an hour's dual in which, because of congestion in the circuit and difficulty in picking up the approach lights in time in the bad visibility, I did only two landings, one normal and one asymmetric. I then went solo. On my first circuit I failed to line up with the approach lights in time, but on my second everything went swimmingly so that I was able literally to grease the wheels onto the runway.

Now that I could put the Lincoln onto the ground as lightly as thistledown, by night as well as by day, I felt thoroughly at home in the old monster. But the night was not yet over. I shared an aircraft with Bob Hodges,[3] whose ham-fistedness scared the wits out of me. He made five abortive stabs at lining up (and sometimes both his speed and height got dangerously low). The sixth worked out all right, but we couldn't have missed the fence by much because we arrived with a hell of a wallop on the grass well short of the runway threshold. I was glad when he decided to return to dispersal because the VHF R/T was playing tricks.

We changed to another Lincoln for me to have a go. I climbed straight up to 2,000 feet and did a full BABS instrument letdown and approach procedure which worked out perfectly, but when I called 'finals' at four miles, flying control instructed me to break off on getting visual contact because the wind had swung round through 180 degrees. I picked up the approach lights at 500 feet, turned off to port and did a steep right handed circuit to line up with the new runway, but the visibility was so bad that it didn't work out at all well. After overshooting I went well downwind and got the navigator to line me up on the BABS back-beam. We crawled in at 400 feet until we picked up the approach lights, and I managed to put the old

---

[3] Later, Air Chief Marshal Sir Lewis Hodges

monster onto the runway with barely a tremor. By then the night was just perceptibly becoming less than pitch black.

After one and a half sweaty hours under the hood doing my instrument rating test in a Lincoln with Flt Lieut Steedman, I got ready for an afternoon trip to West Freugh. As Met was promising some pretty sticky weather I planned the flight meticulously with the navigator. Getting a Lincoln started and airborne took about half an hour; then there was the long laborious climb through cloud into the clear at 10,500 feet, and settling down to a steady cruise with the engineer beside me busy synchronising the Merlins while I had nothing to do but keep height, course and speed accurately as directed by the navigator. This was infinitely more satisfying than a transit trip in a single seater, which was always a misery of anxiety. As captain of a large aircraft I was in my element again; this was what I was born for; the necessary leadership came naturally and without effort.

The Valetta, rather like a big Anson of the later, more flabby marks, was not awfully impressive. Although it was easy enough to fly, the cockpit was unnecessarily complicated by a vast array of switches and levers many of which could have been eliminated if automatic services had been employed. After soloing, I was rostered to go to Belgrade as navigator in one. I was up at 04.30hrs with familiar early morning pre-flight symptoms: eyes red and weeping, tummy empty, head reeling with weariness. Alan Gibb navigated to Northolt.

We were flying in thick, miserable cloud. Northolt GCA was not yet open. Their Eureka beacon [4] was unserviceable. We had, consequently, to do a Gee let-down. As usual I found it impossible to relax in a passenger seat, so I stood at Alan's side - not that I was frightened, but that, being naturally interested in all the symptoms, I could not help projecting myself into the pilot's seat and wondering what exactly was going on at every lurch or alteration of engine note or change of attitude.

After picking up our passengers, the RAF boxing team plus one,

---

[4] A form of radar beacon

I navigated the flight in cloud along the airways as far as Munich; the two and a half hours passed very swiftly indeed. Alan took over from here. It was about 5pm when we got to Zemun airport at Belgrade. The runway being unserviceable, Bob Hodges plonked us down with several horrid lurches on the very rough grass. There was quite a reception committee for us. Protocol kept us out of bed until 1am!

We took off from Zemun a little after 10am, delayed somewhat by a general lack of organisation, though I suppose our departure must have been pretty expeditious because we were State Guests. It was my turn to fly the Valetta home. Just before we entered the corridor that led through the Russian Zone to Schwechat we hit a huge blue-black cumulonimbus sprouting lightning in all directions. The rain was positively solid. Fortunately it didn't last very long, because while it did last I was not a little frightened and confused, and had it been much more turbulent I don't think my instrument flying would have been safe.

Having had a quick lunch at Schwechat, which seemed highly civilised after Zemun, we pushed on VFR[5] to Munich and then IFR[6] through two cold fronts which gave me well over an hour on instruments with moderate clear icing. Although there was a considerable build-up of clear ice on aerials, stone-guards, etc, the anti-icing system kept all the important parts free. Beyond Koblenz, where we broke out of cloud, it became a dreary slog direct to Manby where we landed just after 8pm.

For my Valetta night flying I was paired with George Petty on a calm, warm, cloudless but pretty dark night. I had no trouble at all. When we climbed out of the aircraft at 02.15hrs after four continuous hours of it, the first grey light was beginning to creep among the hangars and the dispersed aircraft. The cold, dew-drenched grass smelled delicious.

One afternoon I had just landed a Valetta at Manby after lunching at Little Rissington, when air traffic control gave me an emergency call to go and search for a ditched aviator about ten miles

---

[5] Visual Flight Rules
[6] Instrument Flight Rules

off Flamborough Head. Someone had reported that he was bailing out of a Sabre. Alex Steedman, my co-pilot, slipped into the driver's seat while I went back to the navigator's table, and off we roared. All I had for navigating was a pencil and a local Gee chart. Nevertheless we carried out a fairly efficient search pattern over calm sea, being joined in time by a Canberra, two Sabres, a Washington and an Anson in the air, and two Air-Sea Rescue launches on the water. We saw nothing.

When our fuel flow-meters showed 500 of our 560 gallons gone, and our fuel contents gauges indicated about 70 gallons left in the tanks, we set course for base 45 miles away. The port motor cut dead for lack of fuel just as we crossed the coast. By operating the crossfeed Alex got it going again and climbed to 3,000 feet and obtained clearance for a direct approach to the runway. Although he did a glide landing from 2,500 feet, both motors stopped as he turned off the runway onto the perimeter track. If we lived, we learned!

I swore never to rely on a fuel gauge in its lower readings after this. Had I been flying the aircraft, we would undoubtedly have turned back earlier, but at this time I was sufficiently confident of Steedman's superior experience with the Valetta to let him go on as late as he did. I certainly didn't realise we were cutting things so fine.

Our final flight on this phase of the syllabus was a transatlantic navigation exercise primarily for the benefit of Alan Gibb and myself (in my capacity as a navigator). John Lawrence was in charge, with George Petty and Lieut Cdr Peter Austin [7] as the 'working' pilots. Once I had got into the Lincoln and had settled myself into the navigator's seat in the 'tunnel' I was visually out of touch with the ground, so that with the exception of a few minutes during our approach to Iceland, and in flight over Greenland, the progress of the flight was for me no more than what odd calculations and lines drawn on a chart could tell me.

We flew to Keflavik at 7,500 feet where a thirty knot head-wind component gave us a groundspeed about 155 knots. We had no Gee; neither the H2S nor the Loran worked; so for navigation I relied on

---

[7] Later, Vice-Admiral Sir Peter Austin

drifts, radio compass bearings and sun position lines. Fairly early on it became evident that we had an appreciable error in our gyro-magnetic compass, so we gave up using it. Of course, that put our air position indicator out of action, but since I very rarely used air position methods I wasn't bothered. At Pete Austin's cry of "Land ho!" I looked out on the starboard bow and saw at a range of some 60 miles the impressive sight of the ice-cap of Vatnajokull with huge black cliffs falling down to the sea.

The airfield at Keflavik was at the tip of the long low peninsula of volcanic ash running out from the Hekla massif, as bleak and windswept a strip of land, utterly devoid of vegetation, as I had seen. When I jumped out of the aircraft I was nearly blown flat by the 40 knot wind.

Flight planning for the next leg was something of a business as the American rescue services demanded the completion of an incredibly detailed clearance form. Shortly after reaching cruising height an astro compass check indicated that the gyro-magnetic compass was ten degrees in error, and this was confirmed by a radar fix from one of the ocean weather ships, so for the rest of the flight we reverted to the standby magnetic compass. We clocked in over Prince Christian beacon on track for Cape Harrison (Labrador) and had an excellent view of the huge, jagged, frost-splintered mountains of black basalt, the precipitous gorges of the fjords, and the glaciers, white with glints of green and heavily crevassed. But I could only afford five minutes to peer over Pete's shoulder at this exciting vista. Within a few minutes of my ETA, we picked up Cape Harrison looming through the sea fog.

As soon as we crossed the Labrador coast I handed the navigation over to Alan and retired to rest. When we came up to the airways intersection at Rougemont we took up our landing stations. Looking round at my five colleagues in the dim cockpit lighting I couldn't help remarking to myself how very old their lined and tired faces looked. Dorval airport appeared as a pool of darkness towards the edge of Greater Montreal's blaze of lights. Where the lights of English cities were diamantine, those of Montreal, like all North

American cities, which made great use of neon signs, were vividly spangled with rubies and emeralds, topaz and blue zircon. As it was now very dark, it was an exciting sight to see.

George Petty put us down with two hearty bounces which put him even with Pete's effort at Keflavik. It was 03.12 GMT, three minutes less than 24 hours since my alarm clock had wakened me at Manby. It was then 23.12 local time. As soon as the engines stopped I wriggled my way aft with no thought but to get out and have a cigarette before unloading. As I jumped out of the rear door I was surprised by a loud cry of "John!" It was Millie Tymms. As soon as I could decently get away they whisked me off to their flat in the city. There followed an absolutely stunning 36 hours.

When the time came to go home, John Lawrence asked me to take over the driving - largely, I think, because I was the only one of us who had not been drinking vast quantities of champagne and whisky at the Tymms' party for us the night before. Nothing loath, I flew the aircraft along the radio ranges all the way to Goose Bay while everybody else had some sound shuteye. At Goose I did a practice GCA and made what proved easily to be the smoothest landing of the whole trip.

When we clambered into the air again we had 3,500 gallons of petrol on board. Alan was navigating. Peter Austin was driving. After we left Labrador behind both John and George went back to sleep leaving me to fill the role of second pilot. I sat there happily for about six hours watching the stars come out and the afterglow move round the northern horizon, seeing the blood red moon rise ahead, and every hour taking star sights to give Alan a fix.

A navigator is a slave to mathematics and the green hieroglyphics on cathode ray tubes, but a pilot, particularly of a Lincoln or a Lancaster, is a Lord of creation perched in a glass-house high above the world. All the time below us was the grey sludge of the sea fog. Peter had the ultra violet lights glowing on the flight instrument panel; I turned the orange spotlights onto the engine instruments; red and blue flames were streaming back from the exhaust stubs aft of the bull-nosed spinners, curling upwards over the

189

leading edges of our broad, black wings. This was my real working world, and I was happy.

Peter handed over to George about 04.00hrs. At 06.30 when the moon was fading and the sun was very low I got a sun-moon fix, our last chance of any astro, but by 07.00hrs I was so weary that I was seeing spots before my eyes. So I retired to my bunk in the rear fuselage and dozed fitfully in chilly discomfort until 09.30 when we made our landfall some four miles south of track. By means of some clever juggling we managed to land at Manby a mere five seconds past 11.30hrs GMT, our scheduled time of arrival.

The next morning I was trying to get to grips with a Meteor 4 again. It was as if having been used to riding a friendly and lazy hippopotamus I had been suddenly put on the back of a thoroughbred stallion raring to get at a mare. The post-takeoff acceleration of the Meteor to climbing speed really caught me by surprise, particularly as there was eight eighths solid cloud from 500 feet to 7,000. Apart from the first sortie, which was for 'familiarisation' in a Meteor 4, all our flying involved ciné-gun exercises. We took off in formation pairs, climbed to about 12,000 feet where one acted as target for 15 minutes while the other did his gyro gun-sight aiming exercises; then we changed over; and on completion of the exercise we returned and landed in formation.

In clear weather it was fun; but with cloud the formation flying was a stiff task and the fuel problem and navigation an everlasting worry. Climbing through cloud, controlled descents, GCAs and formation flying, all of which were full time exercises in Phase 1, were now purely incidental to the gunnery exercises, and of course the mere handling of the aircraft was supposed to be second nature. For me, none of these things was second nature; they needed intense concentration.

My first flight in a Vampire since May involved taking off in formation with George Petty and following him up through 6,000 feet of cloud for the ciné-gun exercises, followed by a controlled descent and landing in formation. Needless to record, I was pretty rough. All the chaps agreed that by the end of the day, after four

190

extremely sweaty sorties, they were more or less on their knees from exhaustion.

Much of my first cross-country in a Vampire at 30,000 feet was above eight eighths cloud, so my navigation consisted in getting check bearings from selected VHF D/F stations. My canopy and windscreen got pretty well iced up internally. As I did my controlled descent for landing the ice melted on the inside, but heavy water vapour formed on the outside of both windscreen and canopy so that I had to complete my landing with very poor forward visibility, but I was so busy doing it that there was no time to think about it.

After I had qualified in gyro gun-sight aiming we started practising the attack procedure. You approached the target on an opposite heading and some 1500 feet above him. Judging just the right moment, you began a diving turn onto him with the object of straightening up as he came into your sights at firing range - 200 yards. If you didn't judge it right you either overran the target and never got him into your sights at all, or you ended up a long way astern of him in a fruitless tail-chase. Until we were proficient we practised this exercise in pairs at 14,000 feet. Subsequently, when I thought I was pretty good, I discovered that quarter attacks between 30,000 and 35,000 feet were a very different kettle of fish.

Although you were hitting relatively high Mach numbers during the attack (around 0.74, at which the Meteor began to show compressibility effects), you were also very near the aerodynamic stall in a steep turn; so that if you misjudged your distances (and it was terrifically difficult to get them right: 3,500 yards for the beginning of the turn in was far enough to make a Meteor target extremely hard to see), you tended to be walking on a knife-edge between compressibility trim problems and spinning out of a stall. Too often I found myself juddering round a tight turn, mushing horribly and slithering away beyond the target.

On the last day of quarter attacks I made two Meteor trips to 30,000 feet. I was by then beginning to feel happier up there and my attacks were at least consistent even if they did always end up as stern chases. The final exercise was an interesting one: tail-chasing

191

down from 30,000 to 10,000 feet with the target aircraft doing steep turns at 0.76 Mach. This meant that my aircraft was often hitting 0.78 to 0.8 Mach, at which speed the nose-up trim on a Meteor (as well as the snaking) was fierce enough to need two hands on the control column. It was a very strenuous business. Accurate aiming was quite out of the question.

My main failing generally in this fighter stuff was a strong reluctance to get close in to the target aircraft, a failing which, no doubt, I could have overcome in time as I gained confidence in my ability to judge closing speeds accurately and to control the aircraft with precision in all attitudes.

In the midst of the jet phase I received the Operation Order for an Arctic flight in the following month. Two Hastings were to go to Resolute Bay (74° 42' North, 94° 10' west), staying 36 hours at Resolute, which is on Cornwallis Island, one of the small group in Barrow Strait. Ted Grant and myself were to be the navigators of one aircraft captained by Philip Heal, with Bob Hodges and Geoffrey Morley-Mower as the working pilots. Since most of the trip was in high latitudes and some of it close to the North Magnetic Pole, where magnetic variation was very large and the directing force weak, special navigation techniques were required. Tactical flying on the jets was therefore interlaced with intensive planning for this exercise.

We used a 1/2 million USAF chart on a modified Lambert Conformal projection with standard parallels in about 75°N and 88°N, and on this I had to construct a rectangular grid based on the Greenwich meridian, together with isogonals and isogrivs.[8] From Keflavik to Resolute we needed to see the sun and the moon all the time. Once the schedule had been fixed by reference to twilight diagrams and planispheres we had to do all the astro precomputations for routine sun-moon fixes. The sun's altitude increased from about 4 degrees to 15 degrees, the moon's decreasing from 30 degrees to 17. Their azimuthal separation was, on average, about 30 degrees.

The drill was something like this. Our track was a great circle from Keflavik to Thule, thence to Resolute. On the Lambert Polar

---

[8] Lines of equal magnetic variation in relation to grid north

chart these tracks are represented by two straight lines bearing about 350 degrees and 340 degrees respectively, relative to a rectangular grid based on the Greenwich meridian. Our intention was to steer entirely by the directional gyro without magnetic monitoring. Every twenty minutes the true heading was measured by astro compass and converted to grid heading; this grid heading was compared with the desired heading and an alteration of course so many degrees to port or starboard was computed; and the alteration was made in relation to the current indications of the pilot's directional gyro, the setting datum of which was never altered in flight, whatever its rate of precession.

Ted Grant and I were to share the plotting; one of us plotting Keflavik to Resolute, the other Resolute to Keflavik. The one who was not plotting would do the astro steering checks and take sextant sights as required.

We flew a dummy run from Manby to Keflavik and back. The Hastings was infinitely more comfortable than the Lincoln; its flight deck was well laid out and spacious, and for those not on duty there were comfortable passenger seats in the fuselage. On the flight to Keflavik I was the navigation plotter, whilst Grant did the astro, rated the precession of the gyros and kept the gyro-astro log. We took some time to settle down to the routine. On the whole however, the navigation worked out satisfactorily We got there and landed five and a half hours after taking off.

We took off again shortly after midnight. This time Grant was plotter, but I had decided that we needed a third hand. I hijacked a navigator on the College staff who was free-riding in the back, and made him do all the astro compass and sextant observations while I sat in the galley doing all the astro computations and keeping the gyro-astro log. I might as well have been a bank clerk!

The work shared thus between a team of three proceeded so smoothly that we decided to do it this way on the long trip. Uneventfully we arrived over Manby on ETA at 05.30hrs only to have the Tower report 100 yards visibility with cloud on the deck, so Heal diverted to Binbrook where it was clear.

193

We began the Resolute flight early in September. Our first sight of Iceland was again the marvellous ice-field of Vatnajokull with its sharp-edged black cliffs. We were off next morning at 07.45hrs GMT (same local time) into a low overcast above which we flew at 8,500 feet. Grant plotted, I did the sextant and astro-compass work and Flt Lieut Cunningham did the computations.

About 40 miles off the Greenland coast the low cloud dispersed, giving us a splendidly sunlit view of the mountains. We made our landfall on track at Cape Nansen, flew up the Christian IV Glacier with the 12,500 feet Watkins range to starboard, and on over the Lindbergh Mountain, an astonishing fence of rock holding back the ice-cap.

The coastal mountains were positively Gothic: fretted and pinnacled, with knife-edge ridges, sheer sides and huge, tumbling ice-falls. The long, sinuous glaciers were heavily crevassed, and where two were joined together they were marked by a thin, sinuous line of moraine down the middle.

The ice-cap as we saw it from 13,000 feet (clearing it here by about 5,000 feet) was level, utterly featureless once it had submerged the coastal ranges, very dazzling, only rarely etched with sastrugi.

We soon entered cloud which, despite a climb to 23,000 feet, we never topped. We were more or less continually in it for three hours. This prevented any sun-moon fixing, but we did manage to get some snap sun checks on our heading. Fortunately our steering gyros had a reasonably steady rate of precession. We broke out of cloud just north of Coburg Island and got a positive pinpoint on the southern tip of Ellesmere Island, rocky, mountainous country with glaciers and snow rather like east Greenland, but on a smaller scale. Devon Island was, like the sea, covered by low stratus.

When, just eight hours after leaving Keflavik, we came over Cornwallis Island we were delighted to see the huts and landing strip just by the lake inland of Resolute Bay; but the windward end of the runway was covered by sea-fog which appeared to us to be moving in. We came down from 8,000 feet like a Meteor and actually rolled into the fog as we completed our landing run. I couldn't help thinking that we were lucky, particularly in view of the rather dismal landing forecast that we had been given.

Resolute was a collection of wooden huts, oil and fuel drums, bulldozers, snowploughs and miscellaneous equipment almost randomly dispersed by the side of a single gravel landing strip running NNW/SSE between Prospect Hill (800 feet) and Cape Martyr. The soil was a sort of limestone shale, varying in colour between pale straw and battleship grey. When we landed it was dappled with old snow. The only vegetation was an occasional moss or lichen about the size of the palm of one's hand; you had to search for it.

At high noon the temperature reached 25°F at most, and even a slight breeze was distinctly chilling. The variety of arctic dress, the colourful bush shirts, the beards and the Huskies at the door all added to the character of the place. The inhabitants, a mixture of RCAF personnel and a civilian construction gang, all under the command of Flt Lieut Trotter, were a tough crowd, by our standards undisciplined, nevertheless friendly, helpful and glad to see us. The Canadian habits of waste, lack of care for equipment and appalling untidiness were very much in evidence.

When we woke up on the next morning we were greeted by low cloud and snow falling lightly but steadily. By tea time there were heavy drifts on the runway.

Owing to a radio blackout which lasted for the next 24 hours we were unable to get any weather forecasts, all of which disrupted our schedule so much that I had to spend a lot of my time working out alternative route plans and diversion schedules.

When we eventually got some fragmentary evening weather reports from Thule, Eureka Sound, Alert Bay and Isaachsen it was decided that we should abandon the planned northern flight via Britannia Lake and Young Sound and return directly to Manby. Trotter and his men did a sterling job ploughing and compacting the snow on the runaway for our departure early the next morning.

Before takeoff the northern weather stations were reporting rapidly falling barometers, the route seemed to be covered by eight eighths cloud all the way, and what scanty information we had of Iceland indicated bad landing conditions there. Philip Heal decided that if we flew direct to Keflavik he would have sufficient fuel to go on to UK if conditions actually turned out to be too bad.

Just after we had passed over Thule, Philip told me that he was going back to land there to pick up some of the crew of the Lincoln 'Aries' which had diverted there a couple of days before with engine and fuel pump trouble after flying over the Pole. Consequently, we continued eastward for a further 30 minutes to bring us down to our permissible landing weight, then turned around and headed for Thule which we spotted from 9,000 feet through a convenient hole in the clouds.

It was a fantastic place, a young city, a fully equipped modern Air Force base with acres and acres of macadam set down in a moraine-filled valley between the bald dome of the ice-cap (which you saw from the runway) and the grey sea on which ice-floes float like the ghosts of huge immobile sheep. This extraordinary place had a 2,000 ft high radio mast in the circuit, a 1,200 foot table-top island in the final approach funnel and pink cliffs on the south and black cliffs on the north side of the valley.

We lost about three hours in refuelling and stocking up with oxygen and drinking coffee. Then with Aries' student crew on board we leapt into the air again and headed for Manby. About half an hour east of Thule the clouds dispersed. We had a peaceful flight over this fantastic ice-cap, dazzlingly white, perfectly flat and absolutely featureless to all four horizons. Our first pinpoint, as the sun was setting behind us, on an arm of Nordvest Fjord, agreed very closely with my reckoning. Next we made an accurate landfall on the northeast of Iceland in Axar Fjord. Although there was low cloud over the sea, the upper air was clear; it was an ebony night with moon and diamantine stars.

After landing at Manby, as we stood in the light of the rising sun smoking our first cigarettes I was struck by the quiet, comfortable beauty of the greensward of the airfield. Resolute was already a distant memory of wind-driven snow, low barren hills, hermetically sealed huts and gargantuan meals shared with huge bearded men in lumber shirts.

Towards the end of November I was scheduled with George Petty, Frank Dodd [9] and Geoffrey Morley-Mower to fly a Lincoln to bomb Fifla, off Malta, at precisely 15.15 GMT one afternoon. The day started for me at 04.00hrs. It was very dark; the rain was pouring down; and it was as cold as the morgue. George Petty captained the Malta flight, Geoffrey Morley-Mower tried his hand at navigating it and I operated the H2S radar, the Gee and Rebecca. We went all the way above cloud at 20,000 feet until I picked up Fifla on the radar. We made a timed descent to 2,000 feet to get below the cloud, and dropped our practice bomb on the target right on 15.15 GMT.

When we landed at Luqa it was chilly and drizzling. Next morning for once we took off at a civilised hour, 11.30hrs local time. On this leg, which we did at 1,000 feet, Frank Dodd navigated and Geoffrey M-M drove. As I had nothing to do, the trip dragged horribly. About an hour before ETA Gibraltar, Spain hove into view - Cape de Gata backed by the Sierra de los Filabres, and, looming through the further haze, the high Sierra Nevada with the soft evening sunlight reflecting palely off the snow in the upper hollows. It was 6.15 in the evening when we landed and four of us were due to go to a cocktail party in the Mess at 6.30 with lots of high brass including Sir Harold Macmillan and the Governor, so we had a hell of a rush.

The next night was clear-skied and the new moon was setting behind the black mountains as I walked out to the Lincoln. At precisely 11pm I called to the chaps to get in. At 11.30pm, to the second as scheduled, I opened the throttles, released the brakes and guided the Lincoln between the parallel rows of runway lights into the air over Algeciras Bay; and as we climbed away through the Straits all the glittering lights of Ceuta, Tangier, Algeciras and Tarifa were spread before us for our delight.

I enjoyed the flight back to Manby enormously. In slow procession through the night the marine lights of the great Capes -

---

[9] Later, Air Chief Marshal Sir Frank Dodd

Trafalgar, St Vincent, da Roca, Finisterre, Vilano - slid past while the brilliant stars wheeled above us. With the automatic pilot in, I sat like some presiding judge in Heaven, monitoring the instruments and gauges and all the activity in the aircraft.

Towards Finisterre we began to run into increasing amounts of scattered cloud heralding the front which we knew lay across our path over the Bay of Biscay. Soon we were flying continuously in cloud at 3,000 feet. I disengaged 'George' and flew manually while, for half an hour, we battled through some fairly intense turbulence. Ushant, seen only on radar, passed close to starboard; then the cloud broke and at 5 in the morning the lights of Plymouth passed under us when, although it was still pitch dark, we began to feel that daylight was at any moment likely to make its imminent arrival apparent.

Over Bristol our VHF R/T packed up. Twenty miles from base we ran under eight eighths of cloud at 3,000 feet which made the darkness blacker than ever. Then Manby 'Pundit' light blinked hospitably at us. In the circuit I flashed my navigation lights; the control tower answered with a green signal lamp; round we came and marvel of marvels, although I held off rather high and dropped her with a solid bang on the runway, I made the best landing of the whole trip. As I got out of the aircraft into the bitterly cold air I realised that I was extremely tired. So, after Customs clearance and breakfast, home to bed.

When we came back to the jets, it was for live gunnery, bombing and rocketry. I was not very good at any, always being reluctant to get right close to the target, especially when diving at the ground. One day I had a heavy flying programme, three Vampire and two Meteor sorties on air-to-ground gunnery and rocket-firing. My scores were appallingly bad; Dempster, Williamson and Petty, the aces, got consistently good scores. Then on the final flight of the day, in a gloomy grey dusk, I leapt hurriedly into the sky, banged off four quick rocket attacks and got the best score of the whole course, nine and a half yards!

By now I enjoyed a thoroughly satisfying sensation of effortless competence and confidence. The Vampire had grown on me; it was a

198

sweet and lovely, delicate instrument to handle. No longer a strange mechanism to be mastered, it was an integral part of myself that performed even as my mind envisioned the act.

One day I carried out three dive-bombing sorties and one high speed cross country at treetop level, all in a Vampire under a cloudless sky. How I enjoyed it all: the brisk march, parachute over the shoulder, across the tarmac to the aeroplanes; the quick, sure external check; the well-known starting-up drill; the rapid taxi-ing out, testing trim, flaps, dive-brakes, fuel cocks and booster pumps, instrument switches, oxygen, hood and harness on the way to the take-off point. The swift run into the air, with the wheels retracting at the very moment of becoming airborne; and, as the speed built up, the confident zoom and turn...and then, at 6,000 feet over the bombing range the quarter roll, turn and eagle-swoop down onto the target, the firm pull out of the dive that greyed the old man's vision, and the steep climbing turn - eight times in quick succession until all bombs were dropped and I sped like a hare back to Strubby for a tight circuit and landing.

The Meteor, although it had far more urge and speed and was a very much better gun platform was, by contrast, a bus to handle. On my last flight in a Meteor 4 I had a most alarming session. I am still not at all clear as to what went wrong. After lunch Rod Harmon and I had set off to do quarter attacks on each other, and I was flying the Meteor 4 which had spring-tab controls and was therefore very light. After our exercise I led Rod back. We ran into thick snow which forced us down to 400 feet with barely half a mile visibility, but I found the aerodrome and we broke formation to land independently. Turning downwind I lowered the undercarriage at the normal 150 knots and immediately got into the most horrible skidding yaw which took quite a bit of juggling to get out of.

I was still in the snow storm. I had such difficulty in controlling the aircraft due to what seemed like rudder overbalance that I just couldn't get round the circuit, and waffled away towards Saltfleet Haven, where luckily the visibility was much better. With fuel running low I made a distress call, asking GCA to try to pick me up and give me a straight run in, and slithered round through 180 degrees towards Mablethorpe.

I checked all round the cockpit but could discover no cause for such behaviour. There was no sign of icing. GCA couldn't see me because of the snow. I was very worried but quite clear-headed, and had decided either to lob down on the beach or climb to 3,000 feet and bail out if I couldn't get lined up with the runway, as fuel was now precariously low.

Over Mablethorpe I slithered round onto 270 degrees. Although the visibility over the airfield had improved, I found myself badly out of alignment to the runway and decided to overshoot and try again. As soon as I raised the undercarriage I found I had full normal control, so I came round in a tight circuit, lined up on final and put the wheels down - and landed safely, a shaken man.

Phil Fargher, one of the fighter instructors, air-tested the aircraft and could find nothing wrong with it, so we concluded that it was all due to my mishandling the controls, as I had done very little Meteor flying in the previous three months.

During February 1953 we were preparing for our Alaskan trip. I was to be in command of the Expedition, John Lawrence the aircraft commander. The Hastings, with two complete crews, was to go via Lajes in the Azores to Elmendorf Air Force Base near Anchorage, drop John Lawrence and my crew off, and go back to Canada with the other crew. After picking us up again later, it was to return across the North Magnetic Pole and via Thule, weather permitting.

When we eventually got airborne on a filthy morning at Manby, my crew was flying as passengers. After some three and a half hours flying, the port outer engine packed up and was feathered. John headed the aircraft towards St Eval, nearly five hundred miles away in the teeth of a 40 knot NE wind. Those who were not already wearing full flying kit put it on; then most of us sat back to doze. Once, when the power settings were changed, everybody popped up like alarmed rabbits to peer out of the windows.

Early on I let my imagination run free to explore the future; when I got as far as letting the Hastings hit the water I found myself very frightened - tummy in mouth, heart pounding, electric shocks in the guts etc. - so I stopped. To keep normal, I had to set up barriers in my mind beyond which trains of thought must not be allowed to run. I could go just so far, and then something warned me that to go further meant hysteria. So the minutes dragged past in a state of worried calmness occasionally disturbed by electric shocks in my belly whenever the note of the engines varied.

An hour later Flt Lieut Adcock (the alternate Captain) came round, quietly and calmly although very pale, asking us all to check our ditching arrangements and stand by, as it looked as if the port inner engine was going to fail as well. He had not got the length of the cabin before it happened.

I estimated that we were at 3,000 feet, having been gradually descending for some time in order to avoid overheating the engines. Everybody quietly but busily set about stowing things in pockets, putting on gloves and helmets and collecting odd bits of safety equipment. Then we all settled grimly in our seats as the sea came closer.

The surface wind was about 40 knots and the sea was very rough. I decided that there was no chance at all of getting away with a successful ditching so preparation for it was a mere formality. At 1,000 feet Lawrence jettisoned 1,200 gallons of fuel. We then began to throw out all items of loose equipment in the cabin: all the arctic survival equipment, rations, spares packs, tool boxes etc. Through the open parachute door the sea looked horribly close. At 500 feet, just before we started to chuck out our personal baggage, the pilot reported that he was now able to hold height. We settled down again with twenty minutes to go to the Scillies.

My face was sweating, my throat dry; some people were pale, some had red faces. I was entirely calm; busying myself with going over and over my escape drill - undo seat harness, jettison escape hatch, go out taking safety rope, two exposure suits and an emergency survival pack straight to the starboard outboard dinghy, and receive stores and personnel as they followed me out. But I was worried. The two starboard engines were going at full bore, and as

201

long as they went we were OK; but why shouldn't they stop as the other two had?

For a very long twenty minutes I was aware of thirst, sweat and a grim acceptance only of the instant of the present. There was no such thing as a past or a future; and I was by then not afraid. If we had to ditch, death was almost certain (I didn't admit this consciously, although at the back of my mind I was pretty sure of it). Meanwhile all of my mind was concentrated on doing my part properly if ditching came. Never was I so glad to see land as when we flew over the Scillies.

Word came back from Lawrence that all was under control; he had managed to clamber up to 1,200 feet, so he was going to try for Culdrose, near Helston, rather than crash-land on the island's tiny aerodrome. Although the sea was just as rough and the two engines had been exceeding their running limitations for nearly an hour, we faced the next 15 minutes with more cheerful spirits. Over Culdrose John decided to take her on to St Eval, where he put her down with no trouble at all.

Most of us agreed that was as near as we had ever come to the Heavenly Gates, and those who had been even closer admitted that it was quite the longest time they had spent in such proximity. We flew back to Manby in a Valetta the next morning.

It was decided to delay the whole programme by one week, in the meantime changing all four engines. This little escapade upset me more than I cared to admit, and I faced the prospect of flying across the Atlantic as a passenger again with considerable dread. All the week the trip hung over twenty unhappy heads like a sword of Damocles. When we were finally ready to go, my nerves were jangling but of course there was nothing one could do except sit tight and quiet.

Once we were airborne and on our way, however, I found myself entirely normal again. I spent my time now reading, now dozing: but dozing was very difficult because there was so much clatter and vibration in the passenger compartment. Forward on the flight deck it was, of course, delightfully smooth. I navigated the Lajes-Argentia

202

leg, a dreary slog into the teeth of a gale and through a turbulent cold front, and made rather a hash of the job. Approaching Argentia we decided that we had not sufficient fuel to carry on to Ottawa so we landed at 11.00 GMT (= 08.30 hrs local).

Argentia was on a small, flat peninsula on the east side of Placentia Bay, having a delightful vista across a wind-flecked sea that was perpetually changing its colour, towards rounded islands of snow-patched, multicoloured rocks. After being held up for three hours by fuel priming problems, we landed at Ottawa about 7pm local time. The Air Attaché, who met us all, informed me that the Tymms would be arriving in Ottawa at 7.30 and would expect me at the Chateau Laurier. I was of course delighted. They gave me a splendid dinner, but Millie packed me off to bed at 11 so I eventually hit the hay 46 hours after leaving it at Manby.

It was not until I found myself at dusk flying over the almost featureless expanse of snow-covered prairie land, with rare clusters of lights scattered sparsely from horizon to horizon, that I began to realise for the first time the true vastness of Canada. The Maritime Provinces had a scale comparable with that of England; Quebec west of the St Lawrence, and all Central Ontario balanced the eye's sense of scale by the wealth of its jungly detail (like Indian architecture); but here in Manitoba and Saskatchewan the slender evidence of man's presence made the horizons seem very far away.

We night-stopped at Edmonton. Next day, when we crossed the Peace River north of Dawson Creek the clouds more or less vanished. Cultivation ended about Grande Prairie. North of that is all wooded plateau deeply scarred by meandering rivers until on the upper reaches of the Liard, a noble stream now frozen in its deep gorge, one began to see signs of the tilted and folded strata which presented an entirely different erosion pattern. The peculiar geography east of the Rockies across the whole of northern Canada derives from the extraordinary lack of gradient.

The white Mackenzie Mountains to the right of our track, a vast unexplored jumble of highlands enclosed in the sweep of the Liard and Mackenzie Rivers, was a stirring sight that put me in mind of

John Buchan's *Sick Heart River;* but the finest sight of all was the subtle chiaroscuro of cloud and sunlit snow on the distant St Elias Mountains west of Whitehorse, seen against a low and dazzling sun.

We began to converge on the jumbled pinnacles of the Wrangel Mountains which form the main barrier between the Gulf of Alaska and the complex upper basin of the Yukon.

The rivers seemed to dash steeply out of the heights on this side of the Rockies and quickly find their natural level in the old glacial valleys where they spread themselves in wide, gravelly bottoms and meander vaguely from lake to lake for hundreds of miles, the surface of the plateau being considerably higher.

At Northway, climbing to 14,000 feet, we turned left to cross the Alaska Range. Unfortunately a lot of thin cloud obscured what otherwise would have been a wonderful view of both the Wrangel Mountains, less than ten miles to port and going up to 16,000 feet, and the Chugach Mountains.

We landed at Elmendorf at 5.30pm after an eight hour trip. Danny Clare, an old chum, was there to meet us with the Chief of Staff in HQ Alaskan Command.

There followed several days of intensive study of the various facilities at the huge Air Force Base and nights of equally intensive hospitality. I was immensely impressed by this view of the United States Air Force on its own stamping ground, and it was not only for the sheer size of its operation. The Americans were at their best among their machines; they looked the part and were impressive in their confident competence.

We spent a day with a jet Fighter Squadron; another with an Air Rescue Squadron; and a third with a weather Reconnaissance Group. Next we flew to Kodiak in the Commanding General's C54. The Naval Air Station at Kodiak lay, one small side bounded by the sea, in a small and exquisite bowl rimmed by dancing mountains, for the most part treeless, deep in alabaster snow as smooth and rounded as a woman's flesh. Within a mile of one of the runways, right on its centreline, a perfect pyramid rose to 2,600 feet; and further away there was another perfect pyramid even higher. The landward side of the runways was so constrained by sheer walls that take-offs had to be made to seaward whatever the wind direction, and there was no possibility of going round again from a baulked final approach.

Kodiak Island is a small Switzerland set in the sea; not a particularly high land, the peaks seldom exceeding 5,000 feet, but one of rhythmical skylines and bold corries; and on that day the snow was dazzling.

At Elmendorf I flew in a C124 (Globemaster) and had some time at the controls while the rest of the party flew in F94s. The C124 was a very fine aircraft indeed; the performance was formidable, coupled with a remarkably short landing and take-off run. There was a lot of turbulence and up in the cockpit some 25 feet forward of the centre of gravity I was shaken about considerably, rather like being in the front of an old Glasgow tram.

General Agee lent us his personal B17, converted to VIP passenger standard, to fly up to Ladd Air Force Base near Fairbanks to undertake the survival course at the Arctic Indoctrination School. We flew under a cloudless, bleached blue sky with limitless visibility and had the most breathtaking views of the 20,300 feet Mount McKinley and its neighbouring massifs.

At Ladd, apart from terrific hospitality, we joined the three-day course in a superheated lecture room and then went 'on the trail'. We RAF seven were dumped with parachutes and emergency rations, as though we had bailed out of an aeroplane, and left to get on with surviving. We made a great joke of it all, to the utter despair of our field instructor who watched from a safe distance.

By day the temperature reached about 25°F, but during the night it quickly dropped to -10°F. One of the biggest dangers in extreme cold, our experience taught us, was of fire; and quickly we adopted as our slogan the Eskimo saying 'White Man him heap big fool, he build big fire and stand long way from it; Eskimo, him feather-plucker, build small fire and sit on it.'

From Ladd I went by car a further 25 miles into the backwoods to Eielson A.F.B. to fly a weather patrol to the North Pole in a B29. On the night we arrived the 'Fabulous 58th' were celebrating their

1,500th Polar Weather Mission. Everyone from the C.O. down treated us right royally. The next morning I joined our B29 in a warm hangar and at 09.15hrs, everything having been put aboard, pre-flight checks done and crew at their stations, she was hauled out and started up. We were airborne five minutes before ten.

As far as Bettles we flew at 10,000 feet above an overcast. Luckily the cloud broke then so that I, flying the aircraft in the first pilot's position, could see something of the Brookes Range, as wild and desolate a conglomeration of peaks and ridges as I have ever seen with neither reason nor order about their disposition. To put an aircraft down among them would be impossible. These mountains, although not particularly high - they average round six or seven thousand feet - are practically impenetrable. North of Umiat, over the barren lands, we ran over more cloud, but between Umiat and Point Barrow the surface is so flat and featureless that it was often difficult to discern what was and what was not low stratus. By the time we reached Point Barrow we were at 500 millibars, that is about 18,000 feet pressure altitude, which in this cold air was about 16,500 feet true, where we stayed for the next ten hours - making contrails most of the time.

I was very impressed by the quiet efficiency with which everybody did their work on a job that was essentially a team effort, particularly between the three navigators, the pilot, the weather observer, the drop-sonde operator and the radio man. Every one of the crew did his best to make the trip interesting and profitable for me. The radio man insisted on making a special effort to provide me with tea: the pity of this was that their coffee was superb!

Beyond Point Barrow the sea ice was solid. During the whole flight I saw very few open leads, but in the south there were many newly frozen ones. As the sun went down we ran under high cirrus which, combined with the long twilight, prevented our getting any astro heading check for over an hour. Shortly after turning at 80° north, 180° west we ran clear of it and were able to make use of Venus near her maximum elongation. On this leg the ice below us was the same pale blue as the sky, the two merging in a featurcless, deep indigo pool of darkness far ahead of us, so that although we were in bright light in cloudless conditions we were nevertheless forced to fly on instruments for lack of a horizon.

Eight hours after taking off we reached our furthest north, 84 degrees, in longitude 150 west, where we turned for Barter Island. Soon we had an indigo night sky filling the port windows and brilliant saffron twilight filling the starboard ones. Three hours later when it was dark we had a magnificent display of the Aurora, a vast curtain of pale green light that hid the stars and stretched in waving bands from horizon to horizon through the zenith. The flight was completed as excellently as it was conducted throughout, with a perfect landing off a practice GCA.

Next I flew from Anchorage as co-pilot of a C47 to Utopia Creek, a fantastic landing strip on the side of Indian Mountain about 80 miles north of the confluence of the Yukon and Tanana Rivers. It was a splendid morning so that I could see the whole expanse of the Alaska Range, like the tumbled waters of a tidal overfall frozen in mid-storm, a sea of stilled, bleached, pointed waves dominated by Mt McKinley, like a great Bass Rock, towering above them.

The gradient of the airstrip at Utopia Creek was one in ten, and according to my altimeter the far end was 350 feet higher than the near end. This had the interesting result that when you were taxi-ing along at a moderate pace your vertical speed indicator showed a climb of 500 feet per minute!

Naturally you always landed uphill and took off down hill. You couldn't overshoot once you were committed on final approach. The take-off was rather like an ugly rush down a ski jump, but of course the acceleration was such that a C47 was airborne almost as soon as it started; the aircraft merely moved horizontally while the ground dived away below it.

On the way back we flew close alongside the main McKinley massif on the east side, a chaotic jumble of chasms and walls and peaks and knife-edges that held me spellbound.

On 12 March the Hastings arrived back full of a lot of dissipated-looking people. It had been our plan to start at 04.30hrs next morning for Resolute Bay, stopping there only long enough to refuel, and to press on non-stop to Manby where we hoped to arrive at lunchtime on Friday; but unfortunately a complex depression over eastern Greenland put a stop to that, and we had to re-plan our return via Winnipeg and Goose Bay.

From 12,000 feet over Skag, the coldest place in North America they say, we could see the whole rampart of frenzied mountains from Big Delta to Skagway, with the giants Kimball, Sanford, Logan and Fairweather standing proudly above the general level. But it was the unknown land away to the east to which my eyes turned, the dimly seen heights of the Ogilvie Range beyond the Yukon. John Buchan had fired my imagination with his tale of those vague, unexplored areas whence spring the Pelly and McMillan Rivers feeding the wide Mackenzie.

Compared with Fairbanks and Anchorage, Winnipeg was as solid and staid as Huddersfield. Even Hudson's Bay House looked like a Yorkshire Mill. As usual when I was in Canada, I felt as if I had come home.

Next morning we leapt into the bright air on time, gaining, in the short moments between leaving the ground and reaching that altitude which puts all earth in plan, an impression of the vast flat expansiveness of the prairies: a horrible horizonless emptiness that makes man and his works seem rather small. I was a passenger all the way home from Winnipeg, so the flight was indescribably boring except for the refuelling stop at Goose Bay; there it was a crisp clear night with lots of snow on the ground and a magical Aurora in the sky. Our touchdown at Manby marked the end of my flying days there.

We had already received notice of our postings – 'E.A. Johnston to Martlesham Heath to command.' Absolutely delighted, I reckoned it was the best posting of them all.

10

Experimental Pilot

ROYAL AIR FORCE MARTLESHAM HEATH HAD A
distinguished history of experimental and test flying going back as far
as 1917. Its hangars, offices and domestic buildings were old, unusual
and full of character. It was now, in 1953, an Air Force Station
domestically administered by an RAF Group HQ, but funded and
operationally controlled by the Ministry of Supply. The function of the
resident RAF unit, 'The Armament and Instrument Experimental Unit'
(AIEU), of which I was to be the commander, was to provide flying
facilities for the Royal Aircraft Establishment's Blind Landing
Experimental Unit (BLEU) and Armament Department, and also for the
Atomic Weapons Research Establishment (AWRE).

BLEU, which had its offices and laboratories at Martlesham, was
administratively a lodger on my station while at the same time being
one of my functional taskmasters. I also controlled jointly with the
U.S.A.F. the aerodrome at Woodbridge where we used the 3,000 yard
runway of triple width, equipped with ILS and high intensity approach
and landing lights, for most of our experimental flying on approach and
landing aids.

Almost my first priority was to fly a Canberra, and I did all my first
circuits and bumps on the original prototype, WD799. The immediate
impression was of power and speed, mainly, I think, because the air
brakes were relatively ineffective below 300 knots and quite useless
below 200. She tended to wallow at circuit speeds and stiffened up
considerably, particularly on ailerons, above about 300 knots, but she
was certainly very easy to fly. Later I took a Mark 2 up to do runs under
radar control at various speeds on the Orfordness range at 20,000 feet.

An indicated 350 knots at 20,000 feet worked out as Mach 0.76, where she was just on the edge of buffeting in a rate one turn. My upper half in the bubble canopy got roasted by the sun while my legs froze with the cockpit cooling going full bore, but she was a gem of an aircraft to handle.

I later flew the Mk 2 to Kinloss at 39,500 feet at 0.78 Mach, just below the onset of compressibility buffet. There was a strong head-wind and all the cirrus was below us. At 40,000 feet she wobbled a bit. The controls were fairly solid but needed only a gnat's-wing thickness of movement, and if you took your attention away from accurate flying she tended to develop a high-frequency snake cum Dutch roll. She was wonderfully quiet and smooth, though.

The Firth of Forth was clear of cloud so that I could see away to the west beyond the Cumbraes to Arran. Over Leuchars I began a gradual let-down clear of cloud. I climbed out of the aircraft at Kinloss after sixty-one minutes' flying.

I discovered that I was taking command of a station which for morale, discipline and efficiency was about as near perfect as could be. Nevertheless I saw many ways in which I could contribute something on the flying side. Despite the hurly-burly of taking over I managed to fly quite a few of the aircraft in my first week. As well as the Canberra I flew the Devon, the Dakota, and the Meteor NF11 which pleased me more than any of the others. She was a delightful aircraft to handle on instruments, light on the controls yet perfectly stable. The most fantastic of all my fleet was the Avon-engined Lincoln. Put two jets in a Lincoln instead of two of its Merlins, and you had an astonishing monster. After pulling the wheels up I wasn't really in control until we reached 6,000 feet climbing at 170 knots!

The flying side of AIEU was organised in three flights. 'A' flight, which I soon renamed 'All Weather Flight' (AW Flight), was engaged on experimental flying for BLEU. Its broad function was in support of the development of automatic approach and landing. The second flight supporting BLEU was 'C' Flight of three Meteor NF11s which I renamed 'Rapid Landing Flight' (RL Flight), for it was devoted solely to the problem of sequencing large numbers of jet fighters into a rapid landing stream in bad weather. 'B' Flight served Farnborough's Armament Department and the Atomic Weapons Research Establishment, and since its work was predominantly but not exclusively related to ballistics trials I renamed it 'Ballistics Trials Flight' (BT Flight). Its work for AWRE was, of course, of the very highest security category.

On the first day of lousy weather, a 400 cloud base with drizzle, I thought I ought to get airborne myself as the RL flight Meteors were operating; so I flew the Viking in the morning on automatic approach work and one of the Meteor NF11s in the afternoon, as tail end Charlie in a rapid landing stream of three Meteor 11s. We made four runs on the ILS pattern under radar spacing control. On one run I had zero error in time of crossing the threshold and on the remaining three runs my worst error was 1.2 seconds. This was on a par with the experts. Apart from showing that the method was a practicable one from the aircrew point of view, these results of mine surprised both the boffins and the regular crews - to their encouragement, I hope.

The Ashton was a version of the old Tudor with four Nene turbojets. Like the Avon Lincoln it was greatly overpowered at low altitudes; and, being a thoroughly bastard aircraft, had some peculiar handling characteristics. On opening up for take-off one held the stick hard forward in order to minimise the strong elevator buffeting which was present over the first 40 knots of acceleration. The elevators took effect quite suddenly somewhere round 100 knots. As the wheels came unstuck there was immediately a marked change of trim, and while they retracted the speed built up very quickly so that one had to climb steeply to avoid exceeding airspeed limits.

In the air she handled very sweetly and smoothly in all three control axes. The main snags were that at low altitude it was very easy to exceed the airspeed limitation of 245 knots and, there being no airbrakes, deceleration was extremely slow. On asymmetric power she was very good. The stall in landing configuration had plenty of warning in the form of buffeting some 2 or 3 knots above the stall, but at all speeds below final approach speed (110 knots) the airspeed indicator oscillated wildly. The airspeed indicator errors above about 130 knots

211

were very large. I found her quite easy to land: a long, low approach with plenty of power, followed by a smart chop of the throttles on round-out, and she sat down smoothly and firmly.

The next novelty was a flight in the Short SA4 ('Sperrin'), the second prototype of our first four-engined jet bomber. Jock Eassie, the firm's test pilot, very kindly let me fly her from the co-pilot's seat. She had nosewheel steering, not, like the Ashton, by means of a tiller control, but by means of the aileron wheel used in the same sense as a car's steering wheel. I found it simple and effective. On the take-off run it was easy to hold her straight by this means despite a fair crosswind component, until at about 80 knots the rudder became effective and the nosewheel steering could be switched out. Shortly after that the nose came up of its own accord and required to be checked by slight counter-pressure on the stick.

She flew off smoothly enough but while she was accelerating to climbing speed (250 knots) I found myself over-manipulating the elevator control which, although very effective, seemed mushy. Indeed at speeds up to 250 knots I found all the controls felt rather mushy, and not awfully well co-ordinated. Largely due to their being power-operated they had an artificial feel.

The rudder was particularly soft and it was very easy to fly with slip on. I climbed her to 20,000 feet for some radar runs over Orford range. After two or three we were asked to open up to 300 knots which we held at about 7,100 rpm on all four Avons. At this speed all controls were much more crisp and she was a delight to handle. Rate one turns, however, demanded accurate flying at nearly 50 degrees of bank. The dive brakes seemed reasonably effective with little change of trim.

After these runs, but before I could do any further handling trials, we discovered that all the hydraulic services had become ineffective. Jock decided, therefore, to return to base and land it himself. The emergency systems dealt with the undercarriage and flaps satisfactorily. He turned onto finals with 30 degrees of bank and full flap at 120 knots, touched down in a very tail-down attitude and, having no brakes, deployed the tail parachute very smartly indeed. Altogether an interesting sortie.

By the beginning of June 1953 I had flown every type on the unit with the exception of the Python-engined Lincoln. The last one to be flown was the Varsity which I enjoyed except for a longitudinal instability in turbulence that was most disconcerting on instruments. In July the Air Training Corps Gliding School based on my Station let me qualify for Gliding Certificate 'C' in a Grunau. Squeezing oneself into the tiny cockpit was like fitting on a tailor-made pair of personal wings For once the winch launch was reasonably comfortable; I went up at 45 knots until at just under 1,000 feet the rate of climb decreased. Almost immediately after casting off at that point I hit a strong thermal in which I circled. In about fifteen minutes I reached 2,300 feet.

Accustomed as I was to powered rates of climb measured in thousands of feet per minute, I was too hasty to take much account of variations of plus or minus fifty feet per minute in rates of climb or descent, which of course are of primary significance in thermal soaring. I must admit that at no time was I comfortable. The controls were at once extremely light and abnormally slow to take effect. While soaring in turbulent thermals one had to make extremely coarse control movements and often, owing to the effects of a bump, the action of the glider seemed to be the reverse of the effect the controls call for - which, of course, was very disconcerting to a power pilot like myself used to crisp feel and rapid response. There were times when I felt distinctly unhappy, almost as though the glider was out of control.

I had some difficulty in making steep turns accurately, probably due to the sluggish aileron response combined with the liveliness of the rudder. The amount of stick movement for aileron control seemed to me to be inadequate: while turning steeply in a thermal I found I needed almost full opposite stick merely in order to keep the bank from steepening; and I then found myself wondering if the small residual amount of stick movement would be enough to level the wings up again.

What worried me most about gliding, as an experienced power pilot, was getting low. Normally at 150 feet I liked to be firmly lined up on my final landing approach. In the Grunau, of course, 150 feet was almost sky high, certainly adequate for a considerable amount of manoeuvring in 'S' turns. If at that height I was overshooting the touchdown point, I tended to stuff the nose down instead of easing it up to lower the airspeed and losing distance by S-turning, even though I knew that with gliders increasing airspeed meant increasing over-the-ground penetration. It was all a question of assimilating a new technique which was diametrically opposed to the powered techniques which were second nature to me.

As Station Commander I was beset by an endless variety of piffling administrative activities. Nevertheless by the end of July I had become familiar with flying the Canberras on automatic approach development and radar runs over the range, a Meteor 7 on assessment trials of the Zero Reader flight director, the Dakota on secondary radar calibration, and the Devon on radio altimeter calibration. By now I was fully at home in the delightful Canberra. The acceleration could be terrific and I still fall into a dream when I remember the sense of power one got from a high speed zoom.

But of course she had her snags. It was so easy in level flight to exceed her speed limitations; she was awfully uncomfortable in the slightest turbulence at high indicated airspeeds; she took ages to decelerate even with the air brakes out; the buffeting and deceleration when you opened the bomb doors had to be felt to be believed; and the nose-down change of trim when you raised the flaps on overshooting could be quite dangerous when you were flying on instruments.

When I returned to Martlesham from leave at the end of August, the first thing I learned was that Harry Maule had crashed Canberra 799, the original prototype. Miraculously both he and the auto-approach boffin Mike Burgan had escaped with only minor injuries. The Court of Inquiry eventually discovered that the cause was a fuel leak which had resulted in complete fuel starvation of both engines at 300 feet during an overshoot from an automatic approach.

In September I had an incident while flying the Avon Lincoln; it was just 'special' enough to demand extra care, to instil a sense of the unusual, although indeed the job was ordinary enough: an oversized 10,000lb bomb to be dropped from 35,000 feet for telemetry. The day was perfect: calm, windless and cloudless with a slight haze at ground

214

level. We wore rather more and heavier clothing than usual because the Avon Lincoln, unpressurised, was very cold at high altitudes; but in the sun on the ground as we settled in and did our pre-starting checks we were sweating freely.

The unfamiliar layout of the engine instruments for the twin Avon installation had me confused at first; it is strange how the mind does not easily register the meaning of unfamiliar instruments in an otherwise familiar cockpit. Merlins started and run up, then Avons, I waved chocks away and taxied out slowly. After a full and particularly deliberate pre-take-off drill I lined up on the runway with a slight feeling of tension because of the heavy load, the short runway and lack of wind, and awareness of being balanced on my mental toes to deal with unexpected handling characteristics as the wheels came off the ground. She came unstuck nicely, but, laden, noticeably sluggish on the elevators in comparison with the response at normal weights. The speed built up slowly to 175 knots for the initial climb. The bomb, half protruding under the belly, created noticeable buffeting. At 20,000 feet, on instructions from the ground radar controller, I levelled off for a dummy run.

Then the range reported that they were not receiving any telemetry signals from the bomb. "Return to base."

"The last time we landed with one of these bombs on," said Jimmy Crawford, the navigator, cheerfully, "it fell off on the runway and wrote off the tailplane."

Should I land on a short runway with the bomb on, or should I jettison many man-months of work?

The security classification of the store prohibited my landing it anywhere but Martlesham. The governing factor, I decided, was the length of runway I should need in this calm air. Before making a decision I throttled back, lowered the wheels and flaps and tried a stall with power on in the approach configuration. At 80 knots there was mild buffetting and considerable sink, but she was still under control. I judged she would take a 100 knot approach speed comfortably and that if I cut the Avons early enough we would just have sufficient runway length. I decided to have a go even if there was no wind.

215

Round the circuit into a long, straight final approach, at 100 feet she was right in the groove. "Cut Avons." She came down nicely over the threshold at just the right height and speed, and then I ruined it all by touching the main wheels a trifle early.

She bounced, and instead of stalling her onto the ground I tried to wheel her on from the bounce: bingo, up she went again, and yet a third time. Then I did the right thing and she touched gently on all three points. With steady braking she came to a halt 50 yards short of the end of the runway. Thereafter there was much joking by the navigator and flight engineer about the strength of the bomb suspension gear.

I flew the Meteor 9, very similar to the Mk 8, fast at low altitudes and reasonably light to handle, on a rocket ballistics job - releasing pairs in level flight at two hundred feet and 300 knots. Two of the rockets on the port side 'hung up'. I did not know whether this accounted for it, but on the way back at 400 knots I found her apt to snake quite quickly.

By now I had pressed the All-Weather Flight into making regular use of bad weather for training flying in the Devon and the Viking. On a day of average cloud base of two hundred feet with drizzle which varied the visibility between one and two thousand yards, I felt that I myself was morally bound to share in the flying, so I took up the Meteor 4 to do some ILS runs at Woodbridge. As she had only fifty minutes safe endurance at low altitude this was perhaps a little foolish, but everything worked out well and I was able to land back at Martlesham without much trouble. I was happier when the next day turned out to be sunny.

Our replacement Canberra, a Mark 4 dual trainer, arrived in November. She handled very sweetly and was reasonably tolerant of fools as I found when I did my first Canberra night landing in a flat calm on the short runway.

I had spent the day at Farnborough. By the time I got to Martlesham Heath it was pitch dark and drizzling, with a cloud base at 900 feet. I made a lousy approach straight off a controlled descent through cloud - far too low, so low that I actually had to climb to miss the fence. I crossed the threshold with power still on, and used up every inch of the runway with screaming brakes. Not a very good effort.

As the years went by and I flew aircraft of ever increasing performance, the cockpit remained much the same but I saw less of the earth and more of cloud, a world of endless variety of vapour and light. When I took off in a Canberra I would be for a minute or two near the earth accelerating up to 330 knots, its climbing speed, but all my attention would be in the cockpit directed towards the airspeed indicator, compass, gyro horizon and altimeter. And then with one backward blip on the trimmer switch we would soar vastly into the low cloud, boring up effortlessly through the grey layers into brilliant light at 10,000 feet. When I began a long fast let-down, decelerating in cloud at 2,000 feet to approach speed and configuration, we might come out of cloud at 1,000 feet, two and a half miles from the runway. Apart from the fleeting impression of cloudscapes and sunlight all my world for that flight was contained in knobs of familiar shape and instrument dials that were now second nature to me.

Coming back in the dark, when the cockpit was bathed in red light, my sense of isolation was increased; even the controller's voice as he talked me down on R/T seemed part of me, as though I was talking to myself in a different voice, no part of men and events that I surveyed in my going to and fro on the ground.

I took the Dakota up for the purpose of calibrating a radio altimeter, doing first a series of shallow descents over the sea from fifty feet to ten, then shallow climbs from ten to fifty. Harry Maule, who had been doing it the day before, reckoned that twenty-five feet was the minimum height to which it was possible to take a Dakota. I should say here that the radio altimeter measured height from the lower extremity of the wheels, so that in this exercise with the wheels retracted I was about four feet higher than the altimeter reading. On my first run I got as low as an indicated seven feet.

This seemed rather low but not dangerously so as the conditions over Harwich Harbour were perfect.

On all runs I had no trouble with ten feet; but on one of them there was some agitation in my Boffin's voice when I got down to an indicated five feet. He was telling the height continuously to the

217

ground controller. Five feet, we were all agreed, was an 'all time low'. I shudder when I look back on it. Frank Alder sitting in the co-pilot's seat was magnificently unperturbed.

Just after I landed I was told that one of the Devons with Harry Maule and F/Sgt Dale on board had crashed at Woodbridge. When I got over there I found that they had landed her with the wheels up. They were doing a series of runs on the 'restricted pilot's vision' experiment. Maule, in the first pilot's seat, had most of his instruments blanked off, his head clamped and his vision restricted through a slit of fixed dimensions. Dale in the second pilot's seat was safety pilot: it was his duty to hand the aircraft over to Maule at two hundred feet on the final approach in the landing configuration. On the last run he handed it over without having lowered the undercarriage. It was infuriating to have lost another aircraft and I was much upset by this lapse of Dale's, for he was a most careful experimental pilot.

Much of my flying was largely 'bus driving', more or less skilled according to the task. The Dakota milk run was perhaps the least demanding: a straight climb outbound to 10,000 feet at thirty miles and let-down on the return, simply to check signal strengths of the pulse data transmission equipment. At the other end of the scale you had blind approach calibrations on ILS under the hood in the Meteor 7. In thick cloud conditions the rapid landing schedule flown by the Meteor 11s required a fair amount of skill and concentration.

Flying the bomb line in the Canberra or SA4 under radar control needed precision of a lower order. Then there was the theodolite checking of the ILS beams which involved flying the Varsity or Viking or maybe Dakota along a path determined by a theodolite operator on the ground. The several paths were only one degree apart in azimuth; this task demanded a lot of precision. Automatic approaches required not so much skill as being on your toes all the time to watch for something going wrong, and the ability to take corrective action quickly. And there was the 'Pilot's Vision Assessment' (PVA), designed to deteriorate progressively the amount and quality of what a pilot could see while landing, until he could no longer cope: both the guinea pig and the safety pilot needed skill and fine judgement.

I was very keen that we should take every opportunity to build up our skill in fog flying. One morning I teamed up with Harry Maule to fly the Devon in fog. Unfortunately we were delayed by trouble with the Woodbridge beam, and when we finally got airborne the ceiling had lifted to 100 feet and runway visibility to 1,500 yards. Once in the air we found our airborne ILS gear was unserviceable. Fortunately Decca was able to talk us down and we made a good run. I, in the right hand seat, flew the approach on instruments with Harry in the left hand seat peering out into the murk. At 150 feet he saw the runway lights, took control and landed nicely, half way up the runway, off a steep S-turn.

I should say the ceiling was well below the safe minimum for the Decca radar and that had I been solo I would not have got in. As it was, it was very easy because of the excellent teamwork between two pilots and thoroughly good, split second judgement by Harry. (Our problem was that Martlesham had no approach lights at that time.)

On another occasion I went fog flying with Alf Camp in the Devon. We took off from Martlesham with about 100 yards visibility and, unfortunately, had trouble with both the automatic pilot and the ILS. By the time we had sorted it out conditions were improving rapidly. The first landing I did at Woodbridge was unusual. Camp in the right hand seat saw the approach lights at 150 feet. I could see nothing at all; but as he called that we were right on the centreline I disengaged automatics and bored on downwards. I saw no lights whatever, but at about fifty feet identified a white marker on the runway which gave me a clue for landing. At that time the meteorological visibility was 150 yards.

Visibility during the next few circuits picked up to about 450 yards on the ground; nevertheless the lights gave very little help indeed to the first pilot, although the second pilot was able to see them from as high as two hundred feet and give him sufficient confidence to carry on down to seventy-five feet where he was able to identify the runway surface. In low visibility the field of view from the cockpit is tremendously important, and the transition from instrument to visual in such low visibilities needed a lot of practice.

In May 1954 I did an hour's circuits and bumps in the Short SA4.

The next day I went up to 12,000 feet in her as co-pilot to Frank Alder; and the following day I flew her myself to 40,000 feet to drop a 10,000lb store, an instructive experience which really earned my five shillings flying pay. I managed to coax her up to 40,000 feet at climbing power, but at maximum continuous power I couldn't hold her there. She stabilised just below 39,000 feet at 145 knots indicated airspeed, which was about 0.59 Mach. At that, I was juggling all the way.

In a 15 degree banked turn with no more than 1.2g indicated, she was on the edge of buffeting and lost as much as 1000 feet per minute. She wallowed laterally; the aileron control tended to be jerky; rudder control was not positive; but elevator control seemed satisfactory. Considering the size and weight of the aircraft, however - we took off at 105,000lb all up - the controls were remarkably good, being fairly light, effective and balanced. The lack of feel and feedback of the servo controls, of course, was a bit disconcerting at first.

The rigmarole of the flyovers and the actual live run was not easy. In the first place one was struggling to keep the aircraft steady on instruments at its maximum height. Vision from the cockpit was extremely poor, and in any case the glare at that height above a carpet of cirrus was such that one had to keep one's eyes inside for comfort. There was considerable chatter on the R/T from other users and a lot of interference from both the electronics in the store and sparking micro-switches in the bomb-door circuit. The ground controller was very bad indeed. It was hard work and an interesting experience, but I didn't like that buffeting, particularly as one had no feedback from the controls by which one could gauge whether there was any aileron or elevator flutter.

We also had a little trouble, slightly disconcerting, with low temperature at the fuel filters and a tendency for jet-pipe temperatures to surge. I must confess that above 30,000 feet there was some psychological effect which magnified small troubles; one felt lonely, helpless and eager to get down to more friendly levels. The 9lb cabin differential pressure, which gave you an environment of 8,000 feet when you were at 40,000, was an excellent invention. The de-misting

220

flow, on the other hand, was entirely inadequate; the windscreens were well and truly iced up for about ten minutes after descending, and only continuous rubbing cleared them.

Although I didn't really like very high altitude flying, I became the specialist pilot on the SA4 and made a number of missions over the range. It seemed ridiculous to fly fifty-five tons of aeroplane at fighter speeds at high altitudes. The servo controls were so light in proportion to the size and weight of the aircraft that they only added to the unreality.

There was a certain amount of delay in the control responses which made precision flying at high altitude rather difficult: I tended to over-control. For small aileron movements the response seemed to be jerky. The elevator was too spongy for precise control; it could have done with a heavier feel. The trimmers, in this aircraft artificial also (in that they merely varied the loading of torque rods in the servo system), were insufficiently positive.

At 40,000 feet the mighty bombardment ship was right against the stops. It needed very careful handling even at climbing power to hold its height. At an indicated airspeed of 160 knots it was only just beyond the peak of the lift-drag curve. Lose 15 knots in level flight and you started going down like a brick.

I made my first bomb release from 25,000 feet near the limiting Mach number (0.78), 325 knots indicated airspeed (about 530 true). When I opened the bomb doors I thought she was going to shake to pieces. The instrument panel was vibrating so much in its mountings that I couldn't read the compass indicator. Still, with all its failings and limitations, the SA4 was at least a comfortable vehicle for high flying with its 9lb cabin pressure differential and automatic cabin heating.

At the beginning of August 1954 I took a specially equipped Devon, heavily laden with spares and boffin gear, to the Swedish Air Force base at Vasteras for three weeks of flight evaluation of a runway approach aid called Barbro. Jimmy Crawford came with me as navigator and F/Sgt Chapple to service the aircraft. We flew IFR along the civil airways to Stockholm, where we cleared customs inbound and collected some duty-free stores from the Embassy before flying direct to Vasteras. Sitting in the cockpit for hour after hour I experienced enormous pleasure in being back in the foreign cruise routine. The journey was uneventful except when, just short of Heligoland, the port engine began to vibrate badly. I diagnosed plug leading, and after I ran it for a few minutes at high rpm it cleared itself - but not before Chapple made the classic remark "I've never experienced it in the air before. It sounds much worse than it does on the ground." We never let him forget it.

At Vasteras I taxied to a parking place by an old Junkers 86 in front of a hangar full of Venoms. We were met by a group of tall, quietly spoken, almost solemn Swedish Air Force Officers among whom was Flight Engineer Torsten Bergens from the Air Board, who had been appointed as our chief guide and mentor: a delightful chap, large, ugly and full of fun and vitality. After lunch, Dennis Platt and Brian White, our boffins in charge of the project, who had flown by BEA to Stockholm, arrived. We had a general discussion about the programme. The CO directed that we should have all the help and priority that we needed, so we adjourned to the control tower to work out ways and means, which were the subject of much debate there, and also again standing by the aircraft, at which my suspicion began to grow that the Swedes spent rather a lot of time just standing around discussing things.

It took Chalky and Dennis some days to be satisfied that the Barbro beacon was up to the standard they required before it was worth starting the flying programme. Although the military controllers were willing to deal with me in English, I took this opportunity to learn from Torsten's No. 2, Capt. Roy Mukov, all the Swedish jargon necessary for working with flying control at the airfield. When we started operating I was able to communicate with the tower entirely in Swedish from asking for 'start-up clearance' to reporting 'engines off' at the end of a sortie. It was merely a courtesy on my part, for the controllers' English was far better than my Swedish.

Most of the military pilots were NCOs and most of the Officers seemed to be administrators. In the Officers' Mess they certainly were rather aloof, but obviously my Swedish call-sign 'Filip Adam' came to be recognised by many of the NCOs, and it was surprising and touching how often I was addressed in hotels, bars and restaurants by complete strangers saying "Hallo Filip Adam, I hope you are enjoying your visit to my country."

Once flying started, the pace was hot. On our first two sorties in the evening the air was clear and perfectly smooth and our airborne equipment worked 100%. The first sortie was a general look at the beam: while Dennis Platt recorded data I flew right round it at three miles radius and made two or three approaches on it. Then we began the theodolite runs.

Chalky's theodolite had marks in it to indicate plus or minus one twentieth of a degree in azimuth. He aligned it along the direction he wanted me to fly, in this case the centreline of the runway, and it was my job to fly the aircraft at 300 to 500 feet under his azimuthal control, keeping within these marks, while Dennis Platt in the back of the Devon operated a paper-recorder on which the received signal strength was recorded, and an automatic observer which photographed the DME indicator, the aircraft attitude and its heading. Whenever I got outside the theodolite limit of plus or minus one twentieth of a degree, recording stopped.

It sounds rather difficult but in fact I soon got the hang of it and with concentration I could maintain the limits for about 80% of the time. The programme involved making several recorded runs at each of a quarter of a degree, half a degree, one degree, two and three degrees to right and left of the centreline. I got the thing down to a fine art and averaged about six minutes per complete circuit, but it certainly demanded intense concentration. We could, of course, only do the job effectively when the air was smooth. Eventually clearance came through from the Air Board to do photographic runs, similar to the theodolite runs except that the position of the aircraft was determined every two seconds by vertical photography. It didn't require quite such accurate flying in azimuth, but the wings had to be kept absolutely level.

Air Traffic Control on this field was little more than embryonic. Nominally our approaches had priority. One morning I was doing my runs just below cloud at 500 feet in rain with Venoms, also on straight-in approaches, flying over us, around us and under us, all of this with tower clearance. On another day while we were operating on runway 19, Harvards were operating gaily on runway 12 right across us. On the last day I made 17 runs to finish the whole job on schedule. I had flown 136 theodolite runs, 40 photographic runs, several demonstration approaches for senior Swedish people and a number of general check flights.

The Managing Director of Swedish Phillips, who invented and made Barbro, came up with us one morning with two of his senior engineers. They arrived in the most splendid Chrysler I had ever seen. Chalky on the ground and I in the air put on a show for them, speaking all our control patter in Swedish: but as Chalky said afterwards, "I don't think they recognised it as their own language."

I slipped quietly away from Vasteras in the Devon at 9am without any formal send-off. We flew non-stop to Manston where we broke cloud at 800 feet in continuous drizzle and landed for Customs and fuel. Within thirty minutes we were airborne again. Martlesham was just as cold and wet, but our welcome there was heart-warming.

Back at Martlesham Heath I discovered a total change of plans for the future of the AWRE project at Woodbridge, and uncertainty about our continuing to use the strip for BLEU's development work. The SA4 was to be transferred to Farnborough. I was sad to make my last flight in her for, as Jock Eassie had said when I first started, "you get attached to the old space-ship." At the end of October I received letters from the Controller of Atomic Weapons (Sir Frederick Morgan) and also Sir William Penney commending our 'outstanding contribution' to the success of the trials of their project at Woodbridge.

I did the first automatic flare-outs in the Varsity. The last had been done in the Devon in 1949 with a different autopilot and a laboratory model radio altimeter. We didn't actually touch down, but used a false datum ten feet above the runway. I maintained manual control of rudder and aileron, the leader cable rig not yet being fully operational. The elevators were controlled by ILS glide-path signals until the radio altimeter assumed authority for the round out. The control was a bit rough, there being a long-period oscillation about the true exponential path, but in principle it worked and we were all very pleased despite one or two quite exciting moments. A couple of days later Alf Camp achieved the Varsity's first touchdown under automatic elevator control.

I was given the opportunity to fly the dual version of the Vampire, the T11 - what the Meteor boys called 'the screaming kiddy-car'. The cockpit was, of course, entirely different from that of the Vampire 5; the view was different; the feel was different: heavier ailerons, spongier rudder (spring tabs) and not quite the same trim changes, so it seemed quite another aeroplane. I had a happy half an hour despite the lack of power as compared with a Meteor.

We laid on a series of automatic ILS demonstrations for Bomber Command. The last day was one of those worrying days when I had to make a decision about the fitness of the weather for myself to fly. If others had been flying the answer would have been an easy NO. At Martlesham and everywhere else in the UK and Western Europe visibility was varying between 500 and 1500 yards with cloud at 150 feet and steady rain.

The conditions were ideal for demonstrating automatic ILS in the Canberra but there was nowhere suitable for diversion in the event of equipment failure in the air. Having already scheduled myself to fly, I now had to make a dispassionate decision without weighting my own fear too much either way. Before announcing my decision I asked Sqn Ldr Stoop, my No. 2, what he would do. "Scrub" was his unhesitating response. I laughed: "For once we agree."

I decided nevertheless to take the Devon to show the visitors some manual ILS at Woodbridge, even though I was a bit doubtful about being able to land back at Martlesham. I think they were quite impressed, for on three approaches to Woodbridge we saw nothing until we were at 120 feet and bang in the groove for landing.

Getting back into Martlesham was a little bit dicey owing to getting very unreliable signals from the glidepath, but with the help of the localiser and the DME [1] we just made it, breaking out of cloud at one hundred feet right over Crown Point with about 800 yards visibility.

---

[1] Distance Measuring Equipment

When one of the Air Ministry's photographers came down to spend the day with us, we gave him a pretty heavy programme of flying and ground shots. The highlight was a mixed formation, Alder leading in the Avon Lincoln, myself No. 2 in the Varsity (an absolute cow for formation flying), Holden No. 3 in the Devon going flat out at 150 knots, and Spittle and Gibson, Nos. 4 and 5 in the Meteor 11 and 9 respectively, barely going fast enough to keep airborne. We were in a stepped down echelon starboard.

It was hard, sweaty work in turbulent air, but I enjoyed being absorbed in exercising my skill and took pleasure in the calculated risk of edging into ever closer formation.

During the summer of 1955 a Whirlwind (S55) flight of No. 22 Squadron became established at Martlesham and I was able to renew my acquaintance with helicopters with some dual. Having opened the throttle to bring the rotor revs up to two hundred, I eased up on the collective pitch control and wobbled rather uncertainly into the air. After two or three minutes of somewhat erratic hovering I got the hang of it enough to traverse sideways some 100 yards in either direction; then by dint of enormous concentration I made her travel some 200 yards along the edge of the runway while rotating some 360 degrees in azimuth. I was rather pleased with this.

Except for the very heavy foot-load on the yaw control and a certain amount of yaw instability I found it surprisingly easy. I did a few circuits and landings. One approached the alighting area from two hundred feet at 60 knots cruising airspeed, then reduced the collective pitch and eased back the cyclic pitch column, maintaining fixed rpm on the throttle and directional control on the rudders (this was rather unstable), the result being that the chopper descended in a tail-down attitude, losing forward speed. The aim was to arrive over the chosen landing spot in hovering flight at about ten feet. Attitude could vary a lot according to the combination of collective pitch, cyclic pitch and throttle setting, so that I usually found on arriving over the landing spot that I had to hover a while in order to correct an excessively tail-down attitude by juggling with the two pitch controls. If I had everything level and steady, the process of lowering the aircraft onto the ground

226

disturbed its equilibrium, so that every landing, though safe, was wobbly.

Indeed 'wobbly' is the only word which rightly describes the way I flew a chopper. I found them very challenging. By dint of concentration I could, after twenty minutes, hover reasonably successfully, fly sideways and backwards, and take off and land safely.

John Charnley [2] took over as Superintendent of BLEU at the beginning of August 1955. He was a large, pleasant type about a year younger than myself, with whom I got on exceptionally well from the first. He was, professionally, a high flyer who had come to us from the Aerodynamics Department of RAE. I bemoaned our lack of fog-flying experience (due to lack of facilities), and I got him interested in working up a Canberra programme for the next winter. He always seemed to pay attention to my views on BLEU's work. He certainly re-focused its programme, which had latterly become somewhat repetitive and aimless.

I argued strongly that BLEU should bring the development of fully automatic landing back into the programme. The Air Ministry was very reluctant to support it, so John, once convinced that 'autoland' was worth going for, cultivated the support of civil aviation with the result, to my delight, that we soon embarked on the exciting project of developing automatic landing for jet aircraft.

In October we began an intensive statistical assessment of ILS sensitivity. In one week I made at least two Meteor 7 sorties each day. I was paired with F/Sgt Spittle. One of us in the front seat was safety pilot; the other, blacked out in the rear cockpit, would take off, fly to Woodbridge and complete two recorded ILS approaches; the safety pilot would then land the aircraft so that we could change places and repeat. After the fourth approach we returned to Martlesham, landed and remained in the aircraft while it was quickly refuelled, then went off to do the same drill all over again. I found this a very pleasant routine but it did tend to make work pile up in the office. To brighten the rear cockpit the ground crew had posted a pin-up girl on the bulkhead screen above the instrument panel. I must confess that by the

---

[2] Later, Sir John Charnley

end of the week I was pretty tired of Cleo Somebody, 'a J. Arthur Rank Starlet', oafishly leering, heavy breasted and advertising it!

It was interesting to discover the accuracy with which a Varsity could be flown at a fixed height. We were recording radio altimeter accuracy by flying along the runway at levels every ten feet down from one hundred feet. At one hundred feet it was impossible to fly accurately level by reference only to the ground. I had to refer to the altimeter as the primary guide, and on the whole plus or minus six feet was practicable. At sixty feet I began to get some assistance from the ground; around forty feet I could maintain height to about the same accuracy by external reference as by using the altimeter. At five feet I could fly accurately plus or minus one foot entirely by external reference.

I continued my helicoptering with the attached flight of 22 Squadron. An interesting exercise, requiring a nice balance of height/speed judgement, control co-ordination and concentration, was low 'overshoots' from auto-rotative approaches. You went into 'engine off' autorotation at about 600 feet, checked as for an auto-rotative landing but brought on engine to maintain rotor revs, and overshot from about five feet.

After going into autorotation (pitch fully fine, throttle closed) you maintained about 40 knots with the cyclic pitch lever, going down like a brick; at two hundred feet you started checking the speed to about 25 knots while you brought the engine revs up to about 2,000 (ie just short of applying drive to the windmilling rotors); by about seventy-five feet you had checked the speed so, with some degree of unnatural willpower, you pushed the nose down to restore a level fuselage attitude; at about thirty feet you started hauling up on the collective pitch lever to check the descent; and as the revs fell to normal you opened the throttle to hold them steady while further increasing the collective pitch to give you hovering flight at five feet.

Throughout this game rotor revs were fairly critical and had to be watched; but you were also hurtling towards the ground! You just hadn't enough pairs of eyes to watch everything. It was a very good exercise.

228

At the first opportunity I took John Charnley up in the Devon in the morning fog to give him some idea of the value of lighting patterns on the ground. Although the fog was thin vertically and dispersing quickly we had two or three useful runs at Woodbridge, getting our first glimpse of lights at about a hundred feet on the glidepath. I liked his eagerness to get airborne to find out things for himself. Subsequently I flew him down to Farnborough to have a look at Calvert's approach simulator.

It was a marvellous stick and string affair. You manipulated the pitch and roll controls of an aeroplane while gazing through a monocular sight which showed with lifelike aspect the flying instruments and the frame of the windscreen. At the appropriate stage of an instrument approach on GCA or ILS the lighting pattern came into view through the windscreen and behaved faithfully in all three planes as it would in real life. You could go through all the motions of descent, check, flare-out and hold-off: the aspect and relative velocities of the lights being so realistic that you could judge your hold-off to a fraction.

You could vary the lighting patterns, cockpit cut-off, slant visual range (up to 500 yards) and aircraft speeds. I did some serious work with it, using 500 yards slant visibility on a standard Calvert lighting pattern with 125 knots approach speed at first, and later 160 knots.

I learned a great deal about the shortcomings of light patterns for judgement of height in low visibility and the effect of approach speed on azimuth guidance with only limited pattern information. The monocular vision didn't seem to make a ha'porth of difference to my performance. After the first few minutes I didn't even notice that I was using only one eye.

Bomber Command was not very happy about Boscombe Down's clearance of ILS in the Valiant, so exceptionally BLEU was asked to do some flight trials. I arranged to go to the OTU at Gaydon to see what facilities they could give my pilots on the Valiant simulator as a preparation for doing the ILS clearance. I took off in the Meteor 9 in thick drizzle, climbed through cloud to a clear lane at 14,000 feet, homed to Gaydon, let down to 2,000 feet and was talked down by their radar to break cloud over the approach lights at three hundred feet above the airfield. Visibility was about 2,000 yards in drizzle. Bob Hodges, now the Chief Instructor, met me. We duly arranged what I had come for, and after watching a crew exercising in the simulator went for lunch, where we joined the AOC 3 Group and a former Cranwell colleague, Brian Young, who had just taken over as Station Commander. I came under very heavy pressure over the ILS clearance fiasco.

After lunch the weather had taken a turn for the worse. Bob, being a very cautious chap, dragged me into a long talk with the forecaster who was so gloomy as to be almost frightening, so that I was glad to get away from him. Climbing away from Gaydon through cloud I collected a lot of airframe icing but got above everything at 15,000 feet and enjoyed my twenty minute trip above the white ocean. Martlesham reported three eighths at three hundred feet, clearing quickly from the southeast, and indeed by the time I got there there was no cloud at all east of the Ipswich-Norwich road.

Before landing I did a couple of barrel rolls and a loop above 6,000 feet out of sheer joy of flying this delightful aircraft (as compared with the much heavier Mark 7s we had). When I landed, Keith Wood told me that while I had been away final agreement had been reached with Boscombe Down that they and we jointly would do the Valiant ILS clearance on Gaydon's aircraft. It now remained for us to get together with Boscombe to decide the method of doing it.

We had been allotted the tail-less Avro 707 Delta, the quarter scale model of the Vulcan, for advanced speed control work in the low-speed regime. At the end of December it was wheeled out of the hangar for Alf Camp to do its air test following the inspection and installation programme. As everything was OK I decided to try my hand in the afternoon. Camp spent half an hour explaining the cockpit to me. Then I went through the intricate business of being strapped into the fully automatic ejection seat, shut the metal canopy and was all on my own with a horribly restricted view of the outside world.

Carefully and methodically I checked around the unfamiliar cockpit, started the engine, engaged the power controls, checked the operation of all services, and taxied gingerly away. I found the brakes very firm and the undercarriage rather harsh. Lined up on the runway I again went carefully round the cockpit rather than rely on a mnemonic. Trim flaps fully out (on each wing there were three control surfaces: an aileron, an elevator and this trim flap which, operating from neutral to about 14 degrees up, was in fact an auxiliary elevator); dive brakes in; artificial feel and power controls engaged; aerodynamic trim OK; artificial trim fully nose down; temperatures and pressures normal; fuel on, fuel pump on; instrument AC supply on; pitot heaters on; and so forth.

Finally, when everything was double checked, "Tower from 01, take-of clearance." I opened up to 10,000 rpm against the brakes, released them, and eased the throttle fully open as she rolled. The stick was a bit heavy, the rudders very light, and I had a tendency to use too much brake in the business of keeping straight.

At about 90 knots the nosewheel lifted off the ground. She flew clear at about 115 knots. As the wheels retracted and speed rose there was a nose-up change of trim which I tried to hold on the 'feel-trim', not very successfully because its operation had quite a lag and there was a small dead spot at the stick neutral position. Subsequently I found the right answer was to retract the trim flaps progressively as the trim changed. Wavering in pitch a little bit, I climbed away, letting the speed build up. As the trim flaps came in there was a sharp nose-down change of trim.

The aircraft had a temporary speed limitation of 250 knots. At 230 knots she was very light and quick to respond to all controls. As there was a fairly thick haze I had to do my precision exercises by instruments. Before going to do a landing at Woodbridge I put down the wheels and flaps to investigate its slow-speed characteristics. She was pretty straightforward down to about 120 knots, when two things happened. First the rate of sink started building up very quickly as speed was reduced further (this was the feature we were interested in), and second the wing tips began to stall, giving a continuous 'Dutch Roll' effect. I didn't go below 110 knots this time, but it seemed to me that between 120 and 110 knots things happened very quickly. I was delighted to find that retraction of the airbrakes at this speed killed any sink almost instantaneously.

Away, then, to Woodbridge for the first landing. Lined up at 140 knots at 800 feet at three miles with wheels down and trim flaps out, I put the air brakes fully out and adjusted the power to let the speed drop progressively to about 120 knots over the threshold. I had been warned that below about thirty feet there was a pronounced ground effect which made a 'check' action of the elevators unnecessary; but I chopped the power rather high, for although I forced myself to hold the stick fixed in anticipation of this round-out, we hit the ground quite firmly, and I imagine the speed must have dropped off rather quickly, allowing a high rate of descent to build up which was only partially killed by the ground effect.

After taking off again I did some more low-speed handling, getting the synchronisation of flaps and trim changes weighed up, before joining Martlesham circuit again. I made two approaches to 120 knots at the threshold to see what the overshoot was like, and found that if you retracted the air brakes and then opened the throttle it was a piece of cake. So, round to the final landing. The Dutch Rolling at 120 knots was very apparent this time; and although I was careful not to close the throttle too early, again I did not notice any marked ground effect at the flare-out. With gentle braking the landing run was of the order of 1,500 yards.

In a fairly active week, flying the 707 stood out most vividly. It was always an interesting experience to master a new aircraft alone and without air instruction, and this being a fairly unique machine added a certain glamour to the occasion. A bright red Delta in the circuit attracted a lot of attention!

Apart from the professional interest in flying a new and advanced type there was the distinction of joining the small band of experimental pilots with Delta experience, and the smug feeling of being in the forefront. It was all rather bogus really, because above its minimum drag speed it was a remarkably easy aeroplane, although undoubtedly the job we were going to do with it would demand a high degree of skill and had a certain element of risk.

For the joint ILS reassessment I detailed Harry Maule and Alf Camp to do our part, both sound and experienced chaps though neither of them had flown a Valiant; but because of the importance of the job I decided that I must do the training exercises and at least one assessment sortie so as to be able to back them up in any subsequent inter-Establishment arguments. Gaydon gave us a quick briefing on Valiant power controls, fuel system and hydraulics before I climbed into the simulator with Flt Lieut Foster as my instructor. All the various knobs and tits which, when read about in Pilots Notes, seemed so confusing, fell easily enough into place, and away we went on a familiarisation 'flight'. After take-off we climbed to 14,000 feet, and straight away I was in difficulty with the pitch control. Even at the end of the day both Harry Maule and I were agreed that it was unnaturally difficult to maintain any pitch stability. Otherwise we found the simulator remarkably realistic - and very hard work.

At 14,000 feet I checked changes of trim with changes of configuration, the effect of powered control trimmers, manual reversion and the effect of manual trimmers. Both trim systems were fierce on rudder and aileron but the pitch trim was remarkably unresponsive in both power and manual, in respect of both tailplane incidence and elevator tabs. In power control the feel was more or less what you would expect of a large aeroplane, much heavier in all three axes than the SA4. In manual, even at low airspeeds, the controls were extremely heavy and the response was very slow. I found the exercise most realistic except for the liveliness in pitch.

After about an hour's general handling I let down into the 'circuit' for an ILS approach. Again I found control in yaw and roll very easy, quite comparable with one of our lighter Lincolns. Control in pitch was at all times difficult. I used the recommended Gaydon technique of flying constant power and increasing flap from 20 degrees to 40 degrees about a mile before intersecting the glidepath, allowing the speed to fall off from 150 knots to 135 in the meanwhile. We used 150 feet above nominal runway elevation as break-off height, but owing to phoney glidepath indications at 400 feet had some difficulty in keeping a good rate of descent on practically all our approaches except the last.

Each of us during the day did about half a dozen ILS runs. Without question we found the pitch control very difficult indeed, and on that basis I felt that about 350 feet was the lowest safe height (although overshooting from 150 feet was a piece of cake provided you didn't let too big a rate of descent build up). I was fairly sure in my mind that in the real aeroplane pitch control would not be so difficult. On the other hand the Boscombe pilots who were watching remarked that they didn't think we would realise such easy and rapid roll and yaw responses as we had been using on the simulator. The atmosphere of verisimilitude was most impressive. Indeed during the later stages of an approach the anxiety load built up quite genuinely and I forgot entirely that I was sitting in a mechanism anchored firmly to the floor of a building on the ground. I could have done with a lot more of it. But undoubtedly after three hours in the simulator I was quite confident to take a Valiant and fly it in any reasonable conditions.

The next morning Foster and I went out to the dispersal and did our external checks. It took nearly twenty minutes to secure ourselves in our seats, then another twenty to do internal checks and start up. I took the first detail in the captain's seat. I ran up to full power on the brakes to check temperatures, pressures and rpm before rolling. The tail took an appalling buffeting. Once the brakes were released the acceleration (at an AUW of 124,000lb) was phenomenal. At 90 knots there was adequate rudder control. With a firm backward pressure on the control column the nosewheel came up at about 100 knots and she flew off smoothly at 125 knots.

The climb away was steep. After wheels and flaps were up I climbed away at 300 knots and discovered that the controls in all three axes were firm and positive. She actually felt like a large, heavy aeroplane as compared with the SA4 which felt more like a Meteor; yet the response to control movement was immediate. I was glad to find none of the control instability in pitch which was so apparent in the simulator, although in every other respect all was just the same.

After a few minutes' general handling at 10,000 feet I let down into the circuit to do ILS. I made eight runs altogether. The air was very calm. The aim of my first run was to get a general idea of the behaviour

234

of the aircraft on the beam. The glidepath gave the impression of being oversensitive. We rode high on it all the way in, and I weaved purposely on the localiser from one and a half dots left to one and a half dots right. Aircraft controllability seemed adequate for maintaining normal localiser limits. I overshot from fifty feet. On my second run I simply flew a normal ILS approach. I found a kink in the localiser beam at seven hundred feet, but the aircraft could cope with it. The rate of descent on the glidepath at 135 knots was nine hundred feet per minute. I went visual at 150 feet and could have landed.

Thereafter I flew a number of approaches skewed left and right on the localiser. Out of eight approaches down to 150 feet, I judged six to have been successful despite my built-in distortions. Once I had got the trick of entering the glidepath properly, and used to the high rate of descent, I found accurate speed-keeping quite simple, although I had a strong tendency to go high on the glidepath at about four hundred feet. Controllability in the localiser plane was jolly good.

Below three hundred feet I saw very little if any of the approach lights due to the forward/downward cockpit cut-off, and below two hundred feet lining up was done on the runway lights. This was a serious limitation for bad weather operation which needed further investigation. We also needed some experience with varying crosswind components. Purely on the ILS side, however, my general impression was that it was safe to fly down to 150 feet IFR on ILS, although at 135 knots the transition time available for a break-off was very small. Given a visual transition altitude of 250 feet there would be a high rate of landing successes.

Although it was a pretty arduous sortie I enjoyed flying the Valiant. I found even landing so large an aeroplane very easy, though it did use up a lot of runway before coming to a standstill. I enjoyed the sense of power, the sense of comfortable isolation in an intimate cockpit so far forward that I could not see the wingtips - a situation that made me feel truly suspended in a bubble in space. It was a fine flying machine.

One foggy day Sqn Ldr Greenland, the new CO of AW Squadron, asked me if I would show him the procedure for ILS at fog-bound London airport in the Devon. The clag top was solid at 1,200 feet, above which was brilliant sunshine. The lower we got over Heathrow the darker it became until we first saw lights at 150 feet by the radio altimeter. Runway visual range [3] was 400 yards; it was genuine smog and very gloomy. I did three quite good approaches, going visual between 150 and 170 feet. On my last, to my horror I saw, very late, a Constellation on the runway ahead, beautifully camouflaged by the murk, and we just managed to scrape over it. For a moment I was a little worried whether I was approaching the correct runway. Not seeing anything at all except the runway lights I had no way of telling whether it was 10L or 10R, other than assuming that the ILS channel selector was correctly set up. The approach controller was more than a little perturbed when I reported it.

Returning to helicoptering after a long absence, I did my first live winchings, both successful if a little imprecise. The more I flew these things the more I was baffled by their aerodynamics. They were bone-shaking contraptions, and I persevered not from any pleasure in flying them but from a professional desire to master the technique.

Towards the end of January 1956 we ran, over several days, a big demonstration programme of Barbro to representatives of Air Ministry and Fighter Command. When it was all over I was very tired and very proud of my chaps. Everything went like clockwork even when we had to put the emergency programme on at short notice on the last morning because of a sudden deterioration of the weather. They were breaking cloud at eighty feet on radio altimeter in drizzle with 1,500 yards visibility. However, we kept the schedule going and luckily the weather cleared completely after lunch. But it was a very worrying morning. I took off my hat very humbly to Harry Maule and Alf Camp, the two demonstration pilots.

I went to work on the Canberra in February doing automatic flare-outs with manual azimuth control. Joe Birkle was with me; he had changed the intermediate form of control between 170 and 50 feet to constant pitch attitude. We were getting extremely smooth flares to a datum twenty feet above the runway which encouraged us to lower it

---

[3] i.e. The maximum distance at which one could see a high intensity sodium light

236

until eventually we did two impressively smooth touches on the runway. This was the first time that we had put a jet aircraft onto the runway under automatic elevator control.

In March Valiant 208 became available at Vickers for automatic approach work. I was invited to Weybridge for its first trial flight. Low cloud and drizzle greeted me in the morning, and as usual at Vickers I sat around in Chief Test Pilot Brian Trubshaw's office while nothing seemed to happen. With Staff Harris driving we eventually got airborne just after ten and bored up through solid cloud to a clear lane at 14,000 feet. As soon as we engaged automatics, however, I discovered snags in the approach coupling; and when we got to Woodbridge I found we weren't receiving any glidepath signal. We did four or five very ropey approaches using manual elevator control, with obvious instability in the roll and yaw channels. Altogether it was a bit of a shambles, but possibly of value as a shakedown trip to give Harris some idea of the procedure for doing recorded runs.

My earlier impression of the quietness and smoothness of the Valiant was confirmed. Although in terms of feel she handled like a 'heavy' aircraft, she was a delight to fly and in our final overshoot she climbed away so rapidly that we were at 16,000 feet before I really caught up with her! Back at Wisley I did a controlled let-down from 16,000 to 800 feet, including a 180 degree turn during the steep descent through fairly turbulent cloud, and was very favourably impressed by her steadiness on instruments. After a short post-mortem it was decided not to attempt to fly again until Monday, when Harry Maule was scheduled to fly her.

The Canberra flare-out was now very satisfactory and the leader cable work in the Varsity had suddenly taken a great stride forward, so we decided to put the whole works together in the Canberra. Up till then we had had nothing but snags and reverses in the automatic landing programme. While the installation programme was under way, I renewed my acquaintance with the Delta 707 after a lapse of three months.

The cockpit was very claustrophobic. Not an easy aircraft to fly accurately at the best of times, she was a real handful below her

237

minimum drag speed (Vi$_{MD}$). At normal cruising speeds some difficulty arose from a certain backlash in the controls, coupled with a sluggishness of elevator trimming - or rather, sluggishness in response to trimming action. I was over-controlling. Below 120 knots, of course, I ran into all the additional excitement of a high angle of attack with rapid build-up of rate of sink, together with dutch-rolling resulting from irregular tip-stalling. Approaches to the runway below 120 knots were going to be very difficult indeed, and somewhat dangerous I feared.

I did some circuits and bumps; perfectly docile on the approach at 121 knots, she became distinctly tricky at 120 knots, and I didn't consider myself sufficiently familiar with her to venture any slower near the ground. At altitude I had her down to 95 knots but she was yawing and rolling really violently with a fantastic rate of descent despite what seemed like an almost perpendicular attitude. I made several more sorties practising slow flying. It needed intense concentration; one was fighting her all the time.

Once, when I hit a slight bump at 100 knots indicated, I very nearly lost control: with full opposite rudder and aileron the starboard wing was still dropping and she was still yawing to starboard. Just when I was about to stuff the stick forward and whip the airbrakes in, she began to recover. The automatic throttle helped a lot although the gearings were not yet quite right.

I went up in the Canberra with Joe Birkle to do some camera-recorded automatic touchdowns. Heading 095 on the downwind leg at Woodbridge I checked that ILS, Leader Cable and autopilot were switched on and did a brief functioning check of the autopilot. It was then time to throttle right back to lose speed for lowering the undercarriage. The wheels came down as we did a wide curve round Orford lighthouse. As we turned onto the ILS localiser beam I put down full flap, simultaneously applying full nose-down trim. Autopilot engaged, height lock on, beam control selected - and in we went under automatic control over Orford village while I checked that the wheels were locked down, all fuel pumps on, and power adjusted round 6,400 rpm to give 110 knots.

As the glidepath needle came down to centre I switched in

238

glidepath control; the aircraft dipped, and I pulled the throttles back some 500 rpm. She rode smoothly down the beam and Woodbridge Tower gave me clearance for 'touch and go.'

The strip loomed out of the haze. I made a final check of configuration before the last act. 'Cameras stand by.' At 300 feet by the radio altimeter I put one hand on the throttles, the other lightly on the control spectacles, thumb poised over the autopilot cut-out button just in case. Just below 300 feet I marked the white light flashing on the monitoring panel, indicating that leader cable guidance had superseded the ILS localiser and that we were on a 'fixed attitude' rate of descent.

At about 75 feet a green light flashed to indicate that the flare-out had been initiated. I now concentrated entirely on looking outside the cockpit to monitor the flare. At an estimated twenty feet I began throttling back.

The flare was smooth, right in the middle of the runway, but she was floating a bit, so I closed the throttles rather more sharply and the main wheels clunked onto the ground. Immediately I disengaged the autopilot and concentrated on keeping the nosewheel clear of the runway while opening up the throttles gently to 7,000 rpm. At this stage, particularly if there was any crosswind, a little clumsiness could lead to a damaged aeroplane. As soon as she was firmly airborne again I selected undercarriage up; when the indicator lights went out I brought the flaps in, leading on the elevator trim and throttling back as the speed built up. Joe read the accelerometer: 0.5g on this touchdown.

And so it went on until Joe said he had had enough and we went back to Martlesham. I made a slow approach to the runway, chopped the throttles 100 yards short of the threshold with 95 knots on the clock, and held off with nose pitched very high. The accelerometer read 0.3g after an immaculate touchdown, and I said to Joe "Nuts to your automatics!"

The aim of the automatic throttle experiments in the 707 was to fly an advanced aeroplane down a glidepath at a speed below the minimum drag speed. She had a Vi_{MD} of 120 knots (rectified). So far all our work on this aircraft had been finding the optimum gearings for the throttle control: the right balance of throttle responses to changes of pitch,

239

airspeed, and long-term changes of flight-path and configuration. The work was done at altitude, mainly in level flight but also with short periods in shallow climbs and descents. In April I did the first flights down a glide-slope, the glide-slope being provided by a man on the ground looking through a theodolite and guiding me by R/T as for GCA.

I did eight approaches altogether, varying the gearings and the selected airspeed, starting at 120 knots (rectified) and working down to 110 knots (rectified). The throttle control worked admirably; not only did it keep the speed within plus or minus two knots, which was what we wanted, but also by taking an onerous task away from me it let me pay far more attention to flying the glidepath accurately. This was the first occasion when a delta wing-form flew an accurate glide-slope at a speed significantly below Vi_{MD}.

At ten knots below, I was beginning to work hard in both longitudinal and lateral control. Longitudinally, because big pitch-up changes (together, of course, with immediate application of full power) were needed to regain the glidepath once you dipped below it; and laterally because you were getting unstable tip-stalling which, though easily corrected by rudder, needed constant attention. I thought that below 110 knots there was such a rapid rise of lateral instability that it would not be safe to operate below 105 knots even though the throttle control might be able to cope with the sink problem.

As a reciprocal gesture for the loan of our Lincoln, Neil McDonald, the Chief Instructor at the Empire Test Pilots' School, let me have a couple of sorties in one of his Hunters. What a delightful aeroplane it was, even though handling it was like balancing on a pinhead with a large rocket attached to it. Tremendous verve, tremendous power and tremendously fast aileron response. The acceleration from take-off was stunning; in no time at all I was at 430 knots, the optimum climbing speed. At altitude I found it difficult to keep up with myself in an aircraft that cruised effortlessly at 0.9 Mach.

I thought the ailerons were too light above 40,000 feet and I didn't like the seesaw pitch trim changes when the airbrakes went out. Otherwise she was a joy to fly.

At full power she was doing 0.94M indicated at 42,000 feet. Obviously I was flying her very gingerly at this stage and felt pretty daring when I pushed the nose down some 30 degrees. At 0.98M indicated the stick suddenly moved forward a couple of inches, and the elevators which had been heavying up quite a bit became virtually ineffective. She wouldn't go any faster than 0.99M indicated which was in fact 1.2M true. I closed the throttles and hauled back with both hands on the stick; the force required was considerable; she came up slowly at first, and then quite quickly as she became subsonic again.

There was nothing at all alarming about it, yet there was enough 'phenomenon' to make one realise how exciting the early development flying of transonic types must have been.

On the morning of October 1st 1956, Andrew Humphrey,[4] John Charnley and I got down to discussing some outstanding policy matters relating to BLEU's programme. We had had an interesting exchange of views on the problems of setting up adequate flight testing facilities within the autopilot industry, on the need for automatic throttle control on the Phase 2 Vulcan either for approach or cruising, and were just settling down to a talk on the glidepath problem when I was called to the telephone. It was my Adjutant, who quietly blasted the whole day and set a blight on the last weeks of my tour at Martlesham. "The AW squadron Canberra has just crashed on final approach to runway 22, this side of Crown Point, and is on fire."

"Christ," I said. "Who is flying it?"

"Les Coe."

I rang off, put my head into John's office, quietly relayed the message to him and fled to my car.

The usual pall of black smoke led me to the scene. I was almost dazed. Everything was over bar the shouting: the flames were under control, the Senior Engineering Officer was in charge, the Doctor was there and one body was just being removed from the shattered nose which had become detached. They said it was a civilian's. A very white-faced Mike Burgan remarked that Joe Birkle was the passenger. The pilot was still jammed in, and the Corporal in charge of the Crash

---

[4] Later, Marshal of the Royal Air Force Sir Andrew Humphrey

Party was shielding him from a small fire by means of a CO_2 spray.

The Doctor said they were both dead. I was unable to recognise either. An AA card in the pilot's pocket confirmed it was Coe; John Charnley identified the other as kindly and solid Joe who had flown with me so often on the automatic landing development programme.

Once the fire was extinguished and the bodies had gone to the mortuary I went to Air Traffic Control to hear eyewitness accounts. At half a mile on finals after what looked a completely normal approach she had simply rolled to port onto her back, veered off to starboard and gone into the ground *'whoomf'*. Johnnie Greenland and I then went to tell the widow. She was out shopping, so we waited in Johnnie's flat next door. When she arrived home she stood outside for a full ten minutes gossiping with a neighbour while we waited - one of the unhappiest ten minutes I have ever spent.

John Downey was appointed President of the Court of Inquiry. It did its work meticulously, exploring in depth all the possible technical reasons for the crash. The evidence pointed incontrovertibly to the cause being a compressor stall in one engine when a large throttle opening was made, but the Court blamed the pilot for approaching the runway at too low an airspeed for the gusty wind conditions obtaining. He was too low and too slow when he had to raise the nose and apply considerable power suddenly.

I took a BT Flight Canberra to a safe height and satisfied myself that a sudden application of asymmetric power at low airspeed with wheels and flaps down would indeed flick the aircraft onto its back in a matter of seconds. If ever there was an unnecessary crash, it was this one.

I quitted my post at Martlesham Heath in the middle of November with a deep dark scar on my mind.

11

Academic Pilot

FORTUNATELY FOR MY SANITY, I HAD ACCESS TO an Anson 19 and a Chipmunk at Bovingdon during my six months as a Student at the Joint Services Staff College between November 1956 and May 1957. Many a time I bored through the dark winter nights on a triangular cross-country flight all alone in the Anson, inevitably ending up with a full GCA, often because the weather conditions demanded it. Having been permitted to remain in Quarters at Martlesham, I found the Chipmunk very handy as a means of weekend transport. She had no navigation aids but was good at flying low and slow through the murk, and weaving along the main roads. At 90 knots I had time for map-reading.

In January 1957 I was promoted to Group Captain and told that my next appointment was to command the RAF Station at Topcliffe in Yorkshire where No.1 Air Navigation School had just been reactivated. It was given two specific functions: the training *ab initio* of the new trade of Radio Navigator for the Javelin All Weather Fighter force, and Refresher Courses for qualified air navigators. Its aircraft were Marathons, Valetta Flying classrooms and Mark 10 Vampire Night Fighters. Because I had not flown Vampires for a number of years I persuaded Flying Training Command to send me first on a Vampire refresher course at No. 4 Flying Training School at Worksop. There, I was as happy as a skylark: flying, watching flying, listening to the wail of turbines on the ground and the harsh pandemonium of R/T in the air.

On my first sortie in a T11 my assigned instructor, Flt Lieut Keith Payne, put me literally 'on my back at 30,000 feet with nothing on the clock' just to show me what would happen. Actually she was just past the vertical in the first part of a loop when he centralised the controls and let go. She seemed to stand still in the air before falling out of the sky with never a flick, although she did a bit of a 'pendulum swing' while the speed started to build up, but at this stage the airspeed indicator was off the scale below 60 knots.

At 34,000 feet, with the whole of North Wales, Anglesey and Lancashire spread out below us, we did some gentle barrel rolls. On my first I didn't get the inverted nose quite high enough, with the result that in the recovery I had to pull some 'g' with sharp buffeting at about 0.7M. Payne demonstrated a spin to the left, into which the aircraft was rather reluctant to go. We lost about 3,000 feet.

"Now you do one to the right," he said. "You will find she is much more lively." Too darn right she was! Nose up, speed down to 120 knots, stick fully back, then full right rudder: she flicked over two complete rolls to starboard with the nose above the horizon, straightened out and hesitated for a second, began a slow spiral with falling nose and then flicked viciously into a fast, steep spin with varying rates of turn and varying pitch angle.

"Now recover."

Full opposite rudder. No effect. Fully forward with the stick. If anything she spun even faster. The ailerons snatched over to the left. I centralised but let the stick come back a bit for a moment. Just as she stopped spinning - indeed, before I realised she was going to, for the recovery was quite sudden - I shoved the stick into the instrument panel again, with the result that she dived past the vertical. Owing to ice on the canopy and a uniform cloud sheet ahead, I was a little disoriented and was a trifle late in initiating recovery from the dive, so that a lot of speed built up and the pullout greyed me out. Exhilarated, I levelled at 18,000 feet having initiated the spin at 28,000.

The density of R/T traffic, despite the abbreviated patter, was higher here on both approach and local frequencies than I had experienced anywhere else. Coping with it on a controlled descent was almost more difficult than flying the aeroplane. I was more out of R/T practice than flying practice. I came to admire not only the high standards of the flying instructors, who had a very considerable

244

workload to deal with; but also the way the young pilots under training coped with it all. They had so much more to bother about than we did: faster and more complicated aeroplanes, intricate procedures, high density R/T, critical navigation and endurance problems, and greater physiological and psychological strains. The split-second teamwork as between the pilots, the local controller, the approach controller and the talk-down final controller when the air was full of traffic was impressive.

On May 27th 1957 a Marathon came down to Martlesham Heath to pick up me and my baggage. As it stood on the tarmac my old colleagues in BT Flight ribbed me about my 'four-engined kiddie car', and that, I concluded later when I knew the machine well, was a just description. Powered by four De Havilland Gypsy Queen engines she looked, and on paper seemed to be, an admirable little navigation trainer. The cabin layout provided two identical pupil navigation stations and a separate one for a navigation instructor. There was also a good radio operator's station. The stations for two pilots were thoroughly well equipped. As I settled into the co-pilot's seat I reckoned that I was going to like flying Marathons.

When we arrived at Topcliffe I did half an hour in the circuit and found it was a very pleasant machine to fly, if somewhat bland. The ailerons and elevators were well harmonised and light, but the rudder was comparatively heavy and, with one outer engine shut down, the foot-load was surprisingly high. Landing was simple. With flaps at 'take-off' I made my final turn into wind at 105 knots, reduced speed progressively to 90 knots and put down full flap just short of the airfield boundary. The main wheels touched sweetly, but I was surprised by the rapidity with which the nosewheel clunked onto the runway despite full up-elevator.

It was with some surprise that I discovered during the next few days that my pilots, who had all converted from Varsitys, disliked Marathons intensely. I had intended to designate a Vampire NF10 as my personal aircraft, but decided quickly that it would be better for their morale if I stuck my name and command pennant on a Marathon instead.

I soon found that running a large, permanent RAF Station was pretty well a full time job even if I did have four Wing Commanders to whom to delegate. Luckily the training programme involved night flying three or four times a week, and this, together with weekend flights to Malta later, was to form the basis of most of my flying while I was at Topcliffe. It was a good way to get to know my station. By day, because I was inevitably the 'Brass-hatted Bullshit King', I found it very difficult indeed to get behind the woodenness of my airmen, most of them north-countrymen; but at three o'clock in the morning after a long flight it was so much easier to slip into the airmen's ready-room in one's flying overalls and beg a cup of coffee while discussing the behaviour of the machine, or to go out to the wireless hut and have a chat with the duty operator about the problems of communication that we had experienced. Then, for a few minutes perhaps, formal barriers dropped and man spoke to man.

Early in September we were told that our role was to change radically. We were to take on the task of training direct-entry Officer Navigators, the so-called 'All-Through' training. Their year-long course involved not only teaching them how to navigate, but also the elements of how to be an RAF Officer. It meant a big expansion programme.

With the onset of winter, airframe icing was beginning to inhibit the operations of the Marathons. Early in November while piloting a navigation exercise over the Scottish Highlands at night I had my first alarming experience of the aircraft's limitations. Flying around 8,000 to 10,000 feet, the airframe picked up some moderate rime icing over a period of time and I found it impossible to maintain height without applying climbing power. Since it was only rime, and not very thick at that, I was distinctly puzzled, but conceded that the ice might have altered the shape of the drag curve and put us into an unstable regime. So on the first suitable occasion I took my Marathon into the air in search of ice.

There was a convenient layer of freezing cloud between 3,500 and 5,000 feet, temperature minus 1 to minus 2 degrees Celcius. The air was very smooth and stable. We picked up a fair amount of glazed ice

246

but it didn't seem to worry the aircraft very much. At +2lb boost, 2,100 rpm, the cruising speed was about 125 knots indicated. A growth of about one inch of ice in something like 5 to 10 minutes knocked the speed down to 110 knots; application of the de-icing boots cleared it sufficiently to lift the speed to about 118 knots. I experienced very rough running due, I assumed, to asymmetric icing of the propeller bosses; and twitching of the ailerons caused by the disturbed airflow from iced-up Eureka blade aerials. The discrepancy from my earlier experience was surprising.

Subsequently I learned of the Marathon's susceptibility to vertical currents which, at those altitudes over Scotland and the Pennines, could be of considerable magnitude; so I leaned to the view that my original trouble was not icing at all so much as a very widespread down-draught.

A month later several of us had tales to tell of a night exercise. I took off at about 19.30hrs and climbed at +5lb boost and 2,600 rpm for my planned cruising height of 5,500 feet. We entered stratocumulus at 2,000 feet. At 4,000 feet slight icing began. It did not affect performance, but I switched on the propeller de-icer pump. At 5,000 feet I encountered slight turbulence and heard precipitation striking the aircraft for about half a minute. This was followed by the noise of ice being flung onto the fuselage from the propellers.

As I was still in cloud at 5,500 feet I decided to continue the climb to get above the tops which had been forecast at 6,000 feet. I went into full de-icing drill: air intakes to 'sheltered air', and wing and tailplane de-icer boots cycled on and off at random over roughly two-minute cycles. The outside air temperature gauge read minus four degrees, and a quick flash of my torch showed about two inches of clear ice on the windscreen wiper blades. There was a gradual increase of airframe buffeting to quite an unpleasant level, and control response, particularly in the rolling plane, became rather sluggish. At 5,700 feet the rate of climb diminished to zero at 110 knots.

I had now been airborne for twenty minutes. I dropped down to my next lower quadrantal cruising height, 3,500 feet, where the temperature was plus two degrees. At normal cruising power the speed was down by nearly twenty knots, and even at full climbing power I was unable to get more than 130 knots in level flight.

After another twenty minutes or so, the ice had not noticeably dispersed, so, being over the Lincolnshire flats, I went down to 2,000 feet where the temperature was plus five degrees. This did the trick. At cruising power the speed swiftly built up to 140 knots. I climbed back to 5,500 feet without any trouble, but later encountered slight clear ice at 5,000 feet which forced me to increase power to the maximum continuous rich setting in order to maintain height.

All of us had similar experiences that night and agreed that, although the aircraft were never uncontrollable, the inability to maintain height above freezing level might have had unfortunate consequences had we not been flying over comparatively low terrain. We also agreed that there was no question of being involved in large standing waves on this occasion. I was more than ever convinced that the Marathon, pleasant little dinky toy that it undoubtedly was, was simply not man enough for the task that the authorities were setting us.

In consultation with my excellent Wing Commander Flying, Don Wylie, I drew up rigorous Standing Orders restricting the operation of Marathons in conditions of forecast icing or standing waves, and sent a paper to Group HQ proving statistically that it was now impossible to fulfil our training task in the planned time. I urged the phasing out of the Marathons and their replacement by Varsitys which had the performance to penetrate and operate well above the danger levels.

The Air Staff huffed and puffed, and the new Senior Air Staff Officer hustled down to teach me my business. At the end of the day I took him back to Manby in my Marathon, letting him fly it. On the way I sneaked into some freezing clouds, and he had the grace to express some surprise at the effect it had on the performance. My AOC backed me to the hilt, with the result that a decision was made to re-equip us with Varsitys as soon as possible.

A short while later, despite my worthy Standing Orders, I was caught out by a dud Met forecast on a night exercise. I ran into quite a bit of icing at 8,000 feet. After rather less than ten minutes, boost was down to under zero due to icing of intake guards, and speed to 100

248

knots despite full anti-icing drill. I estimated the clear ice to have been two inches on leading edges. I only got rid of the stuff by going down to 2,000 feet over the Bristol Channel and getting really warmed up. Interesting - but also, on a very dark night with the mountains of South Wales close by, apt to be fraught with potentially unpleasant consequences.

It was therefore with delight that we received our first Varsity for pilot conversion at the end of February 1958. The Martlesham Varsitys had been stripped and converted into flying laboratories; what we now had was the original crew trainer, designed for the V-Bomber force for operation by two pilots, two navigators and a signaller, with a visual bombing station down a hatch in the belly.

Don Wylie and I flew our first one on a foul day when every approach had to be an instrument approach under radar control to 400 feet. I was surprised to find how vastly superior it was to our Valettas in both performance and feel. Aileron control was both lighter and more positive; elevator control was decidedly crisper. She was much more stable for flying on instruments.

In the previous autumn one of my pilots had been unable to recover from an intentional spin in the Vampire T11. On passing through the mandatory 'bale out' height, still spinning, he jettisoned the canopy prior to ejecting. To his surprise, loss of the canopy destabilised the spin and the aircraft recovered on its own. He had the presence of mind to stay with it, pull out of the dive and land back at Topcliffe, albeit a very shaken man when I met him on the tarmac.

Spinning was temporarily banned while the Central Flying School carried out an intensive programme of investigation with our T11 and others.

In March the ban was lifted. Immediately I flew in the Vampire T11 with John Bull, our check pilot. After the CFS spinning trials I thought I ought to be the first to spin it at Topcliffe.

At 28,000 feet I spun her to the right. She flicked through two full rolls, dropped her nose and spun slowly before settling into a fast, steep, stable spin. I started to recover all right: opposite rudder, pause, stick firmly and fully forward; but the spin stopped far more quickly than I expected. Before my dull wits operated, she flicked into a spin the opposite way. The same happened again. And there I was, five seconds behind the aeroplane, flicking from spin to spin and going down fast. Johnnie Bull had to take control from me to recover at 10,000 feet. I admired his sang froid, but felt an awful fool.

We climbed back to 28,000 feet and this time, initiating my recovery after the 6th turn, came out smoothly. Then Johnnie demonstrated ways of recovering from extreme attitudes near the stall, all requiring firm centralisation of the controls while the aircraft went through an extraordinary series of manoeuvres. I did not enjoy feeling that the aircraft was out of control, even if it was only for ten seconds.

Most of my hours had been flown on the Marathon, partly because it was unpopular and I felt my pilots needed encouragement; and partly because I felt it necessary for establishing my authority as a Marathon operator vis-à-vis the know-alls on the Staffs who thought that we were too wimpish about the problems we faced. Actually I quite enjoyed flying them despite their operational limitations. Nevertheless I also flew the Valetta Flying Classrooms and the Vampire 10s regularly on functional missions.

With the coming of the Varsitys we incorporated overseas flights into the student training syllabus. The plan was for three aircraft to fly to Malta on a Friday, where the crews could enjoy 48 hours of rest and recreation before returning to base on Monday. For destination we chose Takali, smaller, more intimate and friendly than the huge Staging Post at Luqa.

My alarm clock woke me up at 04.30hrs on a wet Friday morning for the proving flight. After breakfast in the Mess I went down to the Varsity Flight with butterflies in my tummy. Even in my fortieth year I could get this wartime feeling of tension before any flight that was out of the ordinary, in this case because of a full load take off in rain under solid low cloud. Having done all the planning and crew-briefing the night before, all that remained for us to do was to take a final look at the weather chart. On the dot of 07.00hrs I opened the throttles.

In chilly blue-grey dampness we roared into the air off runway 21 and turned straight onto a heading for St Catherine's Point, climbing slowly to our planned height of 8,000 feet. We had been routed to Istres via Sète, a point on the coast some 40 or 50 miles west of the mouth of the Rhône.

All the way down the French Fixer Network was almost unintelligible on R/T, and Marseilles control was no different: not our R/T at fault, but the French, who were quite the worst performers I had encountered in Europe. The forecast cloud base at Istres was less than 1,000 feet, so it was with some trepidation that I prepared to do a French controlled descent through cloud. Great, then, was my relief when some 2 minutes before ETA I descried a sharp edge to the low cloud just south of my destination. So I was able to make a VFR descent and arrival at that great, bleak place.

We were airborne again an hour after touchdown. For four hours we hung suspended between blue and blue. There was no wind to ruffle the Mediterranean. Occasionally we made an R/T call to Ajaccio or Elmas or Tunis. Otherwise there was nothing to disturb our pleasant condition of suspended animation in the pilots' seats, though I have no doubt that the navigator was working feverishly all the way. Promptly at 5pm the cliffs of Gozo loomed up and Malta presented its usual delightful prospect in the clear evening light. It was all a wonderful change from life in Station Headquarters!

On the return flight the French Met Man at Istres warned me of 'grandes orages' over the Massif with cumulo-nimbus up to 40,000 feet. I asked "What is the probability of meeting these grandes orages?" "aucune probabilité," he replied. "Il y a une *certitude* de rencontre des grandes orages." Thus fortified I pressed on. Fortunately he was wrong. At 8,500 feet I found a clear lane between stratocumulus and altostratus, but in the end I had to do a BABS into Topcliffe with fracto cumulus at 800 feet, drizzle and a bitingly cold northeast wind.

The advantage of being an aviator was that one frequently had to conquer fear and one had to resign oneself to anxiety. Every time I flew a Vampire with its one engine I was faced with the humiliation of discovering yet again that I was not a bold pilot. Flying one of the student Officers on a low-level map-reading exercise with a tight fuel plan, I waved chocks away immediately after starting up and did my

251

after-starting checks while rolling along the perimeter track. Because we were using runway 14, which happened very rarely, involving a very short taxi, I was caught out and barely managed to complete my pre-take-off checks before turning onto it.

This was the first time I had taken off with full external tanks on this short runway, and even from a fast rolling start it was jolly unpleasant. There was no room whatever for error. I lifted her off at 125 knots, correct for the weight, a bare 50 feet before the end of the tarmac. I turned straight onto an easterly climbing heading through scattered stratoform layers, bursting into clear sunshine over Scarborough at 14,000 feet. We turned southwards, and after a further 20 minutes began a fast let-down through much solider cloud, making contact with the ground at 1,000 feet in drizzle about 5 miles north of Peterborough.

Our track took us at 400 feet above ground level via Downham Market, Wattisham, Coltishall and King's Lynn. Widespread drizzle brought the visibility down to about 1.5 miles, but the vision forward through the wet windscreen was negligible, so I was rather worried about the risk of collisions as we weaved between a number of very active airfields.

Acting Pilot Officer Milligan's map reading and navigation, despite its being his first low-level trip, were faultless. He didn't seem at all put off by the turbulence. At King's Lynn we shot up through solid cloud, not breaking out until 18,500 feet, having collected quite a bit of ice. Ten minutes cruise at that height, then a fast descent to arrive bang over Topcliffe on time. By careful attention to power and speed I had managed to get around the course with a reserve of 400lb of fuel above what had been planned; and the weather at Topcliffe was luckily better than we had expected. Young Milligan was really quite paternal towards the silly old buffer in the driver's seat!

To celebrate my 40th birthday I flew my first Vampire night solo since leaving Manby. It was a really black night and I was very frightened and I didn't enjoy it one little bit. I was apprehensive before flying and I was scared while flying and the whole thing was a victory of willpower over inclination. Trying to analyse this dislike of flying a

Vampire at night (and it was only the Vampire, for I positively enjoyed night-flying normally), I came to the conclusion that it was basically a heightening of my dislike of flying on one engine. One seemed so much more vulnerable when there was no chance of a successful crash-landing in the event of engine failure. My passenger, my batman Clark, loved every moment of it, but he was in fact adding to my worry, because the chances of his being able to parachute down successfully would have been remote.

Psychologically, however, my first night flight with a student navigator in a Vampire was a different kettle of fish. After a dusk take-off under eight eighths overcast at 4,000 feet we burst through into daylight, cloudless, above. Cruising at 32,000 feet up to Leuchars I saw the hard bronze edge of the northern horizon grow pale and fade, and the night soak up from below and envelop us. Through gaps in the low cover, I saw the filigree of lights from Crail to Burntisland, from North Berwick to Glasgow: and indeed so clear was the night that over Carlisle I could see at once the glow of Glasgow, Newcastle and the Leeds-Bradford complex.

Below the cloud on our arrival back at base it was pitch dark, but so clear that every illuminated window could be seen almost individually from 15 miles away. None the less, my landing on runway 03 was a horrid clunk.

These night flights with young trainee navigators in the Vampire 10 kept the adrenaline flowing. With full tip tanks the average high level sortie consisted of a triangular cross-country lasting an hour and a half, and fuel margins were usually tight. When the canopy was completely iced up, we were in a bubble of darkness at 30,000 feet plus, the two of us huddled closely together like twin foetuses in a womb, connected to the seemingly infinitely remote real world only by the fluorescent glow of my flight instruments and the spiky traces on the navigator's cathode ray tube.

Back on the ground there was always a poignant moment after I had cut the high pressure fuel cock, when the turbine was winding down and we were unclipping the oxygen masks from our sweaty faces before the opening of the canopy let the outside world in on us: we would look at each other with an almost conspiratorial smile as though to say "Well, we've made it once again."

Occasionally, of course, the navigator was so inept as to be positively dangerous, and on one occasion I even had to burst out with "Dammit, if I had left it to you we would both be swimming in the North Atlantic by now." The youngster had the grace to reply "Yessir, sorry sir."

On the way back from Malta in a Varsity early in February 1959 we had a minor adventure. Monday at Takali dawned wet, chilly, windy and miserable. The first two hours flying, until we were west of Sardinia, were most unpleasant: much icing, thick cloud, heavy turbulence and some lightning. Barely half an hour out of Malta, indeed, we were struck by lightning while negotiating the lower skirts of a cumulo-nimbus. As we couldn't check the compasses for another two hours there was some slight concern over our navigation, but I had two delightfully efficient student navigators and in the end all worked out well. The P12 magnetic compass proved to have acquired a 15 degree error, the G4B gyro-magnetic about 3 degrees. Apart from losing the trailing aerial there was no ill effect other than the shock to our nervous systems caused by the shattering noise of the strike.

Beyond Sardinia the weather was cloudless until we reached UK which was blanketed by stratus; so on landing at Marham for Customs I had to do a full GCA, and an even more unpleasant instrument approach at Topcliffe where there was heavy icing in the cloud all the way down to 700 feet.

A few days after this my AOC rang me up and told me that I had been selected for the course at the USAF War College at Maxwell Field in Alabama in the autumn prior to taking up a post in the following year with the British Joint Services Mission in Washington DC. Continuing to keep flying right up to the day I left in mid June, I made my last flight in a Vampire T11 to renew my instrument rating. As our own examiner was on leave, I flew over to the Flying Training School at Linton-on-Ouse and subjected myself to a somewhat patronising Flight Lieutenant.

It did a lot for my self-confidence to pass the test before a completely objective examiner instead of one of my own chaps whom I always suspected of being a bit lenient. Quite respectful at the end, the examining pilot's laconic comment as he climbed out of the cockpit to leave me to return to Topcliffe was "Most impressive, sir." Little did I know, but that was to be my last flight as a full-time professional pilot.

The United States Air Force Air University Command at Maxwell Air Force Base in Central Alabama was a small city in itself. It comprised a very busy airfield and a number of postgraduate training schools and colleges; at its summit was the War College at which I joined the 'Class of 1960' on August 1st 1959.

A fleet of aircraft was provided so that all pilots could maintain their proficiency and qualify for their flight pay. As part of the RAF-USAF Exchange Agreement, I was entitled to use these facilities. Having already flown the Dakota I chose to be checked out as a first pilot on the C47, but the authorities were also kind enough to give me a short ground-school course on the systems of the jet T33 to enable me to fly in it as a co-pilot.

I now entered an interesting new world where one flew literally by the book, for the use of the pilot's check list was mandatory for every activity in the cockpit. It came as something of a shock to me, for example, when my check pilot chopped an engine immediately after take-off, to have to call to him to read out the checklist 'actions in the event of engine failure', rather than to perform instinctively the emergency actions of closing down the engine.

Moreover the air traffic control regulations had the iron force of Federal Law.

Apart from doing my checkout on type in the local flying area, all my flying henceforth was done under Federal Aviation Agency (FAA) control on the intensively developed network of airways and upper air routes that criss-crossed the continent. In order to do this I had to attend annually a short course and undertake a tough written examination on FAA regulations as well as a mandatory flight check of various procedures.

One weekend I teamed up in a C47 with a Major Portaluppi, sharing the flying leg by leg for three days. We were just over 28 hours in the air, covering 4,200 nautical miles. We flew airways to Randolph AFB at San Antonio (Texas), night-stopped at Joplin (Missouri), thence to Scott AFB at Belleville (Illinois) and on to Olmstead AFB at Harrisburg (Pennsylvania) for the second night, and flew back the same way in one day.

I was asked to fly a Gooney Bird to Keesler AFB, south of Mobile (Alabama), to pick up a visiting lecturer, three and a half hours on a pitch black but clear night. What a joy and a delight it was to get out of the lecture hall and off the ground. My American colleagues didn't seem to get the same pleasure out of flying, regarding it as a necessary duty for more money. However, I fell happily into the routine of flying somewhere new every other weekend, sometimes in the C47, sometimes further afield in the T33.

The Lockheed T33, the standard jet trainer, was roughly equivalent to the Vampire T11 but with a bit more thrust and range. It was a single engined, tandem dual cockpit machine, the ejector seats of which were probably the most difficult thing to master. One of my colleagues, Lt Col John Archer, took me on my first flight, to visit Lockbourne AFB, near Columbus (Ohio).

On a Friday, as soon as the afternoon College session was finished, off we went to Base Operations to get ready. There was eight eighths stratus at 500 feet, reported solid to 41,000 feet but extending north only as far as Birmingham (Alabama), so we had to file an IFR flight plan and were told there would be a fair amount of delay before we obtained clearance At 16.00hrs we went to the aircraft. At 16.45hrs we climbed in and called air traffic for start-up clearance. It was dark before it came through just after 18.00hrs: and when I pressed the button the engine would not light up. This made me feel foolish. We had to take another aircraft and re-file the flight plan, so we didn't get airborne until 19.20.

By then it really was as dark as the back of the moon and still drizzling from a low ceiling. ATC cleared us by the route we had asked for, and at 24,000 feet we broke out of the cloud into a clear, brilliant, full-moonlit sky. Atlanta Centre then told us to enter a holding pattern south of Birmingham at 24,000 feet for fifteen minutes. John got wild

256

with them with the result that we got clearance for a VFR climb straight through to 37,000 feet.

The T33 was very firm and very quick to respond on elevators; very light and quick on ailerons, but with the heavy load of fuel in full wingtip tanks an absolute swine to control laterally. Neutral stability in the rolling plane made it hard to stop strong rolling oscillations creeping in due to lag in aileron response. As the inertial load of the tip tanks decreased, this tendency died and she became quite a pleasant aircraft to fly by instruments. Between Birmingham and Nashville (Tennessee) all the cloud below us vanished; the rest of the trip was as clear as a bell. Nashville, Louisville, Dayton went by in quick succession, and at one time we could see simultaneously the lights of Cincinnati, Indianapolis, Dayton and Columbus.

At Lockbourne we were met by Colonel Charles Wimberley, commander of the 301st Bomb Wing of Strategic Air Command, equipped with B47 Electronic Countermeasures aircraft and KC95 tankers. After supper and some drinks, we went to bed about midnight. The hospitality at the Base was terrific. Two slightly frail Officers flew home on Sunday afternoon: a lovely flight at 24,000 feet in brilliant weather with the great rivers - the Ohio, Wabash, Tennessee etc. - glinting at enormous distances.

Col Dannacher took me in a T33 on my first trip to the Wild West. After just over two hours of night flying we landed and night-stopped at Connally AFB near Waco (Texas). For the first hour next morning I flew under the hood until Dan called me out to look at the distant massif of the Guadaloupe Peak, the northern gatepost of the pass through to the West. We turned right at Wink, flew up line of the Pecos Valley to Roswell, then northeast over the high plateau of New Mexico to Cannon AFB near Clovis where we landed after a couple of hours in the air.

In a limitless brown plain stretching from horizon to horizon the only noticeable feature was the town itself with its grain elevators and big stockyard which seemed dwarfed by the sheer emptiness of the land. The railroad ran like a ruled line from edge to edge of the horizon. I thought it was rather terrifying.

257

We went through the usual routine: met by the Duty Airdrome Officer with a car, conducted to Base Ops where we spent about an hour planning the next two-hour leg, then sat down to a snack luncheon in the cafeteria-buffet. Having finalised the weather and submitted a flight plan, we went out to the T-Bird, did our pre-flight checks, fitted ourselves in (quite a business because one had to have so much flight documentation to hand), and started up. We backtracked to Roswell climbing to 31,0000 feet, then set course slantwise across to El Paso. From this point onwards the scenery was breathtaking even from our vast altitude.

One could see the whole of the Alamagordo Valley with the famous white sands shining at the top of it. On the port side, across the Rio Grande, was the vast wilderness of the Chihuahua plateau. Over Tucson we swung northwest along the edge of the massif towards Phoenix, where we landed at Williams AFB about 5pm. The air was still warm. The Vale is as flat as a board but the mountains around its eastern and northern edges are pink, steep and rugged.

The first homebound leg was even more exciting, across the intricately dissected highlands northeast of the Roosevelt Reservoir which irrigates the valley floor round Phoenix, and over the astonishing high mesas of western New Mexico and eastern Arizona. Here indeed are wide open spaces. We went on via Albuquerque, Amarillo, and Wichita Falls with a groundspeed of 420 knots to Perrin AFB down in the lowlands of Oklahoma. From Albuquerque we could see the snow-capped peaks of Colorado 150 miles to the north.

What I saw west of Waco/Amarillo impressed me tremendously: the enormous geological features, the great emptiness, the sheer distances. At Perrin we went through the planning routine again but couldn't get anything to eat. Half an hour after we were airborne it was dark; and then home again to land off a radar approach after flying some 3,800 miles.

For my next flight west I chose to go on a navigation refresher in a T29, a sort of magnified Varsity. We got into El Paso International at about 10pm local time and put up at a Motel on the edge of the airport. In bright, wonderfully clear warm sunshine in the morning we flew north at 8,000 feet above sea level, over the great canyons and jumbled buttes and mesas of the deserts of New Mexico, skirting snow-capped Mount Taylor (14,000 feet). I was full of admiration for the Americans for having so effectively conquered this continent, yet remembered too the handful of Britons who conquered much of the world.

This arid quarter of this great land with its sparse scrub, heavily eroded high plateau, was exactly what one had learned to expect from western Movies and TV serials. Having crossed a wonderful peachy-pink desert heavily dissected with fascinating canyons, a land of buttes and mesas of a wide variety of shades of red barely 3,000 feet below us, we turned west by north at Farmington to pick up the Colorado River near Marble Canyon. Over the Grand Canyon we dropped down to 1,000 feet above the level of the plateau. The variety and beauty and utter emptiness of the huge, high plateau area together with the dramatic sight of the stupendous, vividly coloured gash in the earth took my breath away; it was even more impressive than the Rift Valley and the crater of Ngoro Ngoro.

After a night at Las Vegas we flew homewards but lost an engine and made a precautionary landing at Sheppard AFB, Wichita Falls (Texas). A C47 was flown out from Maxwell to pick us up.

Colonel Joe Wiseman and I shared a Gooney Bird to fly to Stewart AFB in Upper New York State. I flew the leg from Andrews AFB near Washington DC through the intensely active New York Air Traffic Control Zone to Stewart. It was murky and dark and Joe had to work extremely hard at navigation and on the R/T with constantly changing IFR sector clearances. It was an interesting example of the complexity of operating in a high density airspace in instrument weather.

In the end they routed us right round to the east of the New York Terminal Control Area, each clearance being only as far as the next beacon or intersection, and I found it rather disturbing to be steering in any direction but where we were destined for, not knowing what was to come next, wholly at the whim of Air Traffic Control.

Joe was phlegmatic. We flew back on Sunday with a fuelling stop at Pope AFB in North Carolina.

In the middle of January 1960 the course spent a week on nuclear

259

weapons studies. Since Federal Law prohibited us four foreigners - the British and Canadians - from taking part, the College made available to us a VIP Gooney Bird with a command pilot, and worked out an interesting schedule of work and play in the Far West. We set off early in the morning of 15th January for Las Vegas via Amarillo, but shortly after leaving the latter we received a 'below minimums' forecast for Las Vegas - low cloud, snow, heavy icing and no suitable diversions. Major Skidmore, the aircraft commander, therefore decided to divert to El Paso International. The next day we flew to Las Vegas.

In this part of the world one could fly for hours on end, hundreds of miles in any direction over completely empty territory. Even the towns are barely larger than villages. After a night's mild fluttering on the gaming tables, it was my turn to fly the Gooney Bird on the leg to Vandenberg AFB on the California coast. Again we passed over some magnificent desert scenery, then the chunky, well-forested Coast Range.

Vandenberg occupied a strip of sandy, heathy wilderness some twenty miles long by eight miles deep, just north of Arguello Point, a most dreary area. We were given an intensive afternoon schedule which included visits to Thor, Atlas and Titan launching sites of various degrees of hardness. The Titan silos were truly titanic: 40 feet in diameter and 165 feet deep with massive galleries at various levels, like something out of H.G. Wells.

After spending a day there we flew to Hamilton AFB outside San Francisco and landed off a GCA into a chilly (42°F), misty, drizzling and overcast afternoon. Then it was my turn again to pilot the Gooney Bird to Los Angeles International where, by contrast, the sun was bright and the temperature a balmy 68°F. We spent a whole day galloping through aeroplane production lines. I had never realised that there were so many aeroplanes in construction at once in the whole world.

On the leg from Los Angeles to Petersen AFB, Colorado Springs, I occupied the right hand seat and navigated and reported along the airways. It was a trip full of scenic interest. Beyond Mormon Springs at the northwest end of Lake Mead the Nevada desert scenery gave way to the dissected plateau type with its tortured gorges, escarpments, canyons, buttes and mesas. Beyond Bryce Canyon it became pines and snow above the 10,000 foot level.

At Hanksville we turned east across the arid, tortuous valley of the Green and Colorado Rivers and scraped over the saddle between the bare white peaks of Mount Peale, and there at last we saw the solid backbone of the Rocky Mountains, the high peaks of Colorado stretching from north to south, dazzling in the sunshine. These are real mountains; this last hour of flight was for me the highlight of the trip. Then suddenly, in an astonishing transition, the mountains dropped like a rampart wall to the level of the snow-covered prairies stretching like a billiard table to the eastern horizon.

At Colorado Springs we spent a day at the Air Force Academy, their 'over the top' version of Cranwell, built, furnished and run on the most lavish lines conceivable. After that we flew quietly back to base.

In April I spent a day on USS *Independence*, one of the huge Forrestal Class of attack carriers. A classmate, Cdr Lou Fields, very kindly fixed me a ride in one of the A3D (Skywarrior) aircraft performing in the morning flying display. The A3D was a fine aircraft, twin jet, transonic. I flew with the Squadron Commander, so we were the first aircraft to be launched from one of the steam catapults. We were flying at about 60,000lb all up, which made her quite a sizeable machine to operate from a carrier deck.

The acceleration seemed to me to be something of the order of 5g, but of course I was prepared for heavy body-loads. What caught me by surprise, however, was the effect when the catapult thrust ceased: one had the impression, for a few moments, of a very marked deceleration, as if the throttles had been cut and the air-brakes extended. I was airborne for about two enormously enjoyable hours. At the end we led a large mixed formations of A3Ds, A4Ds and F8Us over the Carrier. Seen from the lead aeroplane the formation flying was very impressive indeed.

On our first approach for landing we missed the arrester wires and had to do a go-around, but next time we caught on, and the arrival on deck was pretty firm.

As the College Year drew towards its close my final mission as a

261

pilot in the USAF was to take a gaggle of visiting lecturers back to their homes in Sedalia (Missouri), Lincoln and Omaha (Nebraska), and Kansas City (Missouri) in a VIP C47 with Joe Wiseman as my co-pilot. I felt sad about leaving the US Air Force, knowing that although I would be working with them I would never again be part of them, as I surely felt then.

12

An Old Pilot

AIR MINISTRY HAD SELECTED ME FOR A HIGH-SOUNDING but dubious appointment as 'Requirements Interchange Officer' attached to the Director of Operational Requirements at USAF Headquarters in Washington DC. I had an office in the Pentagon and I soon discovered that it was a great grey prison in which I was segregated from the people I was accredited to by a wall of indifference.

My grandiose terms of reference were to make an RAF input into the formulation of USAF Operational Requirements with a view to the long term standardisation of weapon systems. The reality was that no one wanted to know what the RAF thought; and it was left to me to lean against door-posts and seek, from anyone decent enough to chat with me, crumbs of information about what the USAF thought.

Fairly early on, after fruitless approaches to my Director, a Major-General, to seek ways of becoming more integrated into the work of his Staff, I spoke informally to the Head of the RAF Staff on the British Joint Services Mission (BJSM), suggesting that the post was a waste of a Group Captain's time, but he replied that it was a politically necessary post and it was my job to stick it out. So I decided to lump it and enjoy the enormous opportunities for pleasure that social life in Washington offered Isobelle and me. One big disappointment was being debarred from flying USAF aircraft as the result of changes in the Exchange Agreement.

The RAF operated a Heron for the use of the Ambassador and other VIPs. It was based at Andrews AFB with its VIP-qualified pilot and servicing crew. Certain selected Officers on the RAF Staff of BJSM were qualified to fly as co-pilot or to fly it on non-VIP duties, so I decided to become one of their number. In October 1960 the Heron pilot, Flt Lieut Glover, gave me four hours of conversion onto what was a sort of stretched Devon with four engines; it had better aileron response and infinitely better climb.

My first 'operational' trip was to fetch Air Marshal Sir George Mills (the Head of BJSM) back from Idlewild to Washington. I took off in darkness and moderate rain and flew on instruments in thick cloud as far as the Delaware, where it all cleared to a brilliant, full-mooned night, heavily bejewelled as far as the eye could see with the lights of the new York/Long Island/New Jersey complex of cities. I was as happy as a sand-boy. While Glover flew the return trip I did the airways navigation and reporting.

During the next two years or so, I just about managed to maintain proficiency on the Heron. It was not so much the aircraft that was the problem, as keeping up with complex ATC Terminal procedures and the rapid-fire gabble of the controllers on crowded RT channels. There were as often as not several weeks between flights.

Whenever there were VIPs on board, Tom Glover did the piloting; and whenever we were positioning or returning home after dropping, I did it. That way I became quite familiar not only with Idlewild and La Guardia but also many terminals as far north as Ottawa, Toronto and Buffalo, Pittsburgh in the west, and Newport News and Atlanta in the south.

Only once was I captain of the Heron with VIPs on board. Tom was away sick. The Head of the RAF staff at the Embassy, ignoring all the regulations specifying the qualifications for VIP-carrying pilots, asked me to volunteer to fly the British Ambassador and his wife to La Guardia and later bring them, together with the Australian Ambassador and his wife, back from Idlewild to Washington National. Nobody else on the RAF staff felt competent. I accepted the challenge, with the proviso that we should borrow a USAF co-pilot able to translate for me, if need be, the gabble of the New York Terminal controllers.

I spent a full day planning the flight, checking in detail all the relevant FAA regulations and procedures relevant to the flight, and making a number of contingency plans. That evening I had arranged to fly the Heron after dark from Washington National Airport, where it had been having some radio repairs done, to Andrews AFB, in order to check myself out with my first night landing for weeks. Radio trouble and a thunderstorm delayed the job, and on my second landing at Andrews (both were greasers) we suffered a burst tyre. Fortunately no damage was done.

The USAF lent me an excellent young fellow, Captain Kominowski from Texas, who was delightful company, but sometimes his slow Texan drawl was almost as difficult to comprehend as the New Yorkers. After dropping my VIPs off at La Guardia I hopped over to Idlewild where BOAC took us under their wing. Jimmy Stack was there as Deputy Captain of the Queen's Flight, awaiting the arrival of Prince Phillip. As soon as the Royal party departed, my Ambassadors and their ladies climbed aboard the Heron. All went well until we arrived back at Washington at 2am, when I made a very rough landing on a very dark runway, momentarily disoriented after approaching over the brilliant lights of the capital. Needless to say, my final landing at Andrews AFB with no passengers on board was a greaser.

A couple of days later, the Head of the RAF Staff called me over to the Embassy. "His Excellency didn't think much of your landing at Washington National the other night", he said with a straight face. "Your next posting is to Air Traffic Control."

Then he grinned, and told me that I was to take up a planning post in the brand new joint civil-military National Air Traffic Control Service at the end of the year. That was my last flight in the Heron, and in effect my last flight as a professional pilot. I had never been a bold pilot, but from now on I was definitely to be an old pilot.

I arrived in the UK at the end of October 1962 and took up my new job in London a month later. Although I had no time to spare for any flying, I made contact with my old No. 1 Air Navigation School, now at Stradishall in Suffolk, and extracted their consent to let me fly with them as co-pilot on navigation training sorties. With this in mind I managed to arrange a few days' refresher flying on the Varsity at Manby. Whilst I enjoyed it enormously, my performance was a long way below my standard of three years before; my reactions seemed terribly slow, perhaps more because of old age than lack of practice.

Once more, having to tolerate the bumptiousness of Qualified Flying Instructors was a small price to pay for the sheer delight of being back in the daily routine of preparing for flight, being airborne, and crew-room chatter afterwards. Alas, such was the pressure of my work that I did not fly again for a whole year.

One afternoon in March 1964 I travelled by train to Stradishall, where Peter Farlow, an old friend of 8 OTU days, was Wing Commander Flying; and within a couple of hours of my arrival I was happily trussed into the right hand seat of a Varsity off on a navigation exercise. Dusk turned into a very dark night with a brilliant Orion and all his attendants hanging in the sky, and for five happy hours from Stradishall to Inverness and out into the North Sea and back I was once again an active pilot. It confirmed that the cockpit of an aeroplane was my real element.

I got to bed shortly after midnight and, by invitation, arose to go off on a second mission at 09.15. As on the previous night the upper air was perfectly clear and smooth, but the ground below was obscured by low stratus. For another four hours I sat there, fat, bald and happy, floating through the heavens trussed like a dead chicken, and not even the long, dreary journey home could kill my feeling of sheer exhilaration. This was the beginning of a happy and fruitful relationship with Stradishall.

By the spring of 1965 we had so far planned the future UK air traffic control system that I was able to have myself removed from the HQ organisation. With unerring hindsight the authorities had me posted into a job in the field such as I should have had before ever going to the HQ job. Based at Uxbridge, I was to command Military Air Traffic Operations, Southern Region. It was a job that kept me out in the field among flying people. The range of operational problems I had to deal with was extremely interesting, and generally speaking I had ample time (and excuse) to go flying.

In July I fell in love with a mistress whom I knew, sadly, I would never master. It happened like this. . .

266

I was taken for a ride in a dual Lightning Mk 4 by Sqn Ldr Martin, the CO of No. 56 Squadron at Wattisham. Halfway down the runway he lit both afterburners. The acceleration was phenomenal. As soon as she lifted off the runway he held her down, and by the time the landing gear was retracted we were doing 350 knots. At 400 knots he hauled her round in a 4g turn which set my eyeballs popping. Then we went up like a rocket at something like 15,000 feet per minute.

To conserve fuel, he cut the afterburners and handed control over to me, but we still seemed to be climbing more like a rocket than an aeroplane. I levelled at 35,000 feet, and after a few moments Martin brought the afterburners in again. We accelerated smoothly up to Mach 1.6. At that moment the afterburners suddenly cut out. Martin quickly diagnosed a complete failure of the electrical AC systems, so I hauled her round in a 60 degree bank onto the reciprocal heading while he went through the check list switching off radar, Tacan, IFF, autopilot, gun-sights and sundry other things.

Without AC current there was a limitation on engine revs and altitude due to fuel pump problems, so I reduced to 80% power and started coasting downhill. At 1500 feet I handed over to him to complete the GCA approach and landing - with a complete loss of fuel pressure on one engine during the last couple of miles. A hectic sortie! I was floating on air for most of the rest of the day.

The Lightning handled beautifully: stable, crisp, yet smoothly responsive, easy on instruments yet with a tremendous performance, and altogether confidence-building despite being such a complex system.

On a visit to the Central Flying School I was let off in a jet Provost with an instructor. It was pouring with rain from a ceiling between three and four hundred feet, with solid cloud up to 20,000 feet or so. I was allowed to take off, do all the flying and land off a GCA, and didn't comport myself too badly. The Jet Provost was a fairly simple, stable aeroplane that handled quite well on instruments despite a rather heavy aileron breakout force.

On my first visit to Watton to look at our new Air Traffic Control Radar Unit which was taking shape, I lunched with the Station

Commander, his Wing Commander Flying and the CO of 98 Squadron, which did the routine flight checks of all my Air Traffic Control Radar Units. They said they would be happy to let me fly as many of these missions as I wished, if I could get a certificate of qualification on Canberras from the OCU at Bassingbourne as well as a current instrument rating. This prospect tickled my fancy.

In July 1965 I went to make my number at Bassingbourne. They laid on a dual ride for me in a Canberra T4 through all my radar network. I was a bit shaky on my instrument flying, and of course discovered that since the days when I flew them, Canberras had become much more complicated beasts. Being totally out of jet-flying practice, I spent the next two days at Stradishall doing some refresher flying in the Meteor 7. On my last trip I ran short of fuel on a solo cross-country, through running into an adverse jet-stream, and had to put out a 'securité' call to Uxbridge Centre on the distress frequency. They vectored me to Bassingbourne who brought me down on an emergency controlled descent; I landed with less than 10 gallons registering on the gauges.

My AOC enthusiastically supported my project and fixed me a month's Canberra refresher course at Bassingbourne. It started with two interesting days at the Aeromedical Training Centre at North Luffenham, where I battered my ancient body on a pressure-breathing course. This included a rapid decompression from 48,000 feet, followed by a graphic - indeed dramatic - lecture on the ghastly effects of decompression on the human mechanism, as a result of which I imagined all sorts of aches and pains foretelling complete collapse!

My colleagues were two young Flying Officer pilots. I was interested to discern their obvious symptoms of apprehension in the early stages of the course. After the decompression exercise one of them asked me if it had made me feel fatigued. When I replied "Yes, slightly," he said "I feel absolutely battered." So, just approaching my 47th birthday, I could still cope alongside chaps in their early 20s.

I started what was to prove to be my final fling of real flying in the second week of September. The effect of seven days in ground school was to cause a little bit of apprehension, but this disappeared completely once I was in the air. As so often happened this first flight took place in dismal weather. It was raining from a black overcast when we walked out to the aircraft, and by the time we got airborne after half an hour's worth of drills performed according to the lengthy checklist we disappeared into solid cloud at 700 feet. We didn't emerge until 32,000 feet.

Most of the time I was working very hard: switching R/T from local frequency to approach control to Anglia Radar to Humber Radar; oxygen, engine, fuel and electrical checks every 10,000 feet; frequent alterations of heading as directed by radar; listening to my instructor's patter and trying to fly accurately on instruments. I was a little slow and stupid. After general handling in the clear above 32,000 feet, I made a procedural descent back to Bassingbourne into GCA, picking up the approach lights on emerging from cloud at 600 feet and doing my first Canberra landing (a greaser!) in pouring rain. Then off again to do the ILS, after which my instructor, Hugh Mayes, said, "I wish I could do ILS as well as that." For the rest of the day I felt like a man ten feet high.

Next day I reported for Met briefing at 08.30. Even getting dressed for flying had become ritualistic: with serviceability checks of oxygen, microphone, headphones, bone-dome visor, and the garters, knife, and attachments to one's flying overalls, as well as the Mae West with all its gimmicks. Next I was briefed in detail by my instructor for the sortie, an instrument rating dummy run; then out to the aircraft for checks and strapping in and starting up.

Two hours after the Met briefing I opened throttles to roll for a two hour sortie on instruments under the hood. This involved take-off and climb to 40,000 feet with sustained turns on the way up; steep turns on both full and limited instrument panel at 0.72 Mach; then a run on limited panel at maximum permissible Mach number (0.82), recovery to 0.75 Mach and rapid descent to 25,000 feet; stalling in the approach configuration; recovery from unusual attitudes; a controlled descent into GCA followed by an overshoot on one engine (still on limited panel); then a low level GCA and overshoot; and finally, with full panel and both engines, a low level ILS to a landing.

Everything was done under radar control with all the chatter it involves, plus the instructor's advice and the navigator calling out the checks. I just crawled out of the aeroplane when we finally got back to dispersal and shut down at 12.40.

After three dual trips in the Mk 4 I went solo in a Canberra PR Mk 3 for the first time. She had a noticeably higher inertia, and I found it difficult to get rid of speed on final approach. A night dual session was followed by solo on the T4. I was awfully tired and therefore ham-fistedly inaccurate, and sometimes plain stupid, but essentially safe. My last ILS after the instructor had left the aircraft in despair was up to my usual form, and my last circuit and landing were excellent. So back to the Mess for night-flying beer, a late supper and a Scotch before falling into bed.

I enjoyed this concentrated flying enormously, but if it wasn't that I was reliably informed that all Senior Officers who did this course found it extremely tiring, I would have thought myself to be too old for it. Each flight was hard work, packed with high intensity activity. My admiration for the youngsters, for their toughness and professional competence, grew stronger every time I met them on the flight line. If I, with a lifetime of flying experience behind me, found it difficult and tiring, how much more so must it have been for them, fresh from Flying Training School.

A couple of weeks later I went to Watton to establish a basis for flying their Canberras on radar assessments. It was a shattering blow, after so many earlier promises, to have the Station Commander veto the idea on the ground that 98 Squadron had lost 25% of their aircraft due to fatigue problems. His pilots were therefore under-employed. The most he would offer me was one dual trip a month in the T4, which, feeling affronted, I foolishly turned down

Tom Knight, the CO at Gaydon, asked me to have a look at their bad weather recovery procedures which were presenting problems. He gave me a Varsity with a qualified flying instructor and I had a happy time getting in some instrument flying, ostensibly checking the procedures. It was a filthy day with solid low cloud and drizzle. It was hard work, yet I still managed to do creditable instrument approaches down to about 400 feet. Below that I got a little ragged and found it difficult to make the transition to visual adequately for smooth, accurate landings.

This was entirely due to lack of practice.

I made useful friendships at Gaydon and planned to fly with them regularly. When we were asked to have a look at the feasibility of using the Navy cell at Aberporth Radar for controlling crossings of Airway Amber 25 after Mersey Radar closed down, I asked for the loan of a Gaydon Varsity and crew to do the job. Gaydon was willing to play, albeit only a Valetta was available. It was a cool NW airstream situation with about six eighths cumulus, base 2,000 feet, tops 8-9,000 feet, strong gusty winds and crystal-clear visibility such that the brilliant sunlight gave the cloudscapes a tremendously dramatic beauty.

Because of the strong crosswinds at both Gaydon and Brawdy (and I hadn't flown a Valetta for ages), my co-pilot occupied the left-hand seat and did the take-offs and landings as a safety precaution; otherwise I did all the flying. At Brawdy we were met very formally on the tarmac by the Commander, the Commander (Air) and the SATCO.[1] We then had a briefing session before going off to the Wardroom for an early lunch, after which I was introduced to the Captain - none other than Peter Austin of my course at Manby who had been on the epic Lincoln flight to Montreal. The Aberporth trial was both enjoyable and successful.

I celebrated my 48th birthday with the keenest pleasure that had come my professional way for a long time, flying the DH125 Dominie, Stradishall having offered me a couple of days for conversion. In many ways the Dominie was just the aircraft I had been waiting for all my life. For normal operations the cabin was pressurised and air-conditioned to a shirtsleeve environment equivalent to 5,000 feet. She was remarkably stable and, below 30,000 feet, had beautifully co-ordinated controls that were reasonably light yet not too rapidly responsive.

She had a lively performance: the last 10% of engine power gave her a big kick, she cruised at about 0.6 Mach for some 1,000 n.m. or so,

---

[1] Senior Air Traffic Control Officer

and at her maximum Mach No. 0.72, behaved very decently. She had a magnificent complement of communications and navigation equipment for both pilots and the navigators. I wished that I were twenty years younger and three ranks down, just beginning a flying tour on this aircraft.

My first 'functional' sortie in the co-pilot's seat was a three hour flight at 34,000 feet or thereabouts. The wind was over 100 knots from the NW, so it took us nearly two hours to get to Lossiemouth, but a bare 50 minutes to get back. These Dominie trips were most useful to me as a Regional Air Trafficker because they actually used the upper airspace radar control system; but since all the cruising had to be done on autopilot in the interests of the trainee navigators they were a waste of time from the driving point of view.

Just before Christmas I visited RAE Bedford. After lunch BLEU offered me a sortie in their Comet with the Triplex Autoland. Unfortunately it didn't come ready until 4pm, and by the time we were airborne it was dark. They kindly let me fly in the right hand seat. Zala, the pilot, was a very busy man: the autopilot and flight director were not coupling properly onto the ILS beams, which meant that on each approach and flare he was having to go through the drill of recoupling and priming, as well as monitoring the flight and doing all his drills etc., and carrying on a discussion with his Boffin observer. I was filled with admiration for his cool skill in coping with a very high work-load.

On 26th July 1967 I made what turned out to be my last flight as a serving Officer in the RAF. At Brize Norton they were having problems with the pattern approved for high-level let-downs and approaches. In order the better to be able to evaluate the solution, I flew in the right hand seat of a VC10 on a series of approaches and let-downs and was surprised how readily this very large four-engined monster handled like a Dominie in the standard RAF controlled descent pattern, designed originally for jet fighters, so different from the staid procedures used in civil passenger jets.

I had by now been formally notified that I was to retire on my 50th birthday in October 1968. Shortly after flying the VC10 I came to the conclusion that I was not going to play any further part in aviation after

272

quitting the RAF, and decided to give up flying altogether so as to devote more time to preparing myself for civilian life. The Royal Air Force, however, still had one more pleasant surprise for me.

No. 1 Air Navigation School invited me to attend a Passing Out Parade to present the Johnston Memorial Cup, which I had initiated to commemorate my Father (who is the subject of my book *Airship Navigator*) when the School was under my command.

The Passing Out Parade was to take place, quite coincidentally, on the date of my fiftieth birthday. As soon as Isobelle and I arrived at Stradishall we were treated like visiting Royalty. No. 107 Course was passing out, and after the Reviewing Officer had pinned brevets onto bulging chests, the award of the Johnston Memorial Trophy was announced at some length and I was called forward to present it to a very personable young man, Pilot Officer M.D. Beech-Allen, before the Parade performed its evolutions.

After a very good lunch the CO asked me to say a few words. Alas, as I spoke my thanks for the great kindness that they had done me by making me so tremendously welcome on my last day in the RAF, emotion welled up and I almost broke down. However, I ended on a confident note commending to them the Chaplain's text - thrust out from the shore, seek the deep waters - and sat down to what sounded in my ears like thunderous applause.

After lunch the graduating course presented me with a Stradishall tie, a Bowler hat and an umbrella, installed me in a chair at a desk set upon a lorry, and drove me away to the cheers of the assembled Mums and Dads.

So my RAF life ended amongst navigators with whom I had spent so much of it, handing on the torch to a new generation.

A very happy ending indeed.

Index

&

Aircraft Flown

INDEX

Pilot's Vision Assessment (PVA), 218
Pirie, 'Duck', 78
Platt, Dennis, 222, 223
Ponting, Flt Lieut, 124
Pope (USAFB), 259
Popkin, Flt Lieut David, 114, 120 *et seq*, 128, 131
Portaluppi, Major, 255
Porteous, Horace ('Hol'), 55, 57
Pulham, 14, 17 *et seq*

RMS *Queen Mary,* 131

RAF, 18 Group (Training), 140
RAF Squadrons:
   No. 22 Squadron, 228
   No. 58 Squadron, 150, 161
   No. 82 Squadron, 138, 154 *et seq,* 161
   No. 98 Squadron, 268
   No. 209 Squadron, 63
   No. 224 Squadron, 118 *et seq*
   No. 240 Squadron, 61, 72 *et seq*
   No. 540 Squadron, 139, 161
   No. 541 Squadron, 138, 161, 164
Randolph USAFB, Texas, 256
Rebecca, 154, 197
Resolute Bay, 192 *et seq*, 208
Richmond, Colonel, 18
Royal Aircraft Establishment (RAE), 163, 164, 171, 209, 227

St Athan, 79 *et seq*
St Eval, 130 *et seq*, 153 *et seq*, 200, 201
Savage, Michael, 44, 49, 50

Scott, Major G.H., 13, 14, 16, 18, 22
Scott, Mrs Jess, 22, 40, 41
Scott (USAFB), 256
Scragg, Sgt (later Air Vice Marshal Colin Scragg), 28, 148
Selby, Wing Commander John, 164
Shawbury, 150, 165
Sheppard (USAFB), 259
Simons, Sgt, 34, 38
Sinclair, Flt Lieut 'Hooky', 58, 59, 65, 66, 72
Smith, Wing Commander Ruffel, 168
Solar Navigator, 159 *et seq*
Spittle, F/Sgt, 226, 227
Spreckley, Air Commodore, 173, 175
Squire's Gate, 79 *et seq*, 98
Stack, 'Jimmy' (later Air Chief Marshal Sir Neville Stack), 75, 85, 91, 149, 153, 265
Starling, F/O Eric, 80
Steedman, Flt Lieut Alex, 185, 187
Steventon, Don, 178
Stewart (USAFB), 259
Stoop, Sqn Ldr, 225
Stradishall, 265 *et seq*
Straight, Whitney, 23
Strubby, 168, 177 *et seq*
Sutton Bridge, 37, 49 *et seq*
Takali, Malta, 250, 254
ss *Teakwood,* 70
Telecommunications Research Establishment (TRE), 163
Thompson-Hill, Bob, 109
Thomson, Tommy, 84
Thorney Island, 51, 54, 55, 73, 80
Thule, 192, 195 *et seq*, 200
Topcliffe, 243 *et seq*

281

AIRCRAFT FLOWN